Adobe® After Effects® 7

CLASSROOM
IN A BOOK®

www.adobepress.com

Adobe

Adobe Press books are published by Peachpit Press, Berkeley, CA. To report errors, please send a note to errata@peachpit.com.

Printed in the U.S.A.

ISBN # 0-321-38549-7

9 8 7 6 5 4 3 2

Editor: Anita Dennis
Design Director: Andrew Faulkner, afstudio design
Designer: Alison O'Gara, afstudio design
Production: Lisa Fridsma and Dawn Dombrow-Thompson

The editor and design director offer our sincere thanks to the following people for their support and help with this project: Mark Christiansen, Dawn Dombrow-Thompson, Jennifer Domeier, Lisa Fridsma, Takeshi Hiraoka, Steve Kilisky, Todd Kopriva, Jack Lewis, Jill Merlin, Alison O'Gara, Stephen Schleicher, Patrick Siemer, Gordon Studer, Anna Ullrich, Rick Williams, and Christine Yarrow. We couldn't have done it without you.

Getting to Know the Workflow   page 10

Animating a Multimedia Presentation   page 121

Working with Masks   page 203

Performing Color Correction   page 261

Using 3D Effects   page 293

Advanced Editing Techniques   page 363

From the Authors

Welcome to Adobe® After Effects® 7.0 Classroom in a Book. This book represents the collaborative efforts of a talented team of digital animators, digital-video artists, professional illustrators, and 2D and 3D graphic designers. (For biographies, see page 456.) With the help of these gifted individuals, we have created a broad range of creative projects that will help you learn the ins and outs of the industry-standard compositing and animation tool for producing motion graphics and visual effects for film, broadcast, DVD, and the web.

Whether you are a motion graphics novice or an experienced DV artist looking to improve your skills, there is something for you in this book. New and veteran users alike should both take time to get acquainted with the After Effects 7.0 workspace, which has a whole new look and feel, in Lesson 1. Other highlights include Lesson 4, where we combine digital video with an animated, illustrated background to create a dynamic multimedia presentation, and Lesson 11, where we explore the new Timewarp feature that allows you to slow down and speed up footage. Of course, any DV project is only as good as its final output, which is why we cover rendering and output in depth in Lesson 12.

If you have half as much fun completing these lessons as we did creating them, you'll have a blast as you become an After Effects expert. It's all about creativity, so don't hesitate to experiment along the way. Who knows, we may be calling on you to help us with the next edition of this book!

Andrew Faulkner and Anita Dennis

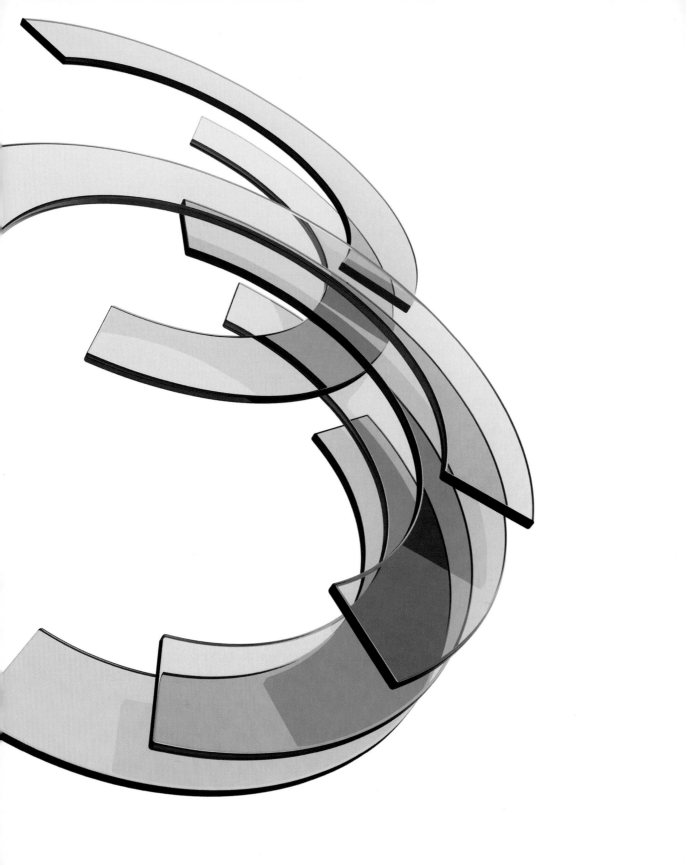

Contents

2   Creating a Basic Animation Using Effects and Presets

3   Animating Text

4 Animating a Multimedia Presentation

5 Animating Layers

| **6** | **Working with Masks** |

| **7** | **Keying** |

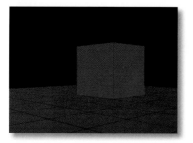

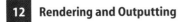

Steve Kilisky
Sr. Product Manager - After Effects
Adobe Systems, Inc.

Adobe®

Greetings from the After Effects team,

Thank you for choosing this book. Whether you are a longtime After Effects user or are just beginning to experiment with time-based design, motion graphics, and creating visual effects, this book has something to help expand your knowledge of After Effects. In addition to covering many new features in After Effects 7.0, Adobe After Effects 7.0 Classroom in a Book *also covers features in After Effects Professional, including motion tracking and motion stabilization. For new users, it will help you get up to speed quickly and help you tap in to the power of After Effects.*

We appreciate your interest and support of After Effects,

Steve Kilisky
Senior Product Manager, After Effects

Getting Started

Adobe® After Effects® 7.0 provides a comprehensive set of 2D and 3D tools for compositing, animation, and effects that motion-graphics professionals, visual effects artists, web designers, and film and video professionals need. After Effects is widely used for digital post-production of film, video, DVD, and the web. You can composite layers in various ways, apply and combine sophisticated visual and audio effects, and animate both objects and effects.

About Classroom in a Book

Adobe After Effects 7.0 Classroom in a Book® is part of the official training series for Adobe graphics and publishing software. The lessons are designed so that you can learn at your own pace. If you're new to After Effects, you'll learn the fundamental concepts and features you'll need to use the program. *Classroom in a Book* also teaches many advanced features, including tips and techniques for using the latest version of this application.

The lessons in this edition include opportunities to use new features, such as producing animations with time-saving presets and behaviors, simplifying tasks using the Adobe Bridge® visual file browser, taking advantage of expanded file-format support, applying new creative effects, editing keyframes using the new Graph Editor, using a redesigned interface with new conveniences, and more.

Prerequisites

Before beginning to use *Adobe After Effects 7.0 Classroom in a Book*, make sure that your system is set up correctly and that you've installed the required software and hardware. You should have a working knowledge of your computer and operating system. You should know how to use the mouse and standard menus and commands, and also how to open, save, and close files. If you need to review these techniques, see the printed or online documentation included with your Microsoft® Windows® or Apple® Mac® OS software.

Installing After Effects

You must purchase the Adobe After Effects 7.0 software separately. For system requirements and complete instructions on installing the software, see the Adobe After Effects ReadMe.html file on the application DVD. You must also have QuickTime 6.5.2 or later installed on your system.

Install After Effects from the Adobe After Effects 7.0 application DVD onto your hard disk; you cannot run the program from the DVD. Follow the on-screen instructions.

Make sure that your serial number is accessible before installing the application; you can find the serial number on the registration card or on the back of the DVD case.

Optimizing performance

Creating movies is memory-intensive work for a desktop computer. After Effects 7.0 requires a minimum of 512 MB of RAM; 1 GB or more is recommended. The more RAM that is available to After Effects, the faster the application will work for you.

OpenGL support

OpenGL is a set of standards for delivering high-performance 2D and 3D graphics for a wide variety of applications. Although After Effects can function without it, OpenGL accelerates various types of rendering, including rendering to the screen for previews.

To get the full benefit of OpenGL in After Effects, you'll need an OpenGL card that supports OpenGL 2.0 and has Shader support and support for NPOT (Non Power of Two) textures. The minimum requirement for using OpenGL with After Effects is a card that supports OpenGL 1.5. When you first start After Effects, it will attempt to determine if your OpenGL card meets the requirements, and it will enable or disable OpenGL as appropriate.

You can view information about your OpenGL card, as well as enable or disable OpenGL in After Effects, by choosing Edit > Preferences > Previews (Windows) or After Effects > Preferences > Previews (Mac OS). Select the Enable OpenGL check box to enable OpenGL; click the OpenGL Info button to learn more about your card.

Note: When you choose Edit > Preferences > Memory & Cache (Windows only), you'll see a check box labeled Prevent DLL Address Space Fragmentation, which is toggled on by default. This gives After Effects access to more contiguous memory on systems with large amounts of RAM; however, it may be incompatible with some OpenGL drivers, which can cause After Effects to crash on launch. Should this occur, this option will become unchecked automatically to prevent further crashes when you launch After Effects.

To learn more about OpenGL support in After Effects, see After Effects Help.

Installing lesson fonts

To ensure that the lessons appear on your system with the correct fonts, you may need to install some font files. The lessons in this book use fonts that come on the After Effects application DVD. If you already have these fonts on your system, you do not need to install them. Otherwise, you can install the After Effects fonts by copying them to the Program Files/Common Files/Adobe/Fonts (Windows) or Library/Application Support/Adobe/Fonts (Mac OS) folder on your hard disk. If you install a Type 1, TrueType, OpenType, or CID font into these local Fonts folders, the font appears only in Adobe applications.

What's on the DVD *

Here is an overview of the contents of the Classroom in a Book DVD.

Lesson files . . . and so much more

The *Adobe After Effects 7.0 Classroom in a Book* DVD includes the lesson files that you'll need to complete the exercises in this book, as well as other content to help you learn more about After Effects and use it with greater efficiency and ease. The diagram below represents the contents of the DVD, which should help you locate the files you need.

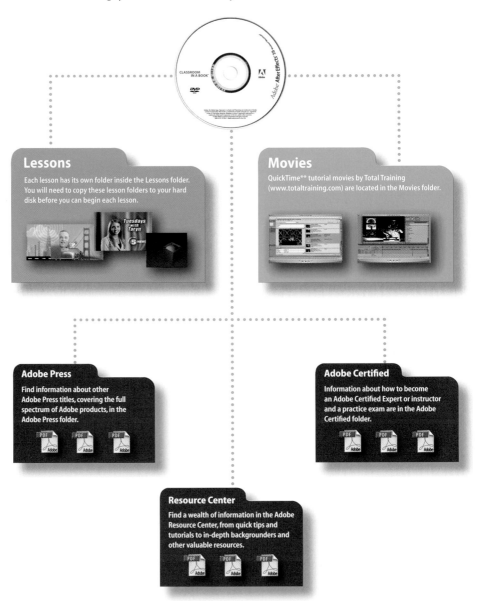

Lessons

Each lesson has its own folder inside the Lessons folder. You will need to copy these lesson folders to your hard disk before you can begin each lesson.

Movies

QuickTime** tutorial movies by Total Training (www.totaltraining.com) are located in the Movies folder.

Adobe Press

Find information about other Adobe Press titles, covering the full spectrum of Adobe products, in the Adobe Press folder.

Adobe Certified

Information about how to become an Adobe Certified Expert or instructor and a practice exam are in the Adobe Certified folder.

Resource Center

Find a wealth of information in the Adobe Resource Center, from quick tips and tutorials to in-depth backgrounders and other valuable resources.

** *The latest version of Apple QuickTime can be downloaded from www.apple.com/support/downloads/.*

Restoring default preferences

The preferences file controls the way the After Effects user interface appears on your screen. The instructions in this book assume that you see the default interface when they describe the appearance of tools, options, windows, panels, and so forth. Because of this, it's a good idea to restore the default preferences, especially if you are new to After Effects.

Each time you quit After Effects, the palette positions and certain command settings are recorded in the preferences file. If you want to restore the palettes to their original default settings, you can delete the current After Effects preferences file. (After Effects creates a new preferences file if one doesn't already exist the next time you start the program.)

Restoring the default preferences can be especially helpful if someone has already customized After Effects on your computer. If your copy of After Effects hasn't been used yet, this file won't exist, so this procedure is unnecessary.

Important: If you want to save the current settings, you can rename the preferences file instead of deleting it. When you are ready to restore those settings, change the name back and make sure that the file is located in the correct preferences folder.

1 Locate the After Effects preferences folder on your computer:

• For Windows XP: .../Documents and Settings/*<user name>*/Application Data/ Adobe/After Effects/7.0.

• For Windows 2000: .../Documents and Settings/*<user name>*/Application Data/ Adobe/After Effects/Prefs.

Note: (Windows only) If you do not see the Prefs file, be sure that the Show hidden files and folders option is selected for Hidden files on the View tab of the Folder Options dialog box.

• For Mac OS: .../*<user name>*/Library/Preferences.

2 Delete or rename the Adobe After Effects 7.0 Prefs file.

3 Start Adobe After Effects.

    You can also press Ctrl+Alt+Shift (Windows) or Option+Command+Shift (Mac OS) while starting After Effects to restore default preferences settings.

Copying the lesson files

The lessons in *Adobe After Effects 7.0 Classroom in a Book* use specific source files, such as image files created in Adobe Photoshop® and Adobe Illustrator®, audio files, and prepared QuickTime movies. To complete the lessons in this book, you must copy these files from the *Adobe After Effects 7.0 Classroom in a Book* DVD (inside the back cover of this book) to your hard disk.

1 On your hard disk, create a new folder in a convenient location and name it **AE7_CIB**, following the standard procedure for your operating system:

• Windows: In the Explorer, select the folder or drive in which you want to create the new folder, and choose File > New > Folder. Then type the new name.

• Mac OS: In the Finder, choose File > New Folder. Type the new name and drag the folder to the location you want to use.

Now, you can copy the source files onto your hard disk.

2 Copy the Lessons folder (which contains folders named Lesson01, Lesson02, and so on) from the *Adobe After Effects 7.0 Classroom in a Book* DVD onto your hard disk by dragging it to your new AE7_CIB folder.

When you begin each lesson, you will navigate to the folder with that lesson number, where you will find all of the assets, sample movies, and other project files you need to complete the lesson.

If you have limited storage space on your computer, you can copy each lesson folder individually as you need it, and delete it afterward if desired. Some lessons build on preceding lessons; in those cases, a starting project file is provided for you for the second lesson or project. You do not have to save any finished project if you don't want to, or if you have limited hard disk space.

If you use After Effects on a computer running Windows 2000, you may need to unlock the files before you use them. This is not necessary if you are using a system running Windows XP or Mac OS.

3 (Windows 2000 only) Unlock the files you copied:

• Right-click the folder that contains the locked files, such as Lessons, and choose Properties from the contextual menu.

• In the Attributes area of the File Properties dialog box, deselect (uncheck) the Read-only check box, and then click Apply.

• In the Confirm Attributes Changes dialog box, select the option Apply Changes To This Folder, Subfolders, And Files.

• Click OK to close the Confirm Attributes Changes dialog box, and click OK again to close the File Properties dialog box.

This final step is not necessary for Windows XP or Mac OS users.

About copying the sample movies and projects

You will create and render one or more QuickTime movies in some lessons in this book. The files in the Sample_Movie folders are low-resolution examples that you can use to see the end results of each lesson and to compare them with your own results. These files tend to be large, so you many not want to devote the storage space or time to copying all the sample movies before you begin. Instead, find the appropriate Sample_Movie folder on the book's DVD and copy the file it contains onto your hard disk as you begin work on a lesson. (You cannot play movies from the DVD.) After you finish viewing the movie, you can delete it from your hard drive.

The files in the End_Project folders are samples of the completed project for each lesson. Use these files for reference if you want to compare your work in progress with the project files used to generate the sample movies. These end project files vary in size from relatively small to a couple of megabytes, so you can either copy them all now if you have ample storage space, or copy just the end project file for each lesson as needed, and then delete it when you finish that lesson.

How to use these lessons

Each lesson in this book provides step-by-step instructions for creating one or more specific elements of a real-world project. Some lessons build on projects created in preceding lessons; some stand alone. All of these lessons build on each other in terms of concepts and skills, so the best way to learn from this book is to proceed through the lessons in sequential order. In this book, some techniques and processes are explained and described in detail only the first few times you perform them.

Note: *Many aspects of the After Effects application can be controlled by multiple techniques, such as a menu command, a button, dragging, and a keyboard shortcut. Only one or two of the methods are described in any given procedure so that you can learn different ways of working even when the task is one you've done before.*

The organization of the lessons is also design oriented rather than feature oriented. That means, for example, that you'll work with layers and effects on real-world design projects over several lessons, rather than in just one chapter, as in the *After Effects 7.0 User Guide*.

Additional resources

Adobe After Effects 7.0 Classroom in a Book is not meant to replace documentation that comes with the program. This book explains only the commands and options actually used in the lessons, so there's much more to learn about After Effects. *Classroom in a Book* aims to give you confidence and skills so that you can start creating your own projects. For more comprehensive information about program features, see:

• The *Adobe After Effects 7.0 User Guide*, which is included with the Adobe After Effects 7.0 software and contains descriptions of many features.

• After Effects Help, which contains all of the information in the user guide and much, much more, and is available from within the application. You can view After Effects Help by choosing Help > After Effects Help.

• The Adobe website (www.adobe.com). If you have a connection to the World Wide Web, you access the website from a web browser or by clicking More Resources in After Effects Help. The Online Resources page of After Effects Help provides links to several useful areas of the Adobe website.

• Adobe Resource Center (http://studio.adobe.com), where you can find a wealth of tips, tutorials, plug-ins, actions, and other design inspiration and instructional content.

Adobe Certification

The Adobe Training and Certification Programs are designed to help Adobe customers improve and promote their product-proficiency skills. There are three levels of certification:

- Adobe Certified Expert (ACE)
- Adobe Certified Instructor (ACI)
- Adobe Authorized Training Center (AATC)

The Adobe Certified Expert (ACE) program is a way for expert users to upgrade their credentials. You can use Adobe certification as a catalyst for getting a raise, finding a job, or promoting your expertise.

If you are an ACE-level instructor, the Adobe Certified Instructor program takes your skills to the next level and gives you access to a wide range of Adobe resources.

Adobe Authorized Training Centers offer instructor-led courses and training on Adobe products, employing only Adobe Certified Instructors. A directory of AATCs is available at http://partners.adobe.com.

For information on the Adobe Certified programs, visit www.adobe.com/support/ certification/main.html.

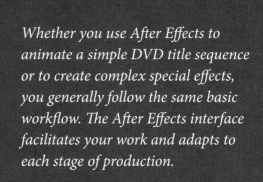

Whether you use After Effects to
animate a simple DVD title sequence
or to create complex special effects,
you generally follow the same basic
workflow. The After Effects interface
facilitates your work and adapts to
each stage of production.

1 Getting to Know the Workflow

Lesson overview

In this lesson you'll learn how to do the following:

- Create a project and import footage.

- Create compositions and arrange layers.

- Navigate the After Effects interface.

- Use the Project, Composition, and Timeline panels.

- Apply basic keyframes and effects.

- Preview your work using standard and RAM previews.

- Customize the workspace.

- Adjust preferences related to the workspace.

- Find topics in After Effects Help.

The basic After Effects workflow adheres to the following five steps: import and organize footage; create compositions and arrange layers; animate elements and add effects; preview your work; and render and output the final composition so that it can be viewed by others. In this lesson, you will create a simple animated video using this workflow, and along the way, you'll learn your way around the After Effects interface.

This lesson will take about 1 hour to complete.

Getting started

Make sure the following files are in the AE7_CIB > Lessons > Lesson01 folder on your hard disk, or copy them from the *Adobe After Effects 7.0 Classroom in a Book* DVD now.

• In the Assets folder: DJ.mov, kaleidoscope_waveforms.mov, pulsating_radial_waves.mov, bgwtext.psd, gc_adobe_dj.mp3

• In the Sample_Movie folder: Lesson01.mov

1 Open and play the Lesson01.mov sample movie to see what you will create in this lesson. When you are done, quit the QuickTime player. You may delete this sample movie from your hard disk if you have limited storage space.

Creating a project and importing footage

When you begin each lesson of this book, it's a good idea to restore the default preferences for After Effects. (See "Restoring default preferences," page 5.) You can do this with a simple keyboard shortcut.

1 Press Ctrl+Alt+Shift (Windows) or Option+Command+Shift (Mac OS) while starting After Effects to restore default preferences settings. When prompted whether you want to delete your preferences file, click OK.

After Effects opens to display an empty, untitled project.

An After Effects project is a single file that stores references to all the footage you use in that project. It also contains compositions, which are the individual containers used to combine footage, apply effects, and, ultimately, drive the output.

Watch the Movie

Total Training: Importing footage

To learn more about the After Effects workspace, including how to import footage items, how to preview footage items in Bridge, and how to import layered Photoshop files into After Effects, see the Total Training movies that are provided on the *Adobe After Effects 7.0 Classroom in a Book* DVD. The QuickTime movies are located in the Movies folder. The movie about importing footage is named ImportingFootage.mov.

About the After Effects workspace

After Effects offers a flexible, customizable workspace. The main window of the program is called the *application window*. The various panels are organized in this window in an arrangement called a *workspace*. The default workspace contains groups of panels as well as panels that stand alone, as shown in the following figure.

A. Application window B. Tools panel C. Project panel D. Composition panel E. Timeline panel
F. Time ruler G. Grouped panels (Info and Audio) H. Time Controls panel I. Effects & Presets panel

You customize a workspace by dragging the panels in the layout that best suits your work style. You can drag panels to new locations, move panels into or out of a group, place panels alongside each other, and undock a panel so that it floats in a new window above the application window. As you rearrange panels, the other panels resize automatically to fit the window.

When you drag a panel by its tab to relocate it, the area where you can drop it—called a *drop zone*—becomes highlighted. The drop zone determines where and how the panel is inserted into the workspace. Dragging a panel to a drop zone results in one of two behaviors: docking or grouping.

If you drop a panel along the edge of another panel, group, or window, it will "dock" next to the existing group, resizing all groups to accommodate the new panel.

If you drop a panel in the middle of another panel or group, or along the tab area of a panel, it will be added to the existing group and be placed at the top of the stack. Grouping a panel does not resize other groups.

You can also open a panel in a floating window. To do so, select the panel and then choose Undock Panel or Undock Frame from the panel menu. Or, drag the panel or group outside the application window.

💡 *Quickly maximize any panel by positioning the mouse pointer over it and pressing the tilde (~) key. (Do not press the Shift key.) Press the tilde key again to return the panel to its original size.*

When you begin a project, the first thing to do is add footage to it.

2 Choose File > Import > File or press Ctrl+I (Windows) or Command+I (Mac OS).

💡 *As with many functions in After Effects, there are many ways to import footage into a project. You can also double-click the Project panel to open the Import File dialog box, or use the File > Import > Multiple Files command to choose files located in different folders. Finally, you can use Bridge to search for, manage, preview, and import footage. For more about using Bridge, see Lesson 2, "Creating a Basic Animation Using Effects and Presets."*

3 Navigate to the Assets folder in your AE7_CIB > Lessons > Lesson01 folder. Shift-click to select all of the files in the folder, and then click Open.

A *footage item* is the basic unit in an After Effects project. You can import many types of footage items, including moving image files, still-image files, still-image sequences, audio files, layered files from Adobe Photoshop and Adobe Illustrator, other After Effects projects, and projects created in Adobe Premiere Pro. As you build a project, you can import footage items at any time.

Because one of the footage items for this project is a multilayer Photoshop file, After Effects asks how you want to import it.

4 In the Bgwtext.psd dialog box that appears, choose Import Kind > Composition to import the layered Photoshop file as a composition. Then click OK. Your footage items appear in the Project panel.

5 In the Project panel, deselect all footage items and then click to select any of the them. Notice that a thumbnail preview appears at the top of the Project panel. Also notice that you can see the file type and size, as well as other information about each item, in the Project panel columns.

When you import files, After Effects does not copy the footage item itself into your project, but rather creates a reference link in the Project panel to the footage item. This saves disk space. If you use another application to modify footage that is used in a project, the changes appear in After Effects the next time you open the project.

To save time and minimize the size and complexity of a project, import a footage item once and then use it multiple times in a composition. You may need to import a footage item more than once, however, such as if you want to use it at two different frame rates.

Enough about importing footage. Now is a good time to save the project.

6 Choose File > Save or press Ctrl+S (Windows) or Command+S (Mac OS). In the Save As dialog box, navigate to the AE7_CIB > Lessons > Lesson01 > Finished_Project folder. Name the project **Lesson01_Finished.aep**, and then click Save.

Creating a composition and arranging layers

The next part of the workflow is to create a composition. A *composition* is where you create all animation, layering, and effects. An After Effects composition has both spatial dimensions and a temporal dimension, called a *duration*, or length in time.

Compositions include one or more footage items—video, audio, still images—arranged in the Composition panel and in the Timeline panel. Simple projects may include only one composition, while elaborate projects may include several compositions to organize large amounts of footage or intricate effects sequences.

You will now create a composition by selecting your footage items and dragging them into the Timeline panel.

1 In the Project panel, Ctrl-click (Windows) or Command-click (Mac OS) to select the Bgwtext composition as well as the DJ, Gc_adobe_dj, Kaleidoscope_waveforms, and Pulsating_radial_waves footage items.

2 Drag the selected footage items into the Timeline panel. The New Composition From Selection dialog box appears.

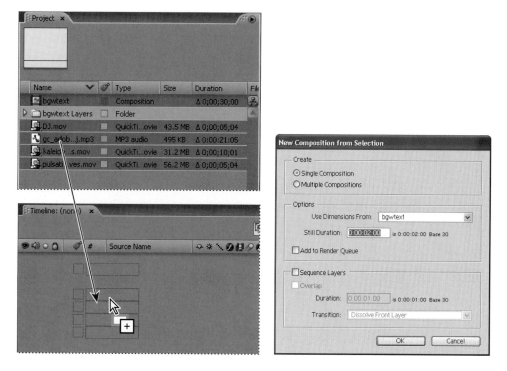

After Effects bases the size of the new composition on the selected footage. In this example, all of the footage is sized identically, so you can accept the default settings.

3 Click OK to create the new composition. The footage items appear as layers in the Timeline panel, and a visual display of the composition, named Bgwtext 2, appears in the Composition panel.

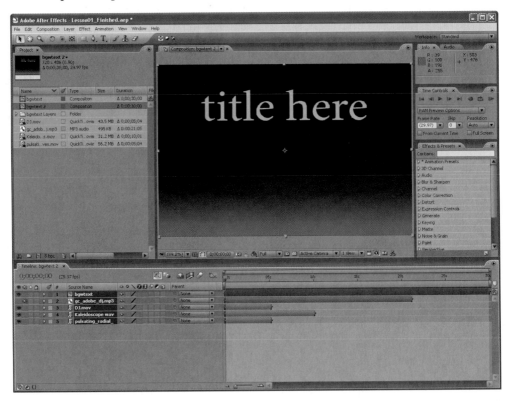

When you add a footage item to a composition, the footage becomes the source for a new layer. A composition can have any number of layers, and you can also include a composition as a layer in another composition, which is called *nesting*.

About layers

Layers are the components you use to build a composition. Any item that you add to a composition—such as a still image, moving image file, audio file, light layers, camera layers, or even another composition—becomes a new layer. Without layers, a composition consists only of an empty frame.

Using layers, you can work with specific footage items in a composition without affecting any other footage. For example, you can move, rotate, and draw masks for one layer without disturbing any other layers in the composition, or you can use the same footage in more than one layer and use it differently in each instance. The layer order in the Timeline panel corresponds to the stacking order in the Composition panel.

In this composition, there are five footage items and therefore five layers in the Timeline panel. Depending on the order in which the elements were selected when you imported them, your layer stack may differ from the one shown in the preceding figure. The layers need to be in a specific order as you add effects and animations, however, so let's take care of that now.

4 Drag Bgwtext to the bottom of the layer stack if it is not already there. Drag the other four layers so that they're in the order shown in the following figure.

From this point forward in the workflow, you should be thinking about layers, not footage items. To that end:

5 Click the Source Name column title in the Timeline panel to change it to Layer Name.

6 Choose File > Save to save your project so far.

About the Tools panel

As soon as you create a composition, the tools in the Tools panel in the upper-left corner of the After Effects application window become active. After Effects includes tools that allow you to modify elements of your composition. Some of these tools—the Selection tool and the Hand tool, for example—will be familiar to users of other Adobe products, such as Photoshop. Others will be new. The following image identifies the tools in the Tools panel for your reference.

A. Selection **B.** Hand **C.** Zoom **D.** Rotation **E.** Orbit Camera
F. Pan Behind **G.** Rectangular Mask **H.** Pen **I.** Horizontal Type
J. Brush **K.** Clone Stamp **L.** Eraser

You can hover the mouse pointer over any tool, and a tooltip will appear that identifies the tool and its keyboard shortcut. A small triangle in the lower-right corner of the tool indicates that one or more additional tools are hidden beneath it. Click and hold the tool, and the hidden tools will appear. Drag over the tool you want to use and release the mouse button to select it.

Adding effects and modifying layer properties

Now that your composition is set up, you can start having fun—applying effects, making transformations, and adding animation. You can add any combination of effects and modify any of a layer's properties, such as size, placement, and opacity. Using effects, you can alter a layer's appearance or sound, and even generate visual elements from scratch. The easiest way to start is to apply any of the hundreds of effects included with After Effects.

Note: This exercise is just the tip of the iceberg. You will learn more about effects and presets in Lesson 2, "Creating a Basic Animation Using Effects and Presets," and throughout the rest of this book.

Preparing the layers

You'll apply the effects to duplicates of selected layers—the DJ layer and the Kaleidoscope_waveforms layer. This is a good practice because it leaves the original layers intact in case you need them later.

1 Select layer 1, DJ.mov, in the Timeline panel and then choose Edit > Duplicate. A new layer with the same name appears at the top of the stack, so layers 1 and 2 are now both DJ.mov.

2 Select layer 2 and rename it to avoid confusion: Press Enter (Windows) or Return (Mac OS) to make the name editable and type **DJ_with_effects**. Then press Enter or Return again to accept the new name.

3 Select the Kaleidoscope_waveforms layer and make two duplicates. Then, rename the duplicates **kaleidoscope_left** and **kaleidoscope_right**.

Use the keyboard shortcut Ctrl+D (Windows) or Command+D (Mac OS) to duplicate the layers quickly.

4 Drag if necessary to rearrange the layers in the Timeline panel so that they're in the following order:

Adding a radial blur effect

Now you will add an effect—a radial blur—to the DJ. The Radial Blur effect creates blurs around a specific point in a layer, simulating the effects of a zooming or rotating camera.

1 Select the DJ_with_effects layer in the Timeline panel. Notice that layer handles appear around the layer in the Composition panel.

2 In the Effects & Presets panel at the right side of the application window, type **radial blur** in the Contains field. After Effects searches for effects and presets that contain the letters you type, and displays the results interactively. When you type the *B*, the Radial Blur effect, located in the Blur & Sharpen category, appears in the panel.

3 Drag the Radial Blur effect onto the selected layer in the Timeline panel. After Effects applies the effect and automatically opens the Effect Controls panel in the upper-left area of the workspace.

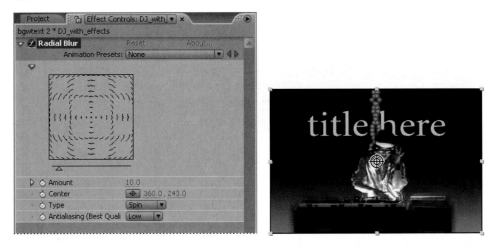

Now, customize the settings.

4 In the Effect Controls panel, choose Type > Zoom.

5 Move the center point of the blur lower by dragging the center cross hair (⊕) down in the Composition panel until it's over the keyboard. Notice that as you drag, the Center value updates in the Effect Controls panel. The left and right values are *x* and *y* coordinates, respectively. Center the blur at approximately 375, 450.

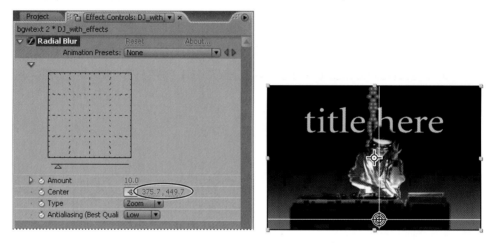

💡 *You can also type the* x *and* y *values directly into the coordinate fields in the Effect Controls panel, or you can position the mouse pointer over the fields so that you can see the pointy-finger icon (👆) and then drag right or left to increase or decrease the values, respectively.*

6 Finally, increase the Amount to **200.0**.

Adding an exposure effect

To punch up the brightness of this layer, you will apply the Exposure color-correction effect. This effect lets you make tonal adjustments to footage and simulates the result of modifying the exposure setting (in f-stops) of the camera that captured the image.

1 Locate the Exposure effect in the Effect & Presets panel by doing one of the following:

• Type **Exposure** in the Contains field.

• Click the triangle next to Color Correction to see a list of color-correction effects in alphabetical order.

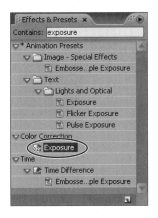

2 Drag the Color Correction Exposure effect onto the DJ_with_effects layer name in the Timeline panel. After Effects adds the Exposure settings to the Effect Controls panel under the Radial Blur effect.

Make sure to select the Color Correction Exposure effect, not the Lights and Optical Exposure effect that is a text animation preset.

3 In the Effect Controls panel, click the downward-pointing triangle next to the Radial Blur effect to hide those settings so that you have a better view of the Exposure settings.

4 For Master Exposure, enter **1.60**. This will boost the highlights in the layer to simulate an overexposed image.

Transforming layer properties

The DJ looks smashing, so now let's turn our attention to the kaleidoscope waveforms that are part of the background. You will reposition the copies you created earlier to create an edgy effect.

1 Select the Kaleidoscope_left layer (layer 5) in the Timeline panel.

2 Click the right-pointing triangle to the left of the layer number, and then click the next right-pointing triangle to open the layer's Transform properties: Anchor Point, Position, Scale, Rotation, and Opacity.

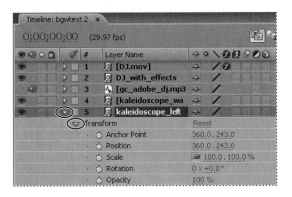

3 If you can't see the properties, scroll down the Timeline panel using the scroll bar at the right side of the panel. Better yet, select the Kaleidoscope_left layer name again and press P. This reveals only the Position property, which is the only property you want to change for this exercise.

With any layer selected in the Timeline panel, you can reveal any single Transform property for it quickly by pressing a keyboard shortcut: For example, P reveals Position, A reveals Anchor Point, S reveals Scale, R reveals Rotation, and T reveals Opacity.

Let's move this layer to the left about 200 pixels.

4   Change the *x* coordinate for the Position property to **160.0**. Leave the *y* coordinate at 243.0.

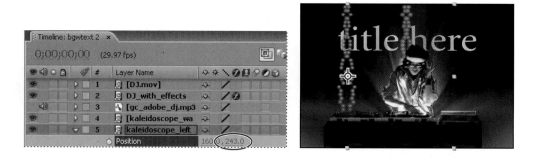

5   Select layer 6, Kaleidoscope_right, and press P to reveal its Position property. You will move this layer to the right.

6   Change the *x* coordinate for the Kaleidoscope_right Position property to **560.0**. Leave the *y* coordinate at 243.0. Now you can see the three waveforms—left, center, and right—in the Composition panel, hanging like a beaded light curtain.

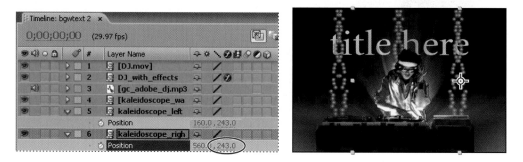

To contrast the left and right waveforms with the center waveform, reduce their opacity.

7 Select the Kaleidoscope_left layer in the Timeline panel and press T to reveal its Opacity property. Set it to **30%**.

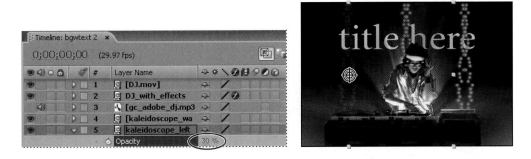

8 Select the Kaleidoscope_right layer in the Timeline panel, press T to reveal its Opacity property, and set it to **30%**.

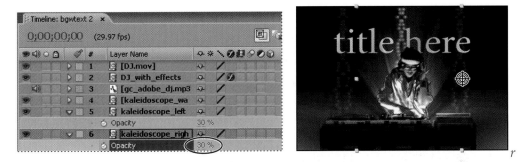

Your composition should now resemble the preceding image.

9 Choose File > Save to save your work so far.

Animating the composition

So far, you've started a project, created a composition, imported footage, and applied some effects. It all looks great, but how about some movement? After all, After Effects is all about motion graphics. So far, you've only applied static effects.

In After Effects, you can make any combination of a layer's properties change over time using conventional keyframing, expressions, or keyframe assistants. You'll explore many of these methods throughout the lessons of this book. For this exercise, you will animate the Position property of a text layer using keyframes, and then use a preset animation so that the letters "rain down" on-screen.

About the Timeline panel

Use the Timeline panel to animate layer properties and set In and Out points for a layer. (In and Out points are the points at which a layer, or footage item, enter and exit the composition.) Many of the Timeline panel controls are organized in columns of related functions. By default, the Timeline panel contains a number of columns and controls, as shown in the following figure:

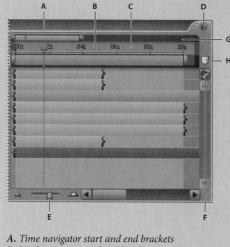

A. *Timeline panel name* **B.** *Current time* **C.** *Switches/Modes column* **D.** *Layer Bar/Graph Editor area*
E. *Audio/Video Switches column* **F.** *Source Name/Layer Name column* **G.** *Timeline panel switches*
H. *Composition button*

The time graph portion of the Timeline panel (the right side) contains a time ruler, markers to indicate specific times, and duration bars for the layers in your composition.

A. *Time navigator start and end brackets*
B. *Work area start and end brackets* **C.** *Time ruler*
D. *Timeline options* **E.** *Zoom slider* **F.** *Comp button*
G. *Navigator view* **H.** *Comp marker bin*

Note: When you click the Graph Editor button ( ), the layer bars in the time ruler switch to the Graph Editor. You'll learn more about the Graph Editor in Lesson 5, "Animating Layers."

Before delving too deeply into animation, it helps to understand at least some of these controls. The duration of a composition, a layer, or a footage item is represented visually in the time ruler. On the time ruler, the current-time indicator indicates the frame you are viewing or editing, and the frame appears in the Composition panel.

The work area start and end brackets indicate the part of the composition that will be rendered or previewed. When you work on a composition, you may want to preview or render only part of a composition. Do this by specifying a part of the composition time ruler as a work area.

A composition's current time appears in the upper-left corner of the Timeline panel. You can go to any time by dragging the current-time indicator in the time ruler or by clicking the current-time field in the Timeline panel or Composition panel, typing a new time, and clicking OK.

For more information about the Timeline panel, see After Effects Help.

Preparing the text composition

For this exercise, you will work in a separate composition.

1 Click the Project panel to bring it forward and then double-click the Bgwtext composition in the Project panel to open it as a composition in its own Timeline panel.

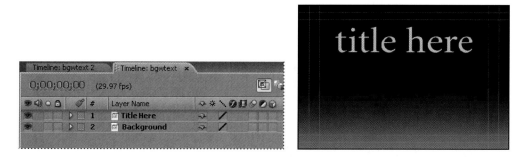

This composition is the imported, layered Photoshop file. The layers, Background and Title Here, appear in the Timeline panel. The Title Here layer contains placeholder text that was created in Photoshop. You must first make the layer editable.

2 Select the Title Here layer (layer 1) in the Timeline panel and then choose Layer > Convert to Editable Text.

Note: If you get a warning about missing fonts, just click OK.

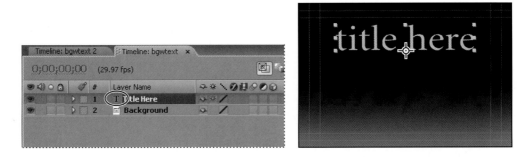

A T icon appears next to the layer name in the Timeline panel, indicating that it is now an editable text layer. The layer is also selected in the Composition panel, ready for you to edit.

Adding the text

You'll start by replacing the placeholder text with real text. Then, you'll animate it.

1 Select the Horizontal Type tool (T) in the Tools panel, and then drag over the placeholder text in the Composition panel to select it. Then, type **Substrate**.

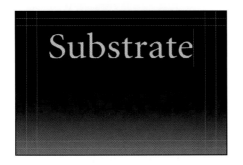

Note: After Effects offers robust character and paragraph formatting controls, but the default settings—whatever typeface appeared when you typed—should be fine for this project. You'll learn more about type in Lesson 3, "Animating Text."

Animating with Position keyframes

Now, you're ready to roll.

1 With the Title Here layer still selected in the Timeline panel, press P to reveal its Position property.

2 Make sure you're at the first frame of the animation by doing one of the following:

• Drag the current-time indicator all the way to the left of the time ruler, to 0:00.

• Press the Home key.

About timecode and duration

The primary concept related to time is duration, or length. Each footage item, layer, and composition in a project has its own duration, which is reflected in the beginning and ending times displayed in the time rulers in the Composition, Layer, and Timeline panels.

The way you view and specify time in After Effects depends on the display style, or unit of measure, that you use to describe time. By default, After Effects displays time in Society of Motion Picture and Television Engineers (SMPTE) timecode: hours, minutes, seconds, and frames. Note that the figures are separated by semicolons in the After Effects interface, but other time display styles (including this book) use a colon.

To learn when and how to change to another system of time display, such as film frames or feet and frames, see After Effects Help.

3 Using the Selection tool (▸), drag the text layer down and off the bottom of the Composition panel, out of the viewing area. Press Shift after you start dragging to constrain the operation to the vertical axis.

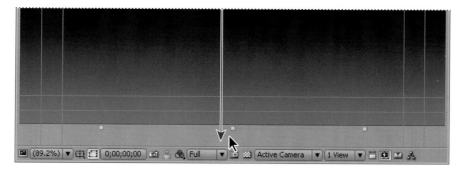

4 Click the stopwatch icon (⏱) for the layer's Position property to create a Position keyframe. Notice that an orange diamond appears in the Position bar for the layer in the time ruler, indicating this new keyframe.

Keyframes are used to create and control animation, effects, audio properties, and many other kinds of change that occur over time. A keyframe marks the point in time where you specify a value, such as spatial position, opacity, or audio volume. Values between keyframes are *interpolated*. When you use keyframes to create a change over time, you must use at least two keyframes—one for the state at the beginning of the change, and one for the state at the end of the change.

5 Go to 3:00 by doing one of the following:

• Drag the current-time indicator to the right in the time ruler so that it's positioned at 3:00.

• Click the Current Time field in the Timeline panel or Composition panel, type **300** (for 3 seconds) in the Go To Time dialog box, and press Enter (Windows) or Return (Mac OS).

Now you can drag the Substrate title to its final on-screen position, but since you dragged it off-screen in step 3, you need to zoom out to grab it.

6 With the Title Here layer still selected in the Timeline panel, select the Zoom tool (🔍) and Alt-click (Windows) or Option-click (Mac OS) to zoom out so that you can see the text layer on the pasteboard of the Composition panel.

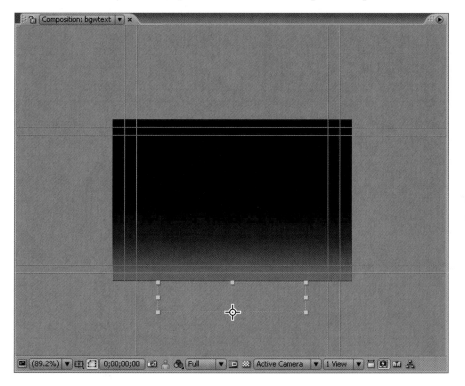

7 Switch back to the Selection tool (▶) and drag the text layer up in the Composition panel, to the top quarter of the viewing area. Press Shift to constrain the drag operation to the vertical axis. Your final Position values should be approximately 359, 158.

💡 *Instead of zooming and dragging, you could also type the values into the text layer's Position fields in the Timeline panel.*

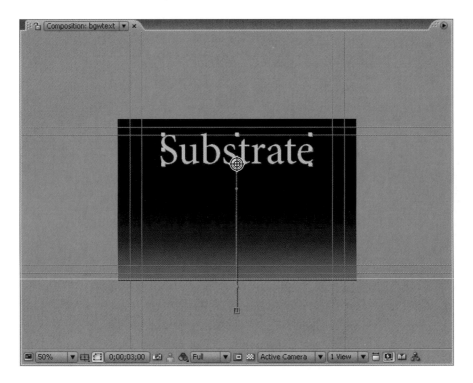

After Effects automatically creates a second keyframe at this position.

8 Zoom back in to the composition by choosing Fit Up To 100% from the Magnification Ratio pop-up menu in the lower-left corner of the Composition panel.

If you're wondering about the blue lines at the top, bottom, and sides of the Composition panel, these indicate title-safe and action-safe zones. Television sets enlarge a video image and allow some portion of its outer edges to be cut off by the edge of the screen. This is known as overscan. The amount of overscan is not consistent between television sets, so you should keep important parts of a video image, such as action or titles, within margins called *safe zones*. Keep your text inside the inner blue guides to ensure that it is in the title-safe zone, and keep important scene elements inside the outer blue guides to ensure that they are in the action-safe zone.

Adding ease in

Even though this is a simple animation, you'll learn good animation practices right away by adding ease-in controls using the Easy Ease feature. Easing into (and out of) animations keeps the motion from being too sudden or robotic.

1 Right-click (Windows) or Control-click (Mac OS) the Position keyframe at 3:00 and choose Keyframe Assistant > Easy Ease In. This makes the text ease to a smooth stop.

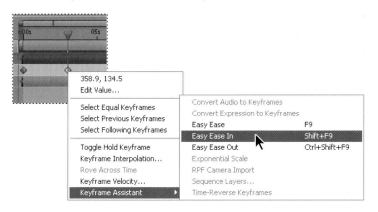

Adding an animation effect

So far, the text is moving on-screen. After it arrives, you don't want it to just sit there, so now apply an animation preset to bring it to life.

1 With the Title Here layer still selected in the Timeline panel, go to 2:10, the point at which the text is almost at its final position. Remember, you can go to the time by dragging the current-time indicator or by clicking the Current Time field in the Timeline panel or Composition panel.

2 In the Effects & Presets panel, type **raining** in the Contains field to quickly locate the Raining Characters animation presets.

3 Drag the Raining Characters Out effect onto the word *Substrate* in the Composition panel to apply it to the text layer.

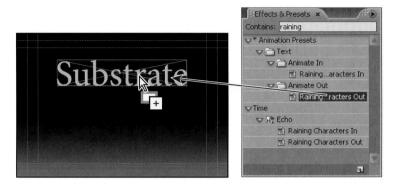

The Effect Controls panel opens for you to customize the effect, but the default settings are fine for this project.

4 Choose File > Save to save your work so far.

Previewing your work

You're probably eager to see the results of your work. After Effects provides several methods for previewing compositions, including standard preview, RAM preview, and manual preview (for a list of manual preview controls, see After Effects Help). All three methods are accessible through the Time Controls panel, which appears on the right side of the application window in the standard workspace.

Using standard preview

Standard preview (commonly called a *spacebar preview*) plays the composition from the current-time indicator to the end of the composition. Standard previews usually play more slowly than real time. They are useful when your composition is simple or in its early stages and doesn't require additional memory for displaying complex animations, effects, 3D layers, cameras, and lights. Let's use it now to preview the text animation.

1 In the Bgwtext Timeline panel, make sure that the video switch (👁) is selected for the layers that you want to preview—the Title Here and Background layers, in this case.

    💡 *Click the pasteboard of the Composition panel if desired to hide the animation vector for this preview.*

2 Press the Home key to go to the beginning of the time ruler.

3 Do one of the following:

- Click the Play/Pause button (▶) in the Time Controls panel.

- Press the spacebar.

4 To stop the standard preview, do one of the following:

- Click the Play/Pause button in the Time Controls panel.

- Press the spacebar.

Using RAM preview

RAM preview allocates enough RAM to play the preview (with audio) as fast as the system allows, up to the frame rate of the composition. Use RAM preview to play footage in the Timeline, Layer, or Footage panel. The number of frames played depends on the amount of RAM available to the application.

In the Timeline panel, RAM preview plays either the span of time you specify as the work area, or from the beginning of the time ruler. In the Layer and Footage panels, RAM preview plays only untrimmed footage. Before you preview, check which frames are designated as the work area.

Let's preview the entire composition—the animated text plus graphic effects—using a RAM preview.

1 Click the Bgwtext 2 Timeline panel to bring it forward.

2 Make sure that the video switch (👁) is turned on for all of the layers in the composition, and deselect all layers.

3 Set the work area to the time span you want to preview: The work area start bracket should be at 0:00, and the work area end bracket should be at 10:00.

4 Drag the current-time indicator to the beginning of the time ruler, or press the Home key.

5 Click the RAM Preview button (▦▶) in the Time Controls panel or choose Composition > Preview > RAM Preview.

A green progress bar indicates as frames are cached to RAM. When all of the frames in the work area are cached, the RAM preview plays back in real time.

You can interrupt the caching process at any time by pressing the spacebar, and the RAM preview will play back just the frames that have been cached to that point.

6 To stop the RAM preview, press the spacebar.

The more detail and precision you want to see, the more RAM is required for RAM preview. You can control the amount of detail shown in either the standard or RAM preview by changing the resolution, magnification, and preview quality of your composition. You can also limit the number of layers previewed by turning off the video switch for certain layers, or limit the number of frames previewed by adjusting the composition's work area.

About OpenGL previews

OpenGL provides high-quality previews that require less rendering time than other playback modes. It provides fast screen previewing of a composition without degrading resolution, which makes it a desirable preview option for many situations. When OpenGL does not support a feature, it simply creates a preview without using that feature. For example, if your layers contain shadows and your OpenGL hardware does not support shadows, the preview will not contain shadows. You can view information about your OpenGL card, if you have one, as well as enable or disable OpenGL, by choosing Edit > Preferences > Previews (Windows) or After Effects > Preferences > Previews (Mac OS). See Getting Started or After Effects Help for more information about OpenGL.

Exporting your composition

When you're finished with your masterpiece—as you are now—you can render it at the quality settings you choose and create movies in the formats that you specify. You will learn more about exporting compositions in subsequent lessons, especially in Lesson 12, "Rendering and Outputting." If you'd like to skip ahead to Lesson 12 and render this project, you're welcome to do so. Otherwise, you can just save it, and we'll continue getting acquainted with the After Effects workspace.

1 Choose File > Save to save your project.

Customizing the workspace

Perhaps in the course of this project, you resized or repositioned some panels, or opened new ones. As you modify the workspace, After Effects saves those modifications, so the next time you open the project, the most recent version of the workspace is used. However, you can choose to restore the original workspace at any time by choosing Window > Workspace > Reset "Standard."

Alternatively, if you find yourself frequently using panels that aren't part of the Standard workspace, or if you like to resize or group panels for different types of projects, you can save time by customizing the workspace to suit your needs. You can save any workspace configuration, or use any of the preset workspaces that come with After Effects. These predefined workspaces are suitable for different types of workflows, such as animation or effects work.

Using predefined workspaces

Let's take a minute to explore the predefined workspaces in After Effects.

Note: If you closed the Lesson01_Finished.aep project at the end of the previous exercise, open it—or any other project—to complete the following exercise.

1 Choose Window > Workspace > Animation. After Effects opens the following panels at the right side of the application window: Info and Audio (grouped), Time Controls, The Smoother, The Wiggler, Motion Sketch, and Effects & Presets.

2 Choose Window > Workspace > Paint. The Paint and Brush Tips panels open and the Composition panel is replaced by the Layer panel, for easy access to the tools and controls you need to paint in your compositions.

Saving a custom workspace

You can save any workspace, at any time, as a custom workspace. Once saved, new and edited workspaces appear in the Window > Workspace submenu. If a project with a custom workspace is opened on a system other than the one on which it was created, After Effects looks for a workspace with a matching name. If After Effects finds a match (and the monitor configuration matches), it uses that workspace; if it can't find a match (or the monitor configuration doesn't match), it opens the project using the current local workspace.

1 Close the Paint and Brush Tips panels by clicking the small *x* next to their panel names.

2 Choose Window > Effects & Presets to open that panel, and then drag it into a group with the Time Controls panel.

3 Choose Window > Workspace > New Workspace. Enter a name for the workspace and click OK to save it, or click Cancel if you don't want to save it.

Controlling the brightness of the user interface

You can brighten or darken the After Effects user interface. Changing the brightness preference affects panels, windows, and dialog boxes.

1 Choose Edit > Preferences > User Interface Colors (Windows) or After Effects > Preferences > User Interface Colors (Mac OS).

2 Drag the User Interface Brightness slider to the left or right and watch the change on-screen.

3 Click Default to restore the default brightness level.

4 Click OK to save the new brightness setting or Cancel to leave your preferences unchanged.

Using After Effects Help

For complete information about using After Effects panels, tools, and other application features, refer to After Effects Help. After Effects Help includes all the topics in the printed user guide, and more. Help topics are updated periodically, so you can always be sure to have the most recent information available.

Note: *A PDF version of the complete Help content, optimized for printing, is also provided on the DVD in the product box.*

After Effects Help is easy to use, because you can look for topics in several ways:

- Scanning the table of contents.

- Jumping to related topics using text links.

- Searching for keywords.

- Using the index.

First you'll look for a topic using the Contents palette.

1 Choose Help > After Effects Help.

Note: *You can also open After Effects Help by pressing F1.*

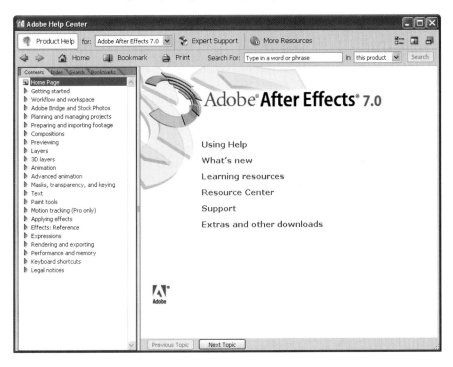

The Adobe Help Center opens, with a navigation pane on the left side of the floating window.

You can return to this location at any time by clicking the Home button (⌂) at the top of the Adobe Help Center window.

The Contents tab of the navigation pane of the Adobe Help Center window lists the contents by topic, like the table of contents of a book.

2 Click the right-pointing triangle to expand the topics 3D Layers > 3D Layers Overview.

3 Select About 3D Layers to read about 3D layers in After Effects.

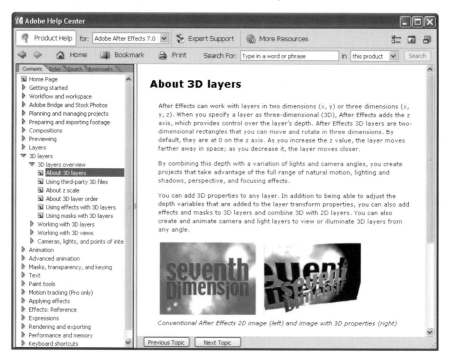

Some Adobe Help Center topics include links to related topics. Links appear as red, underlined text. The mouse pointer changes to a pointing-finger icon (👆) when positioned over a link. You can click any text link to jump to that related topic.

4 Scroll down to the bottom of the About 3D Layers topic, and then click the About Layers text link.

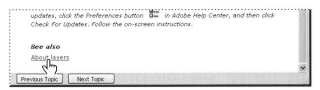

5 Click the Next Topic button a couple of times to see more information about creating layers.

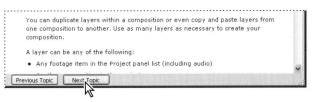

Searching and bookmarking Help topics

You can also search Help topics using words or phrases. In fact, you can search Help for one product or for all Adobe products that are installed on your system. If you find a topic that you may want to view again, you can bookmark it for quick retrieval.

1 At the top of the Adobe Help Center window, type one or more words in the Search For box. For example, type **preset effects**. Leave the In box set to This Product—meaning After Effects. Then, click Search. Topics matching the search words appear in the Search tab of the navigation pane at left, listed in order of relevance.

Note: If you searched multiple products, the results would be grouped by product, then listed in order of relevance.

2 To view a topic, click its title.

3 If this is a topic you think you'll need to return to again, click the Bookmark button () at the top of the window.

4 In the New Bookmark dialog box, accept the default name, and then click OK.

5 Click the Bookmarks tab in the navigation pane to see your bookmark listed there. You can also search for a topic using the index.

6 Click the Index tab of the navigation pane to view an alphabetical list of letters.

7 Click a letter, such as *P,* to display index entries for that letter.

Index entries appear alphabetically by topic and subtopic, like the index of a book. You can scroll down the list to see all the entries that begin with the letter *P*.

8 Click any entry to open the topic about it. If there is more than one entry for a topic, click the triangle to expand visibility for all of the entries, and then click the entry that you want to read.

By default, the Adobe Help Center opens in Full view, which gives access to Product Help, Expert Support, and More Resources. Switch to Compact view by clicking the Compact View button (🖳*) when you want to see only the selected Help topic and to keep the Adobe Help Center window floating on top of the After Effects workspace. Click the Full View button (*🖥*) to return to Full view.*

Checking for updates

Adobe periodically provides updates to software and to topics in Adobe Help Center. You can easily obtain these updates through Adobe Help Center, as long as you have an active Internet connection.

1 Click the Open Preferences Dialog button (▤) in the upper-right corner of the Adobe Help Center.

2 In the Preferences dialog box, notice the Check For Updates button. To check for updates, you would click this button and then follow the on-screen directions to download and save them. For now, however, click Cancel. Then, click Cancel again to close the Preferences dialog box.

3 Choose Adobe Help Center > Close (Windows) or Adobe Help Center > Quit Adobe Help Center (Mac OS).

Using Adobe online services

Another way to get information about After Effects and to stay abreast of updates is to use Adobe online services. If you have an Internet connect and a web browser installed on your system, you can access the Adobe Systems website (www.adobe.com) for information about After Effects and other Adobe products.

1 In After Effects, choose Help > Online Support.

Your default web browser launches and displays the Adobe After Effects Support page on the U.S. Adobe Systems website. You can explore the site and find such information as tips and techniques, galleries of artwork by Adobe designers and artists around the world, the latest product information, and troubleshooting and technical information.

2 Close your browser.

Congratulations. You've finished Lesson 1. Now that you're acquainted with the After Effects workspace, you can go to Lesson 2 to learn how to create and animate compositions using effects and preset animations, or you can proceed to another lesson in this book.

Review

▶ **Review questions**

1 What are the five components of the After Effects workflow?

2 What is a composition?

3 Describe two ways to preview your work in After Effects.

4 How can you customize the After Effects workspace?

▶ **Review answers**

1 Most After Effects workflows involve following these five steps: import and organize footage; create compositions and arrange layers; animate elements and add effects; preview your work; and export the final composition.

2 A composition is where you create all animation, layering, and effects. An After Effects composition has both spatial dimensions and a temporal dimension, called a *duration*, or length in time. Compositions include one or more footage items—video, audio, still images—arranged in the Composition panel and in the Timeline panel. Simple projects may include only one composition, while elaborate projects may include several compositions to organize large amounts of footage or intricate effects sequences.

3 Two ways to preview your work in After Effects are to use a standard preview or a RAM preview. A standard preview plays your composition from the current-time indicator to the end of the composition, usually more slowly than real time. It is useful when your composition is simple or in its early stages and doesn't require additional memory for displaying complex animations or effects. A RAM preview allocates enough RAM to play the preview (with audio) as fast as the system allows, up to the frame rate of the composition.

4 You can customize the After Effects workspace by dragging the panels in the layout that best suits your work style. You can drag panels to new locations, move panels into or out of a group, place panels alongside each other, and undock a panel so that it floats above the application window. As you rearrange panels, the other panels resize automatically to fit the application window. You can save custom workspaces by choosing Window > Workspace > New Workspace.

After Effects lets you hit the ground running with a variety of effects and preset animations. You can use them to create great-looking animations quickly and easily.

2 Creating a Basic Animation Using Effects and Presets

Lesson overview

In this lesson you'll learn how to do the following:

- Use Bridge to preview and import footage items.
- Work with the layers of an imported Illustrator file.
- Apply drop shadow and emboss effects.
- Apply a text animation preset.
- Adjust the time range of a text animation preset.
- Precompose layers.
- Apply a dissolve transition effect.
- Adjust the transparency of a layer.
- Render an animation for broadcast use.
- Export an animation in Flash format for the web.

In this lesson, you will continue to learn the basics of the After Effects project workflow, including learning new ways to accomplish basic tasks and learning how to render a final composition. You will create a simple newscast identification graphic for a fictional TV station, Channel 5. You will animate the newscast ID so that it fades to become a watermark that can appear in the lower-right corner of the screen during other TV programs. Then, you will export the ID for use in broadcast output and in Flash format for the web.

This lesson will take about 1 hour to complete.

Getting started

Make sure the following files are in the AE7_CIB > Lessons > Lesson02 folder on your hard disc, or copy them from the *Adobe After Effects 7.0 Classroom in a Book* DVD now.

- In the Assets folder: 5logo.ai, ggbridge.jpg
- In the Sample_Movie folder: Lesson02.mov

1 Open and play the Lesson02.mov sample movie to see what you will create in this lesson. When you are done, quit the QuickTime player. You may delete this sample movie from your hard disk if you have limited storage space.

Setting up the project

When you begin the lesson, restore the default application settings for After Effects. See "Restoring default preferences," page 5.

1 Press Ctrl+Alt+Shift (Windows) or Command+Option+Shift (Mac OS) while starting After Effects. When asked whether you want to delete your preferences file, click OK.

After Effects opens to display a blank, untitled project.

2 Choose File > Save As or press Ctrl+Shift+S (Windows) or Command+Shift+S (Mac OS).

3 In the Save Project As dialog box, navigate to the AE7_CIB > Lessons > Lesson02 > Finished_Project folder.

4 Name the project **Lesson02_Finished.aep**, and then click Save.

Importing footage using Bridge

In Lesson 1, you learned how to import footage by using the straightforward File > Import > File command. However, After Effects also offers another, more powerful and flexible way to import footage for a composition: using Bridge. You can use Bridge to organize, browse, and locate the assets you need to create content for print, the web, television, DVD, film, and mobile devices. Bridge keeps native Adobe files (such as PSD and PDF files) as well as non-Adobe application files available for easy access. You can drag assets into your layouts, projects, and compositions as needed; preview assets; and even add metadata (file information) to assets to make files easier to locate.

In this exercise, you will jump to Bridge to import the still-image file that will serve as the background of your composition.

1 Choose File > Browse or press Ctrl+Alt+Shift+O (Windows) or Command+ Option+Shift+O (Mac OS).

To open Bridge directly, choose Adobe Bridge from the Start menu (Windows) or double-click the Bridge icon in the Applications > Adobe Bridge folder (Mac OS).

Bridge opens, displaying a collection of panels, menus, and buttons.

2 Using the Folders panel in the upper-left corner of Bridge, navigate to your AE7_CIB > Lessons > Lesson02 > Assets folder. To navigate, click the arrows (Mac OS) or plus signs (Windows) to open nested folders. You can also double-click folder thumbnail icons in the content area on the right side of the Bridge window.

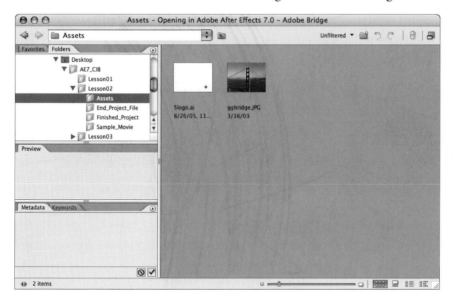

The Bridge content area updates interactively. For example, when you select the Assets folder in the Folders panel at left, thumbnail previews of the folder's contents appear in the content area at right. Bridge displays previews of image files such as those in PSD, TIFF, and JPEG formats, as well as Illustrator vector files, multipage Adobe PDF files, QuickTime movie files, and more.

3 Drag the thumbnail slider at the bottom of the Bridge window to enlarge the thumbnail previews. Optionally, cycle through the various views by clicking the Filmstrip View (⌨) and Details View (⬛≡) buttons. Finally, return to Thumbnails view (⬛⬛).

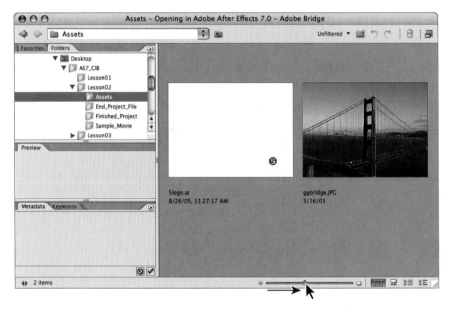

Note: *See After Effects Help to learn more about customizing the Bridge workspace and about using Bridge to search for and manage files.*

4 Select the ggbridge.jpg file in the content area, and notice that it appears in the Preview panel on the left side of the Bridge window. In addition, information about the file, including creation date, bit depth, and file size, appears in the Metadata panel.

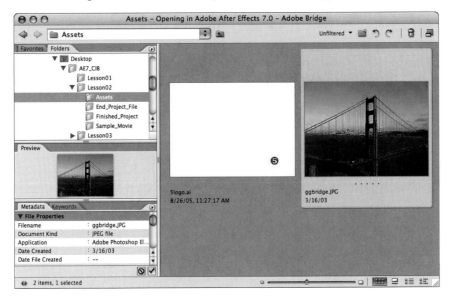

5 To place the ggbridge.jpg file in your After Effects project, do one of the following:

• Right-click (Windows) or Control-click (Mac OS) the ggbridge.jpg thumbnail and choose Place In After Effects from the context menu.

- Drag the thumbnail to the Project panel in After Effects.

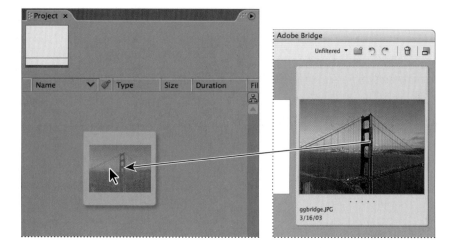

Bridge returns you to After Effects when you place the file. Leave Bridge running in the background for now.

Creating the composition

Remembering the workflow you learned in Lesson 1, the next step to building the TV news ID is to create a new composition. In Lesson 1, you created the composition based on footage items that were selected in the Project panel. You can also create an empty composition, and then add your footage items to it.

1 Create a new composition by doing one of the following:

- Click the Create A New Composition button (⊞) at the bottom of the Project panel.

- Choose Composition > New Composition.

- Press Ctrl+N (Windows) or Command+N (Mac OS).

2 In the Composition Settings dialog box, do the following:

• Name the composition **Channel_5_News**.

• Choose NTSC D1 from the Preset pop-up menu. NTSC D1 is the resolution for standard-definition television in the United States and some other countries. This preset automatically sets the width, height, pixel aspect ratio, and frame rate for the composition to NTSC standards.

• In the Duration field, type **300** to specify 3 seconds.

• Click OK.

After Effects displays an empty composition named Channel_5_News in the Composition panel and in the Timeline panel. Now, add the background to it.

3 Drag the ggbridge.jpg file from the Project panel to the Timeline panel to add it to the Channel_5_News composition.

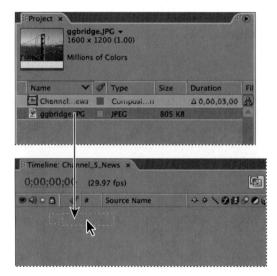

4 Make sure the Ggbridge layer is selected in the Timeline panel and then choose Layer > Transform > Fit To Comp to scale the background image to the dimensions of the composition.

The keyboard shortcut for fitting a layer to a composition is Ctrl+Alt+F (Windows) or Command+Option+F (Mac OS).

Importing the foreground element

Your background is in place. Now you will add the foreground object, which is a layered vector graphic that was created in Illustrator.

1 Press Ctrl+Alt+Shift+O (Windows) or Command+Option+Shift+O (Mac OS) to jump to Bridge.

2 Select the 5logo.ai file in the AE7_CIB > Lessons > Lesson02 > Assets folder and drag it to the After Effects Project panel.

3 In the 5logo.ai dialog box that appears, choose Import Kind > Composition and Footage Dimensions > Layer Size. This imports the layers in the Illustrator file with their original dimensions, which makes them easier to manipulate and speeds their rendering.

4 Click OK.

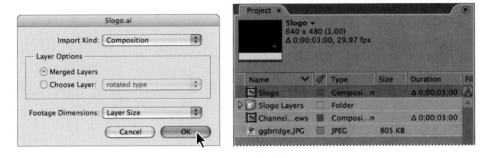

The Illustrator file is added to the Project panel as a composition named 5logo. A folder named 5logo Layers also appears. This folder contains the three individual layers of the Illustrator file. You can click the triangle to open the folder and see the contents if you'd like.

5 Drag the 5logo composition file from the Project panel into Timeline panel above the Ggbridge layer.

You should now see both the background image and the logo in the Composition panel and in the Timeline panel.

Note: You can close Bridge now if you'd like. You won't be using it again during this lesson.

Working with imported Illustrator layers

The Channel 5 logo graphic was created in Illustrator; your job in After Effects is to add text and animate it for the station's newscast. To work with the layers of the Illustrator file independently of the background footage, you will open the 5logo composition in its own Timeline and Composition panels.

1 Double-click the 5logo composition in the Project panel to open it in its own Timeline and Composition panels.

2 Select the Horizontal Type tool (T) in the Tools panel and click in the Composition panel to the left of the Channel 5 logo.

3 Type **NEWS**, all capitals, and then select all of the text you just entered.

4 Choose Window > Character to display the Character panel.

5 In the Character panel, make sure you're using a sans serif typeface such as Myriad Pro and that the Font Size is set to **30** pixels. Leave all other options in the Character panel at their defaults.

6 Choose Window > Paragraph to display the Paragraph panel.

7 Click the Right Align Text button (≣). Leave all other options in the Paragraph panel at their defaults.

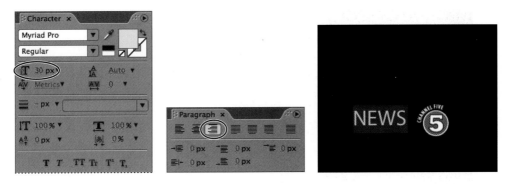

Note: You will learn more about setting type options in Lesson 3, "Animating Text."

8 Switch to the Selection tool (▶) and drag to position the text in the Composition panel so that it looks like the following figure. Notice that when you switch to the Selection tool, the generic Text 1 layer name in the Timeline panel changes to the text you typed, News.

> 💡 *Choose View > Show Grid to make the nonprinting grid visible to help your positioning. Choose View > Hide Grid when you're done.*

Applying effects to a layer

Now you will return to the main composition, Channel_5_News, and apply an effect to the 5logo layer. This will apply the effect to all of the layers nested in the 5logo composition.

Applying and controlling effects

You can apply or remove an effect at any time. Once you've applied effects to a layer, you can temporarily turn off one or all the effects in the layer to concentrate on another aspect of your composition. Effects that are turned off do not appear in the Composition panel and typically are not included when the layer is previewed or rendered.

By default, when you apply an effect to a layer, the effect is active for the duration of the layer. However, you can make an effect start and stop at specific times, or make the effect more or less intense over time, by using keyframes or expressions, which you'll learn more about in Lesson 4, "Animating a Multimedia Presentation," and Lesson 5, "Animating Layers."

You can apply and edit effects on adjustment layers just as you do to other layers. However, when you apply an effect to an adjustment layer, the effect is applied to all layers below it in the Timeline panel.

Effects can also be saved, browsed, and applied as animation presets.

1 Switch to the Channel_5_News Timeline panel and select the 5logo layer. The effect you create next will be applied only to the logo elements, and not to the Golden Gate Bridge background image.

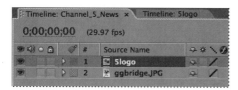

2 Choose Effect > Perspective > Drop Shadow. A soft-edged shadow appears behind the nested layers of the 5logo layer—the logo graphic, the rotated type, and the word *news*—in the Composition panel.

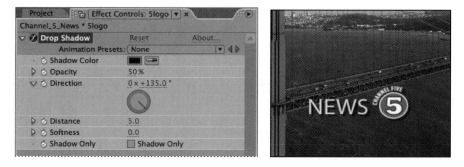

You can customize the effect using the Effect Controls panel, which appears over the Project panel when you apply an effect.

3 In the Effect Controls panel, reduce the drop shadow's Distance to **3.0** and increase its Softness to **4.0**. Remember, you can set these values by clicking the field and typing the number, or by dragging the blue, underlined value.

It's a nice effect, but the logo will stand out even more if you apply an emboss effect. In addition to using the Effect menu to locate effects, you can use the Effects & Presets panel.

4 Make sure the 5logo layer is selected in the Channel_5_News Timeline panel, and then open the Stylize category in the Effects & Presets panel.

5 Drag the Color Emboss effect into the Composition panel. The Color Emboss effect sharpens the edges of objects in the layer without suppressing the original colors. The Effect Controls panel displays the Color Emboss effect below the Drop Shadow effect.

6 Choose File > Save to save your work.

Applying a preset animation

Now that you've positioned the news logo and applied some effects to it, it's time to do some animation. You will learn several ways to animate text in Lesson 3. For now, you'll use a simple animation preset that will fade the word *news* onto the screen next to the Channel 5 logo. This means that you need to work again in the 5logo composition so that you can apply the animation to only the News text layer.

1 Switch to the 5logo Timeline panel and select the News layer.

2 Go to 1:10, which is when you want the text to start fading in.

3 In the Effects & Presets panel, navigate to Animation Presets > Text > Blurs, and then drag the Bullet Train animation preset onto the News layer in the Timeline panel or in the Composition panel. The text disappears in the Composition panel, but don't worry: You're looking at the first frame of the animation, which happens to be blank.

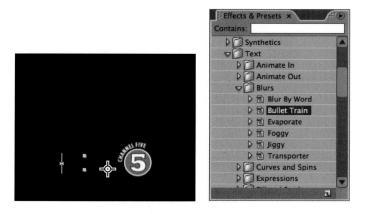

4 Drag the current-time indicator to 2:10 to manually preview the text animation. The text speeds in, letter by letter, until the word *news* is fully on-screen at 2:10.

Precomposing layers for a new animation

The news ID is coming along nicely, and you're probably eager to preview the complete animation. Before you do, however, let's add one more effect (a dissolve) to all of the logo elements except to the word *news*. To do this, you need to precompose the other three layers of the 5logo composition: Rotated Type, 5 Logo, and Crop Area.

Precomposing is a way to nest layers within a composition. Precomposing moves the layers to a new composition. This new composition takes the place of the selected layers—something that does not occur in ordinary nesting. When you want to change the order in which layer components are rendered, precomposing is a quick way to create intermediate levels of nesting in an existing hierarchy.

1 Shift-click to select the Rotated Type, 5 Logo, and Crop Area layers in the 5logo Timeline panel.

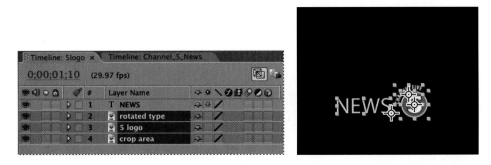

2 Choose Layer > Pre-Compose or press Ctrl+Shift+C (Windows) or Command+Shift+C (Mac OS).

3 In the Pre-Compose dialog box, name the new composition **dissolve_logo** and make sure the Move All Attributes Into The New Composition option is selected. Then, click OK.

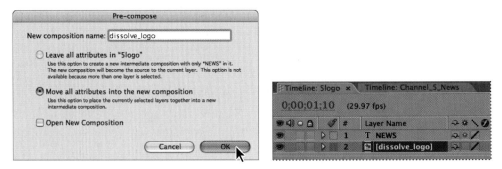

The three layers are replaced in the 5logo Timeline panel with a single layer, Dissolve_ logo. This new, precomposed layer contains the three layers that you selected in step 1, and you can apply the dissolve effect to it without affecting the News text layer and its Bullet Train animation.

4 Make sure the Dissolve_logo layer is selected in Timeline panel and press the Home key to go to 0:00.

5 In the Effects & Presets panel, open the Animation Presets > Transition – Dissolves category and drag the Dissolve – Vapor animation preset onto the Dissolve_logo layer in the Timeline panel or in the Composition panel.

💡 *You can locate the vapor dissolve preset quickly by typing **vap** in the Contains field of the Effects & Presets panel.*

The Dissolve – Vapor animation preset includes three components—a master dissolve, a box blur, and a solid composite—all of which appear in the Effect Controls panel. The default settings are fine for this project.

6 Choose File > Save.

Previewing the effects

It's time to preview all of the effects together.

1 Switch to the Channel_5_News Timeline panel and press the Home key to make sure you're at the beginning of the time ruler.

2 Make sure the Video switch (👁) is selected for both layers of the Channel_5_News Timeline panel.

3 Click the Play button (▶) in the Time Controls panel or press the spacebar to watch the preview. Press the spacebar to stop playback at any time.

Adding transparency

The effects and preset animation make the news ID look great, but there's one more task to complete. You will add some transparency so that the ID can be viewed subtly in the lower-right corner of the TV screen, as many TV stations display logos to emphasize their brand. You can do this easily in After Effects by adjusting the opacity.

1 Still in the Channel_5_News Timeline panel, go to 2:24.

2 Select the 5logo layer and press T to display its Opacity property. By default, the Opacity is 100%—fully opaque. Click the stopwatch icon (⌚) to set an Opacity keyframe at this location.

3 Press the End key to go to the end of the time ruler (2:29) and change the Opacity to **40%**. After Effects adds a keyframe.

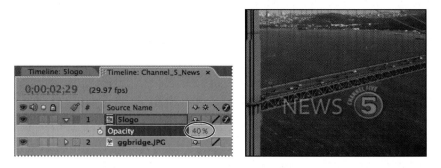

Now, the logo appears on-screen, the word *news* flies in, and it all fades to 40% opacity.

4 Watch a preview of your composition by clicking the Play button in the Time Controls panel, by pressing the spacebar, or by pressing 0 on your numeric keypad. Press the spacebar to stop playback when you're done.

5 Choose File > Save to save your project.

Rendering the composition

Finally, you're ready to prepare your Channel 5 news ID for output. When you create output, the layers of a composition and each layer's masks, effects, and properties are rendered frame by frame into one or more output files or, in the case of a sequence, into a series of consecutive files.

Making a movie from your final composition can take a few minutes or many hours, depending on the composition's frame size, quality, complexity, and compression method. When you place your composition in the render queue, it becomes a render item that uses the render settings assigned to it. As After Effects renders the item, you are unable to work in the program.

After Effects provides a variety of formats and compression types for rendering output; the format you choose depends on the medium from which you'll play your final output or on the requirements of your hardware, such as a video-editing system. You will prepare this animation for two formats so that it can be used for broadcast purposes as well as on the World Wide Web.

Note: For more about output formats and rendering, see Lesson 12, "Rendering and Outputting."

Rendering broadcast-quality output

You'll start by rendering the composition so that it can be used on the air.

1 Do one of the following to add the composition to the render queue:

• Select the Channel_5_News composition in the Project panel, and then choose Composition > Add to Render Queue. The Render Queue panel opens automatically.

• Choose Window > Render Queue to open the Render Queue panel, and then drag the Channel_5_News composition from the Project panel onto the Render Queue panel.

2 Choose Maximize Frame from the Render Queue panel menu so that the panel fills the application window.

3 Click the triangle to expand the Render Settings options. By default, After Effects renders compositions at the Best Quality and Full Resolution. The default settings are fine for this project.

4 Click the triangle to expand the Output Module options. By default, After Effects renders a lossless movie, which is fine for this project. However, you need to identify where to save the file.

5 Click the blue, underlined words *Not Yet Specified* next to the Output To pop-up menu.

6 In the Output Movie To dialog box, accept the default movie name (Channel_5_News), select the AE7_CIB > Lessons > Lesson02 > Finished_Project folder for the location, and then click Save.

7 Back in the Render Queue panel, click the Render button. After Effects displays a progress bar in the Render Queue panel as it renders the file.

After Effects provides an audio alert when the render is complete.

8 When the render is complete, choose Restore Frame Size from the Render Queue panel menu to restore your workspace.

Exporting a composition for the web

The production manager at Channel 5 wants to use this news ID on the station's website, as well as on TV. For that, you need to export the composition in Macromedia Flash (SWF) format. The SWF format is a widely used vector graphics and animation format for the web. It is a compact, binary format that can contain audio and vector objects. web browsers with the Flash Player plug-in can play SWF files.

Before exporting to Flash, you need adjust the composition a bit for online display.

1 Select the Channel_5_News composition in the Project panel, and then choose Composition > Composition Settings.

2 In the Basic tab of the Composition Settings dialog box, choose Preset > Web Video, 320 x 240, and then click OK.

After Effects applies the new web-appropriate resolution—320 x 240 pixels—to the composition. As a result, both the background and 5logo layers are about twice as big as the composition, which is smaller than it was originally, has a different aspect ratio, and has a different frame rate (15 fps). So you need to reposition and resize the layers for the new output medium, including centering the logo in the composition.

3 Select the Ggbridge layer in the Channel_5_News Timeline panel and press Ctrl+Alt+F (Windows) or Command+Option+F (Mac OS) to fit the layer to the composition size.

4 Go to 2:12, which is when the logo starts to fade at the new frame rate.

5 Select the 5logo layer in the Timeline panel, and then press P to reveal its Position property.

6 Change the Position values to **–4.4, –26.1** to center the logo in the composition.

Now, you're ready to export the composition to Flash format.

7 With the Channel_5_News composition selected in the Project panel, choose File > Export > Macromedia Flash (SWF).

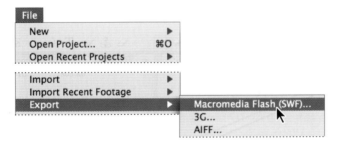

Note: After Effects also offers the File > Export > Flash Video (FLV) command, which allows you to create video content that can be published online and viewed using Flash Player on a wide variety of operating systems.

8 In the Save File As dialog box, accept the default filename (Channel_5_News.swf), select the AE7_CIB > Lessons > Lesson02 > Finished_Project folder for the location, and then click Save.

9 In the SWF Settings dialog box, set JPEG Quality to Medium. This preserves image quality nicely but also reduces the file size somewhat. Leave all other settings at their defaults, and then click OK.

After Effects displays a progress bar as it exports the file to Flash format.

Note: After Effects exports text layers to SWF as vector graphics. Some layer types and layer switches are not supported, such as 3D Layers, 3D Cameras, and 3D Lights. Nested layers are rasterized. For more on SWF export, see After Effects Help.

After Effects exports the composition to SWF and also saves a report in HTML to the same folder as the SWF file.

10 In the Finder, go to the AE7_CIB > Lessons > Lesson02 > Finished_Project folder.

11 Double-click the HTML file to open it in your default web browser, and preview the Flash file by clicking the link on the page. This Flash animation could be used as part of a splash screen on the TV station's website, or as part of an ad, for example.

Congratulations. You've created a broadcast news show ID and watermark. You'll use this ID again in Lessons 6 and 7, when you will learn to use masks and to perform keying.

Review

▶ **Review questions**

1 How do you use Bridge to preview and import files?

2 What is *precomposing*?

3 How do you customize an effect?

4 How do you modify the transparency of a layer in a composition?

▶ **Review answers**

1 Choose File > Browse or use the keyboard shortcuts Ctrl+Alt+Shift+O (Windows) or Command+Option+Shift+O (Mac OS) to jump from After Effects to Bridge, where you can search for and preview image assets. When you locate the asset you want to use in an After Effects project, drag it to the Project panel or right-click (Windows) or Control-click (Mac OS) and choose Place In After Effects from the contextual menu.

2 *Precomposing* is a way to nest layers within a composition. Precomposing moves the layers to a new composition. This new composition takes the place of the selected layers—something that does not occur in ordinary nesting. When you want to change the order in which layer components are rendered, precomposing is a quick way to create intermediate levels of nesting in an existing hierarchy.

3 After you apply an effect to a layer in a composition, you can customize its properties in the Effect Controls panel. This panel opens automatically when you apply the effect, or you can open it at any time by selecting the layer with the effect and choosing Window > Effect Controls.

4 To modify the transparency of a layer, you can reduce its opacity. Select the layer in the Timeline panel, press T to reveal its Opacity property, and enter a value lower than 100%.

Your type doesn't need to sit still while your audience is reading it. In this lesson, you'll learn several ways to animate type in After Effects, including using time-saving methods unique to text layers.

3 Animating Text

Lesson overview

In this lesson, you'll learn to do the following:

- Create and animate text layers.
- Stylize text using the Character and Paragraph panels.
- Animate text using presets.
- Preview animation presets in Bridge.
- Customize an animation preset.
- Animate text using keyframes.
- Animate layers using parenting.
- Edit and animate imported Photoshop text.
- Use a text animator group to animate selected characters on a layer.
- Apply a text animation to a graphic object.

After Effects offers many ways to animate text. You can animate text layers by manually creating keyframes in the Timeline panel, by using animation presets, or by using expressions. You can even animate individual characters or words in a text layer. This lesson takes you through several different animation techniques, including some that are unique to text, while you design the opening title credits for an animated documentary called *The Pond*.

This lesson will take 1½ to 2 hours to complete.

Getting started

Make sure the following files are in the AE7_CIB > Lessons > Lesson03 folder on your hard disk, or copy them from the *Adobe After Effects 7.0 Classroom in a Book* DVD now:

- In the Assets folder: credits.psd, dragonfly.ai, Lilypad.mov, pondbackground.mov

- In the Sample_Movie folder: Lesson03.mov

1 Open and play the Lesson03.mov sample movie to see what you will create in this lesson. When you are done, quit the QuickTime player. You may delete this sample movie from your hard disk if you have limited storage space.

Setting up the project

When you begin this lesson, restore the default application settings for After Effects. See "Restoring default preferences," page 5.

1 Press Ctrl+Alt+Shift (Windows) or Command+Option+Shift (Mac OS) while starting After Effects. When asked whether you want to delete your preferences file, click OK.

After Effects opens to display a blank, untitled project.

2 Choose File > Save As or press Ctrl+Shift+S (Windows) or Command+Shift+S (Mac OS).

3 In the Save Project As dialog box, navigate to the AE7_CIB > Lessons > Lesson03 > Finished_Project folder.

4 Name the project **Lesson03_Finished.aep**, and then click Save.

Importing the footage

You need to import two footage items to begin this exercise.

1 Double-click an empty area of the Project panel to open the Import File dialog box.

2 Navigate to the AE7_CIB > Lessons > Lesson03 > Assets folder on your hard disk, Ctrl-click (Windows) or Command-click (Mac OS) to select the Lilypad.mov and pondbackground.mov files, and then click Open.

Creating the composition

Now, you'll create the composition.

1 Press Ctrl+N or Command+N to open the New Composition dialog box.

2 In the Composition Settings dialog box, name the composition **Pond_Title_Sequence**, make sure the NTSC DV preset is selected, and set duration to **10:00**, which is the length of the pond background movie.

3 Click OK.

4 Drag the Pondbackground.mov and Lilypad.mov files from the Project panel to the Timeline panel, making sure that Lilypad is above Pondbackground in the layer stack.

Now, position the Lilypad layer in the composition.

5 With the Lilypad layer selected in the Timeline panel, press the P key reveals its Position property.

6 Change the Position values to **170.0, 480.0** to move the lily pad to the lower-left corner of the composition.

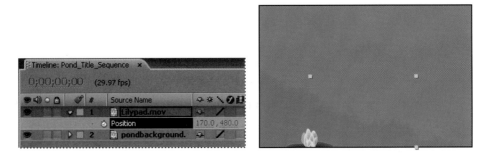

7 Select the Lilypad layer again and press U to hide its Position property, and then choose File > Save.

Now you're ready to add the title text to the composition.

About text layers

With After Effects, you can add text to layers with flexibility and precision. You can create and edit text directly on-screen in the Composition panel and quickly change the font, style, size, and color of the text. You can apply changes to individual characters and set formatting options for entire paragraphs, including alignment, justification, and word wrapping. In addition to all of these style features, After Effects provides tools for easily animating specific characters and features, such as text opacity and hue.

After Effects provides a wide range of text controls accessible through the Tools, Character, and Paragraph panels. You can add horizontal or vertical text anywhere in a composition. After Effects uses two types of text: point text and paragraph text. Point text is useful for entering a single word or a line of characters; paragraph text is useful for entering and formatting the text as one or more paragraphs.

In many ways, text layers are just like any other layer in After Effects. You can apply effects and expressions to text layers, animate them, designate them as 3D layers, and edit the 3D text while viewing it in multiple views. As with layers imported from Illustrator, text layers are continuously rasterized, so when you scale the layer or resize the text, it retains crisp, resolution-independent edges. The main differences between text layers and other layers are that you cannot open a text layer in its own Layer panel, and that you can animate the text in a text layer using special text animator properties and selectors.

Creating and formatting point type

When you enter point text, each line of text is independent—the length of a line increases or decreases as you edit the text, but it doesn't wrap to the next line. The text you enter appears in a new text layer. The small line through the I-beam marks the position of the text baseline.

1 In the Tools panel, select the Horizontal Type tool (**T**).

2 Click anywhere in the Composition panel and type **the Pond**. Then, press Enter on the numeric keypad to exit text-editing mode and to select the text layer in the Composition panel.

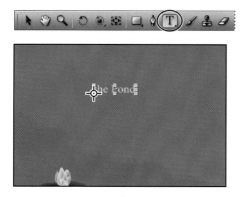

Note: If you press Enter (Windows) or Return (Mac OS) on the regular keyboard instead of on the numeric keypad, you'll begin a new paragraph.

*You can also select another tool, such as the Selection tool (*k*), to exit text-editing mode.*

Now, you can format the text.

Using the Character panel

The Character panel provides options for formatting characters. If text is highlighted, changes you make in the Character panel affect only the highlighted text. If no text is highlighted, changes you make in the Character panel affect the selected text layers and the text layers' selected Source Text keyframes, if any exist. If no text is highlighted and no text layers are selected, the changes you make in the Character panel become the new defaults for the next text entry.

1 Choose Window > Workspace > Text to open the Character and Paragraph panels and to close the Info and Audio panels, which you don't need right now.

💡 *To open the panels individually, you can choose Window > Character or press Ctrl+6 (Windows) or Command+6 (Mac OS) to open the Character panel; and choose Window > Paragraph or press Ctrl+7 (Windows) or Command+7 (Mac OS) to open the Paragraph panel. To open both panels, select the Horizontal Type tool and then click the Toggle The Character And Paragraph Panels button in the Tools panel.*

2 In the Character panel, click the arrow to the right of the font name to see a pop-up menu of available fonts.

3 Choose Myriad Pro from the Font Family pop-up menu. If you don't have Myriad Pro, then choose another heavy sans serif typeface, such as Verdana.

💡 *Select the font name in the Font Family pop-up menu, and then press any letter on the keyboard, such as C. The Font Family menu jumps to the first font on your system that starts with that letter, and the text in the Composition panel takes on the newly selected font.*

4 Make the Font Size **72** pixels.

5 Set the Font Style to Bold or click the Faux Bold button (**T**) in the lower-left corner of the panel. If you can't see the Faux Bold button, expand the Character panel by dragging its bottom edge downward.

6 Leave all other options at their default settings.

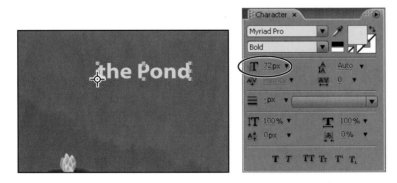

Using the Paragraph panel

You use the Paragraph panel to set options that apply to entire paragraphs, such as the alignment, indentation, and leading. For point text, each line is a separate paragraph. You can use the Paragraph panel to set formatting options for a single paragraph, multiple paragraphs, or all paragraphs in a text layer. You just need to make one adjustment in the Paragraph panel for this composition's title text.

1   In the Paragraph panel, click the Center Text button (≣). This aligns horizontal text to the center of the layer, not to the center of the composition.

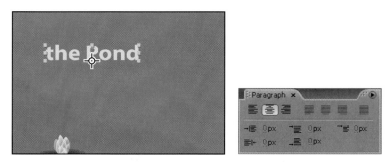

Positioning the type

To precisely position layers, such as the text layer you're working on now, you can display rulers in the Composition panel and use guides and grids for visual reference without having them appear in the final rendered movie.

1   Select the The Pond text layer in the Timeline panel.

2   Choose Layer > Transform > Fit To Comp Width. This scales the layer to fit it to the width of the composition.

Now, you can position the text layer using a grid.

3 Choose View > Show Grid and then View > Snap to Grid.

4 Using the Selection tool (↖), drag the text vertically in the Composition panel until the base of the letters sits on the horizontal grid line in the center of the composition. Press Shift after you start dragging to constrain the movement and help you position the text.

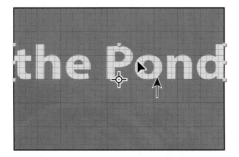

5 When the layer is in position, choose View > Hide Grid to turn off visibility of the grid.

This project isn't destined for broadcast TV, so it's OK that the title and the lily pad extend beyond the title-safe and action-safe areas of the composition at the beginning of the animation.

6 Choose Window > Workspace > Standard to close the Character and Paragraph panels, which you don't need for the next exercise, and then Choose File > Save to save your project.

Using a text animation preset

Now you're ready to animate the title. The easiest way to do that is to use one of the many animation presets that come with After Effects. After applying an animation preset, you can customize it and save it to use again in other projects.

1 Press the Home key to make sure the current-time indicator is at the beginning of the time ruler. After Effects applies animation presets from the current time.

2 Select the The Pond text layer.

Browsing presets

You already applied an animation preset in Lesson 2, "Creating a Basic Animation Using Effects and Presets," and you learned to find effects and presets in the Effects & Presets panel. But what if you're not sure which preset you want to use? To help you choose the right animation preset for your projects, you can preview them in Bridge.

1 Choose Animation > Browse Presets. Bridge opens and displays the contents of the After Effects Presets folder.

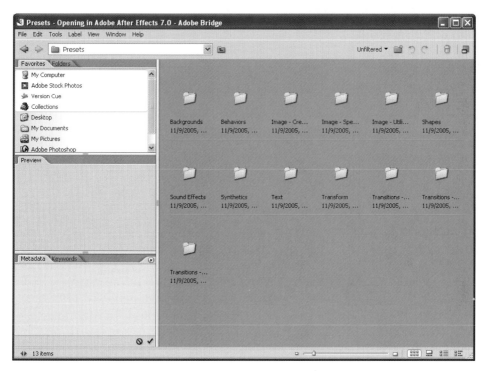

💡 *You can also preview—but not apply—animation presets by choosing Help > Animation Preset Gallery.*

2 In the content area, double-click the Text folder, and then the Blurs folder.

3 Click to select the first preset, Blur By Word. Bridge plays a sample of the animation in the Preview panel.

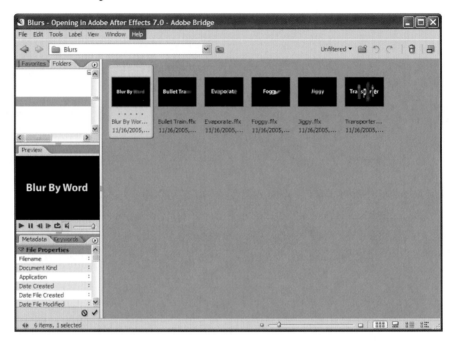

4 Select a few other presets and watch them in the Preview panel.

5 Preview the Evaporate preset and then double-click its thumbnail preview or right-click (Windows) or Control-click (Mac OS) and choose Place In After Effects. After Effects applies the preset to the currently selected layer, which is the The Pond layer.

Nothing appears to change in the composition. This is because at 0:00, the first frame of the animation, the letters haven't evaporated yet.

Note: Leave Bridge open in the background. You'll use it again later in the lesson.

Previewing a range of frames

Now, preview the animation. Although the composition is 10 seconds long, you only need to preview the first few seconds when the text is animated.

1 Drag the work area end bracket from the right side of the time ruler panel to 3:00 to preview the first 3 seconds of the clip.

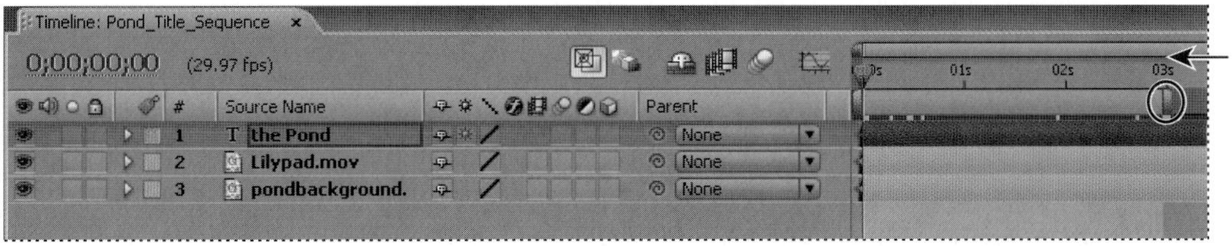

2 Press 0 on the numeric keypad or click the RAM Preview button (▮▮▶) in the Time Controls panel to watch a RAM preview of the animation.. The letters appear to evaporate into the background. It looks great—but you want the letters to fade in and remain on-screen, not disappear into the murky depths of the pond. So you will customize the preset to suit your needs.

3 Press the spacebar to stop the preview, and then press the Home key to make sure the current-time indicator is back at 0:00.

Customizing an animation preset

After you apply an animation preset to a layer, all of its properties and keyframes are at your fingertips in the Timeline panel.

1 Select the The Pond text layer in the Timeline panel and choose Animation > Reveal Modified Properties, or press UU. After Effects reveals all of the properties that were modified by the Evaporate preset.

2 Click the Offset property name to select both of its keyframes. The Offset property lets you specify how much to offset the start and end of the selection.

3 Choose Animation > Keyframe Assistant > Time-Reverse Keyframes. This switches the order of the two Offset keyframes so that the letters are invisible at the beginning of the composition, and then emerge into view.

4 Drag the current-time indicator from 0:00 to 3:00 to manually preview the edited animation. Much better. The letters now fade in to rather than disappear from the composition.

5 Click the arrow in the Label column for the The Pond layer (or select the layer and press U) to hide its properties.

6 Drag the work area end bracket to the end of the time ruler, and then choose File > Save to save your project.

Animating with scale keyframes

The The Pond text layer was scaled to more than 200% when you applied the Fit To Comp command to it earlier in this lesson. Now, you'll animate the layer's scale so that the type gradually shrinks down to its original size.

1 Make sure the The Pond layer is selected in the Timeline panel.

2 Go to 3:00.

Soloing a layer

You can isolate one or more layers for animating, previewing, or rendering by *soloing*. Soloing excludes all other layers of the same type from the Composition panel. Soloing is useful for speeding up refreshing, previewing, and rendering for final output. You'll solo the The Pond layer now as you animate its scale.

1 Click the Solo box in the Switches column for the The Pond layer in the Timeline panel.

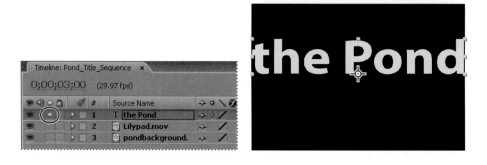

Creating the scale keyframes

Now, you're ready to animate the title using good old-fashioned Scale keyframes.

1 With the The Pond text layer selected in the Timeline panel, press the S key to reveal its Scale property.

2 Click the stopwatch icon (⏱) to add a Scale keyframe at the current time, 3:00.

3 Go to 5:00.

4 Reduce the layer's Scale values to **100.0, 100.0%**. After Effects adds a new Scale keyframe at the current time.

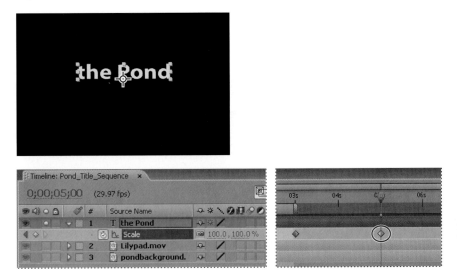

Previewing the scale animation

Now, preview the change.

1 Drag the work area end bracket to approximately 5:10, shortly after the scale animation ends.

2 Click the Solo icon (◉) to unsolo the The Pond layer.

3 Press the 0 key on the numeric keypad to watch a RAM preview of the animation from 0:00 to 5:10. The movie title fades in and then scales to a smaller size.

4 Press the spacebar when you're ready to stop the preview.

💡 *After Effects includes some scale text preset animations, with which you can experiment. They're located in the Presets > Text > Scale folder.*

Adding Easy Ease

The beginning and end of the scale animation are rather abrupt. In nature, nothing comes to an absolute stop. Instead, objects ease into and out of starting and stopping points.

1 Right-click (Windows) or Control-click (Mac OS) the Scale keyframe at 3:00 and choose Keyframe Assistant > Easy Ease Out. Notice the keyframe diamond changes to a left-pointing icon.

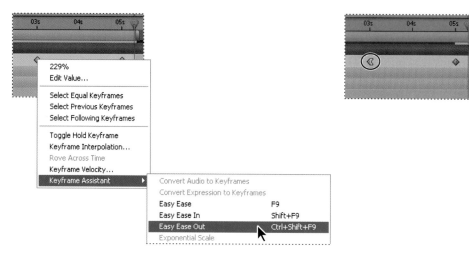

3 Right-click (Windows) or Control-click (Mac OS) the Scale keyframe at 5:00 and choose Keyframe Assistant > Easy Ease In. This keyframe diamond changes to a right-pointing icon.

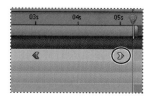

4 Press the 0 key on the numeric keypad to watch another RAM preview. Much better!

5 Press the spacebar when you're done watching the preview, and then select the The Pond layer in the Timeline panel and press S to hide its Scale property.

6 Choose File > Save.

Animating using parenting

The next task is to make it to appear as if the virtual camera is zooming away from the composition. The text scale animation you just applied gets you halfway there; you have to animate the lily pad's scale, as well. You could manually animate the Lilypad layer, but an easier way would be to take advantage of parenting relationships in After Effects so that you don't have to animate the lily pad independently.

1 Press the Home key to go to the beginning of the time ruler.

2 In the Timeline panel, choose 1. The Pond from the Parent pop-up menu for the Lilypad layer. This sets the The Pond text layer as the parent of the Lilypad layer, which in turn becomes the child layer.

As the child layer, the Lilypad layer inherits the Scale keyframes of the The Pond (parent) layer. Not only is this a quick way to animate the lily pad, but it also ensures that the lily pad scales at the same rate and by the same amount as the text layer.

Now, preview again.

4 Press 0 on the numeric keypad to watch a RAM preview of the animation. Between 3:00 and 5:00, both the text and the lily pad scale down in size, making it seem like the camera is zooming away from the scene.

5 Press the spacebar to stop playback when you're ready.

6 Press the Home key to return to 0:00, and extend the work area end bar to the end of the time ruler.

7 Choose File > Save.

About parent and child layers

You use parenting to assign one layer's transformations to another layer. Parenting can affect all transform properties except opacity. A layer can have only one parent, but a layer can be a parent to any number of 2D or 3D layers within the same composition. You cannot animate the act of assigning and removing the parent designation—that is, you cannot designate a layer as a parent at one point in time, and then designate it as a normal layer at a different point in time. Parenting layers is useful for creating complex animations such as linking the movements of a marionette, or depicting the orbits of planets in the solar system.

Once a layer is made a parent to another layer, the other layer is called the *child layer*. Creating a parenting relationship between layers synchronizes the changes in the parent layer with the corresponding transformation values of the child layers. For example, if a parent layer moves 5 pixels to the right of its starting position, then the child layer also moves 5 pixels to the right of its position. You can animate child layers independently of their parent layers. You can also parent using null objects, which are hidden layers.

For more on parent and child layers, see After Effects Help.

Animating imported Photoshop text

If all text animations involved just two short words, such as *the Pond*, life would be easy. But in the real world, you must often work with longer blocks of text, and they can be tedious to enter manually. That's why After Effects let's you work with imported text from Photoshop or Illustrator. Just as with imported graphics or images, you can preserve text layers and edit and animate them in After Effects.

In the following exercise, you will import more text for this title sequence from Photoshop and continue to animate it.

Importing the credits

Some of the remaining text for this composition is in a layered Photoshop file, which you'll import now.

1 Double-click an empty area in the Project panel to open the Import File dialog box.

2 Select the credits.psd file in the AE7_CIB > Lessons > Lesson03 > Assets folder. Choose Import As > Composition – Cropped Layers, and then click Open.

3 Drag the Credits composition from the Project panel into the Timeline panel, placing it at the top of the layer stack.

Because you imported the credits.psd file as a composition with layers intact, you can work on it in its own Timeline panel, editing and animating the various layers independently.

Editing imported text

Once you've imported text from Photoshop, you need to make it editable in After Effects so that you can control the type and apply animations. And if you have a sharp eye, you've noticed some typos in the imported text. So, first clean up the type.

1 Double-click the Credits composition in the Project panel to open it in its own Timeline panel.

2 Shift-click to select both of the layers in the Credits Timeline panel, and choose Layer > Convert To Editable Text. (Click OK if you get a missing-font warning.) Now the text layers can be edited, and you can fix the typos.

3 Select layer 2 in the Timeline panel.

4 Using the Horizontal Type tool (**T**), click in the Composition panel and type an *e* between the *t* and *d* in the word *animated*. Then, change the *k* to a *c* in *documentary*.

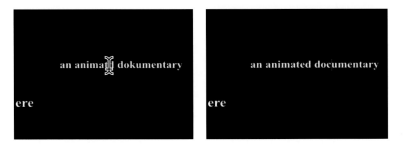

Note: You may notice that the layer name does not change in the Timeline panel when you correct the spelling in the layer. This is because the original layer name was created in Photoshop. If you want the layer name to accurately reflect the text in the layer in After Effects, you can change the layer name: Select the an animatd dokumentary layer in the Timeline panel, press Enter (Windows) or Return (Mac OS), type the new name, and press Enter or Return again.

5 Switch to the Selection tool (➤) to exit text-editing mode. Now, make sure the text uses the same font family as you used for the title text.

6 Shift-click to select both layer 2 and the Your Name Here layer in the Timeline panel.

7 Choose Window > Character to open the Character panel.

8 Set the Font Family to the same typeface you used for the words *the Pond*. Leave all other settings as they are.

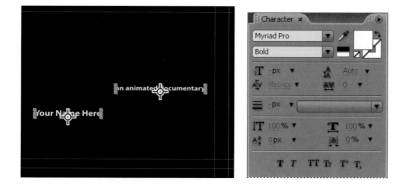

9 Close the Character panel.

Animating the subtitle

You want the letters of the subtitle, "an animated documentary," to fade on-screen from left to right under the movie title. The easiest way to do this is to use another text animation preset.

1 Go to 5:00. You will start the animation at this time, which is when the title and lily pad have finished scaling to their final size.

2 Select the subtitle's layer in the Timeline panel.

3 Press Ctrl+Alt+Shift+O (Windows) or Command+Option+Shift+O (Mac OS) to jump to Bridge.

4 Navigate to the Presets > Text > Animate In folder.

5 Select the Fade Up Characters preset and watch it in the Preview panel. This will work nicely.

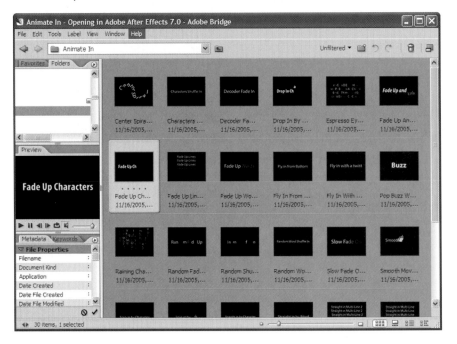

6 Double-click the Fade Up Characters preset to apply it to the subtitle layer in After Effects.

7 With the an subtitle layer selected in the Credits Timeline panel, press UU to see the properties modified by the preset. You should see two keyframes for Range Selector 1: one at 5:00, and one at 7:00. You still have a lot of animation to do in this composition, so you will speed up the effect by 1 second.

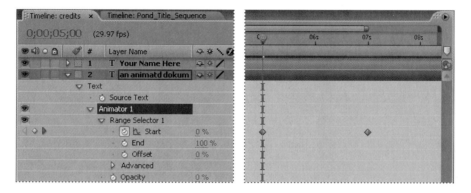

8 Go to 6:00, and then drag the second Start keyframe to 6:00, too.

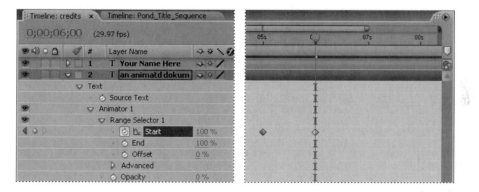

Preview this new animation quickly.

9 Drag the current-time indicator across the time ruler between 5:00 and 6:00 to see the letters fade in.

10 When you're done, select the subtitle layer and press U to hide the modified properties. Then, choose File > Save to save your work.

Animating text using a path preset

By now you should be understanding how versatile and convenient preset text animators can be. You'll use another type of text animation preset next to animate the words *directed by* along a motion path. After Effects includes several animation presets that animate text along a prebuilt path. These presets also provide placeholder text with formatting when you apply them, so in this exercise, you will enter and format your text *after* you apply the preset.

1 Switch to the Pond_Title_Sequence Timeline panel.

2 Deselect all layers, and then go to 5:00.

3 Press Ctrl+Alt+Shift+O (Windows) or Command+Option+Shift+O (Mac OS) to jump to Bridge.

4 Navigate to the Presets > Text > Paths folder.

5 Double-click the Pipes preset. Bridge returns you to After Effects, where the preset automatically creates a new layer, Pipes, with a predefined path that zigzags across the composition. The text on the path is obscured by the movie title. Don't worry. You'll fix that in a minute.

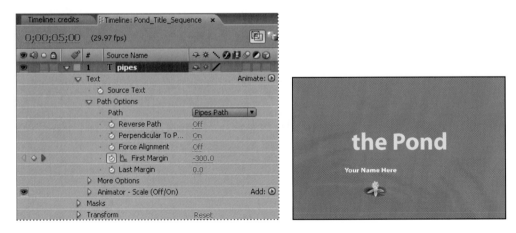

Customizing the preset path

Now, you need to change the placeholder word *pipes* to *directed by*.

1 In After Effects, go to 6:05, when the word *pipes* is visible—and horizontal—on-screen.

2 Double-click the Pipes layer in the Timeline panel. After Effects switches to the Horizontal Type tool (**T**) and selects the word *pipes* in the Composition panel. Type **directed by** to replace it. Press Enter on the numeric keypad when you're done. After Effects updates the Timeline panel with the new layer name.

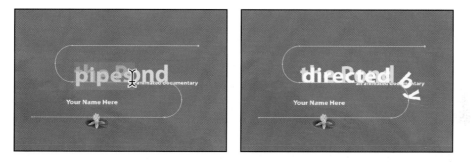

Now, format the text.

3 Open the Character panel, and do the following:

- Set the Font Family to Minion Pro or other serif typeface.

- Set the Font Style to Regular.

- Set the Font Size to **20** pixels.

- Leave all other settings at their defaults.

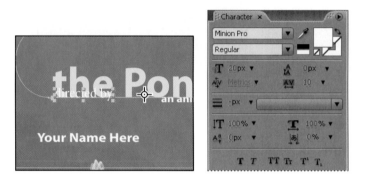

There, that's better.

4 Close the Character panel.

Preview the path animation quickly.

5 Drag the current-time indicator across the time ruler between 5:00 and 8:00 to see how the words *directed by* move on-screen—and then off-screen. You'll fix the text so that it stays on-screen, but now is a good time to adjust the position of the path in the composition so that it doesn't interfere with the movie title.

6 Using the Selection tool (➤), double-click the yellow motion path in the Composition panel to select it.

7 Drag the path down until the words *the Pond* are centered in the top curve and the lily pad is centered in the lower curve.

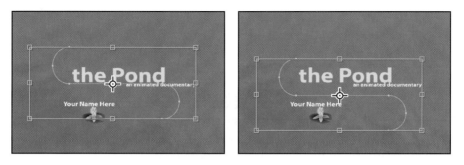

8 Press Enter (Windows) or Return (Mac OS) to accept the change.

You will be working with this animated path again later in the lesson, attaching a dragonfly graphic to it so it appears to be pulling the text on-screen. But first, finish animating the credits.

9 Select the Directed By layer in the Timeline panel and hide its properties. Then, choose File > Save to save your work.

Animating type tracking

Next, you'll animate the appearance of the director's name in the composition. This time, you'll use a text animation tracking preset. By animating tracking you can make words appear to expand outward as they appear on-screen from a central point.

Customizing placeholder text

Currently, the director's name is simply a layer with placeholder text—Your Name Here. Before you animate it, change it to your own name.

1 Switch to the credits Timeline panel and select the Your Name Here layer.

Note: It doesn't matter where the current-time indicator is located when you edit the text of this layer. Currently, the text is on-screen for the duration of the composition. That will change once you animate it.

2 Using the Horizontal Type tool (T), replace *Your Name Here* in the Composition panel with your own name. Use a first, middle, and last name so that you have a nice long string of text to animate. Press Enter on the numeric keypad when you're done.

Note: *Again, the layer name doesn't change, because it was named in Photoshop.*

Applying a tracking preset

Now you will animate the director's name with a tracking preset so that it starts to appear on-screen shortly after the words *directed by* reach the center of the composition.

1 Go to 7:10.

2 Select the Your Name Here layer in the Timeline panel.

3 Jump to Bridge and go to the Presets > Text > Tracking folder. Locate the Increase Tracking preset and double-click it to apply it to the Your Name Here layer in After Effects.

> 💡 *If you're tired of jumping to Bridge and don't care to preview the preset, simply type* **Increase Tracking** *in the Contains field of the Effects & Presets panel. Then, double-click it to apply it to the selected layer in the Timeline panel.*

4 Drag the current-time indicator across the time ruler between 7:10 and 9:10 to manually preview the tracking animation.

Customizing the tracking preset

The text expands on-screen, but you need the letters to initially be so close they're that they're on top of each other, and then expand to a reasonable, readable distance apart. You also want it the animation to occur faster. You can adjust the Tracking Amount to fix both of these problems.

1 Select the Your Name Here layer in the Timeline panel and press UU to reveal the properties that were modified by the preset.

2 Go to 7:10.

3 Under Animator 1, change the Tracking Amount to **–5** so that the letters are squeezed together.

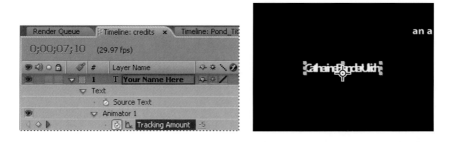

4 Click to select the Tracking Amount keyframe at 9:10, and then delete it. This leaves a second (final) Tracking Amount keyframe at 8:10, set to 0.

5 Drag the current-time indicator across the time ruler between 7:10 and 9:10. The letters expand as they appear on-screen and stop animating at 8:10.

Animating the letters' opacity

Let's take the animation of the director's name a little farther having it fade on-screen as the letters expand. To do this, you'll animate the layer's Opacity property using plain old keyframes.

1 Select the Your Name Here layer in the Credits Timeline panel.

2 Press T to reveal only its Opacity property.

3 Go to 7:10 and set the Opacity to **0**. Then, click the stopwatch icon (⏱) to set an Opacity keyframe.

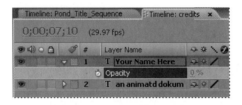

4 Go to 7:20 and set the Opacity to **100%**. After Effects adds a second keyframe. Now, the letters of the director's name should fade as they expand on-screen.

Watch another manual preview to see the change you made.

5 Drag the current-time indicator across the time ruler between 7:10 and 9:10 to see the letters of the director's name now fade in as they spread out.

6 Right-click (Windows) or Control-click (Mac OS) the ending Opacity keyframe and choose Keyframe Assistant > Easy Ease In.

7 Choose File > Save.

Using a text animator group

Next, you will animate part of the director's name—the middle name. To do that, you'll use a text animator group. Text animator groups let you animate individual letters within a block of text in a layer. Creating a text animator group will allow you to animate only the characters in your middle name without affecting the tracking and opacity animation of the other names in the layer.

About text animator groups

A text animator group includes one or more *selectors* and one or more *animator properties*. A selector is like a mask—it specifies which characters or section of a text layer you want an animator property to affect. Using a selector, you can define a percentage of the text, specific characters in the text, or a specific range of text.

Using a combination of animator properties and selectors, you can create complex text animations that would otherwise require painstaking keyframing. Most text animations require you to animate only the selector values—not the property values. Consequently, text animators use a small number of keyframes even for complex animations.

Text animator groups animate a character's position, shape, and size-related properties relative to each character's own anchor point. The text property Anchor Point Grouping lets you reposition each character's anchor point relative to its word, line, or entire text block. In addition, you can control the alignment of the anchor point relative to the anchor point group and the font with the Grouping Alignment property.

For more about text animator groups, see After Effects Help.

1 Go to 8:10.

2 Click the triangle in the Label column of the Timeline panel to hide the Opacity property for the Your Name Here layer. Then, click the triangle again to see the layer's Text property group name.

3 Next to the Text property name, click the Animate pop-up menu and choose Skew. A property group named Animator 2 appears in the layer's Text properties.

Before continuing, rename this generic animator to something more intuitive.

3 Select Animator 2, press Enter (Windows) or Return (Mac OS), and rename it **Skew Animator**. Then, press Enter or Return again to accept the new name.

Timeline: Pond_Title_Sequence	Timeline: credits ×
0;00;08;10 (29.97 fps)	

Now, you're ready to define the range of letters that you want to skew.

4 Expand the Skew Animator's Range Selector 1 properties. Each animator group includes a default range selector. Range selectors let you constrain the animation to particular letters in the text layer. You can add additional selectors to an animator group, or apply multiple animator properties to the same range selector.

5 While watching the Composition panel, drag the Skew Animator's Range Selector 1 Start value up (to the right) until the left selector indicator (⋈) is just before the first letter of your middle name (the letter *B* in Bender, in our example).

6 Drag the Skew Animator's Range Selector 1 End value down (to the left) until its indicator (⋈) is just after the last letter of your middle name (the *r* in Bender, in our example) in the Composition panel.

Now, any properties that you animate with the Skew Animator will only affect the middle name that you selected (Bender, in our example).

Skewing the range of text

Now, make that middle name shake and shimmy by setting Skew keyframes.

1 Drag the Skew Animator's Skew value left and right, and notice that only the middle name (Bender, in our example) sways. The other names in the line of text remain steady.

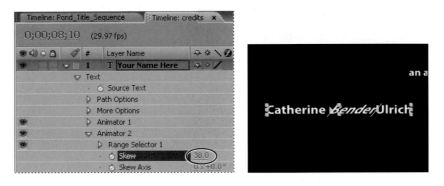

2 Set the Skew Animator's Skew value to **0.0**.

3 Go to 8:05 and click the stopwatch icon (⏱) for Skew to add a keyframe to the property.

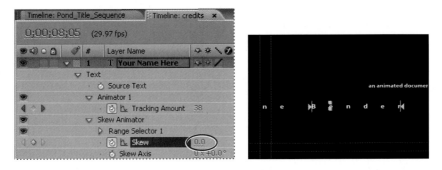

4 Go to 8:08 and set the Skew value to **50.0**. After Effects adds a keyframe.

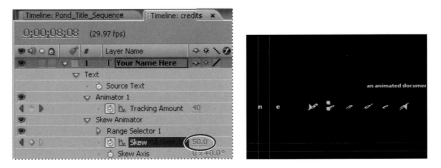

5 Go to 8:15 and change the Skew value to **–50.0**. After Effects adds another keyframe.

6 Go to 8:20 and change the Skew value to **0.0** to set the final keyframe.

7 Click the Skew property name to select all of the Skew keyframes. Then, choose Animation > Keyframe Assistant > Easy Ease. This adds an Easy Ease to all keyframes. That's it. Now, preview your work.

8 Drag the current-time indicator across the time ruler from 7:10 to 8:20 to see how the director's name fades in and expands on-screen, and the middle name rocks side to side while the other names are unaffected.

9 Select the Your Name Here layer in the Timeline panel and press UU to hide its properties.

> 💡 *To quickly remove all text animators from a text layer, select the layer in the Timeline panel and choose Animation > Remove All Text Animators. To remove only a particular animator, select the animator name in the Timeline panel and press Delete.*

Preview the entire composition

Now is a good time to preview the entire composition so far.

1 Switch to the Pond_Title_Sequence Timeline panel.

2 Press Home to go to the beginning of the time ruler.

3 Press 0 on the numeric keypad to watch a RAM preview.

4 Press the spacebar when you're done to stop playback.

5 Choose File > Save to save your work.

Cleaning up the path animation

Currently, the words *directed by* fade in and out as they wind along the Pipes path preset. Let's fix it so that the words are opaque for the entire animation, and they come to a rest just above your name.

1 With the Directed By layer selected in the Timeline panel, press the U key to display the animated properties for the layer.

2 Click the stopwatch icon (⏱) for the Range Selector 1 Offset property to delete all of its keyframes.

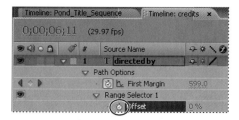

3 Depending on where the current-time indicator is located in the time ruler, the resulting value for Range Selector 1 Offset may or may not be set to 0%. Set it to **0%** if it is not. Now, *directed by* will be visible throughout the composition.

Now, to make the text stop animating above your name, you need to modify the First Margin property.

4 Select the last keyframe for the First Margin property in the Timeline panel and delete it. Because the middle keyframe (now the last keyframe) is set to Easy Ease, the words *directed by* come gently to rest above the lily pad.

5 Go to 6:14 and change the First Margin value to **685.0**.

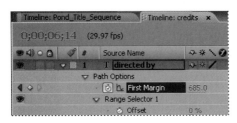

You also need to adjust the mask shape so the path starts and ends off-screen.

6 Using the Selection tool (⬏) in the Composition panel, Shift-drag the mask control point at the top of the S-shaped curve to the right and off-screen.

7 Click the mask control point at the end of the S-shaped curve and drag the control point off to the left side of the screen. Press Shift after you start dragging to constrain the movement and keep the path horizontal.

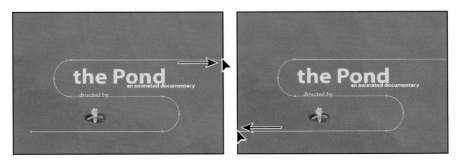

8 Watch a manual preview from about 5:00 to 6:20 to see the corrected path animation.

9 Select the Directed By layer in the Timeline panel and press U to hide its properties, and then choose File > Save.

Animating the dragonfly

To cap off this project, you'll use a mask from a text layer to animate a nontext layer. Specifically, you'll use the mask shape for the *directed by* path to create a motion path for a dragonfly graphic. This will make it appear as if the dragonfly is pulling the *directed by* text on-screen. You need to start by importing the dragonfly graphic and adding it to your composition.

1 Double-click an empty area in the Project panel to open the Import File dialog box.

2 In the AE7_CIB > Lessons > Lesson03 > Assets folder, select the dragonfly.ai file, choose Import As > Composition – Cropped Layers, and then click Open.

3 Drag the Dragonfly composition from the Project panel to the top of the layer stack in the Pond_Title_Sequence Timeline panel.

Copying the mask shape

Now you're ready to copy the mask shape from the path of the Directed By layer to the Dragonfly layer.

1 Go to 5:00.

2 Select the Directed By layer in the Timeline panel and press M to display its Mask Shape property.

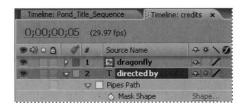

3 Click the Mask Shape property name to select it, and then choose Edit > Copy.

4 Select the Dragonfly layer, and then press P to display its Position property.

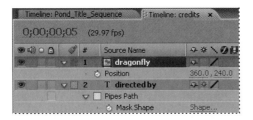

5 Click the Position property name to select it, and then choose Edit > Paste. After Effects copies the Position keyframes from the Directed By layer to the Dragonfly layer.

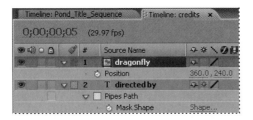

Orienting the dragonfly

Unfortunately, the dragonfly is flying backward, but that's easy to fix.

1 With the Dragonfly layer selected in the Timeline panel, choose Layer > Transform > Auto-Orient.

2 In the Auto-Orientation dialog box, select Orient Along Path, and then click OK. Now, the dragonfly is facing forward as it flies.

3 Select the Dragonfly layer in the Timeline panel and press U to hide its Position property.

Coordinating the text and dragonfly timing

Next, you need to coordinate the timing of the dragonfly's motion with the words *directed by* so that the words correctly trail behind the dragonfly.

1 Select the Directed By layer and press U to display its Path Options in the Timeline panel.

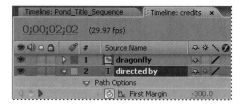

2 Go to 5:09 and change the First Margin value to **127.0**. After Effects adds a new Easy Ease keyframe.

3 Go to 5:18 and change the First Margin value to **373.0**. Once again, After Effects adds a keyframe, and the text moves behind the dragonfly.

4 Go to 5:25 and change the First Margin value to **559.0**.

5 Go to 4:24 and drag the first First Margin keyframe to that position.

6 Manually preview the corrected path animation by dragging the current-time indicator across the time ruler from about 4:20 to 7:10. The words follow the dragonfly and come to rest above your name, while the dragonfly continues to fly along the path and off-screen.

7 Select the Directed By layer and press U to hide its Path Options property, then press the Home key to go to the beginning of the time ruler.

Adding motion blur

To finesse the composition and make the movement look more natural, you'll finish up by applying motion blur.

1 In the Timeline panel, turn on motion blur for all of the layers *except* the Pondbackground and Credits layers.

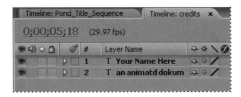

You don't need to add a blur to the Pondbackground layer, but what about the Credits layer? You need to turn on motion blur to the layers in the Credits composition.

2 Switch to the Credits Timeline panel and turn on motion blur for both layers.

3 Switch back to the Pond_Title_Sequence Timeline panel and now turn on motion blur for the Credits layer. Then, click the Enable Motion Blur button (⬤) at the top of the Timeline panel so that you can see the motion blur in the Composition panel.

4 Press 0 on the numeric keypad to watch a RAM preview of the entire, completed animation.

5 Choose File > Save.

Give yourself a pat on the back. You just completed some hard-core text animations. You can render the composition now if you'd like. If so, see Lesson 12, "Rendering and Outputting," for instructions on rendering. Otherwise, continue with Lesson 4, "Animating a Multimedia Presentation."

Watch **the** Movie

Total Training: Animated Text

The series of Total Training movies that are provided on the *Adobe After Effects 7.0 Classroom in a Book* DVD includes a tutorial on animating text. To learn more about converting Photoshop layers into editable text, previewing and applying text animation presets, and applying motion blur to animation effects, see the QuickTime movie AnimatedText.mov located in the Movies folder on this book's DVD.

Review

1 What are some similarities and differences between text layers and other types of layers in After Effects?

2 Describe two ways to preview a text animation preset.

3 How can you assign one layer's transformations to another layer?

4 What are text animator groups?

▶ **Review answers**

1 In many ways, text layers are just like any other layer in After Effects. You can apply effects and expressions to text layers, animate them, designate them as 3D layers, and edit the 3D text while viewing it in multiple views. The main differences between text layers and other layers are that you cannot open a text layer in its own Layer panel, and that you can animate the text in a text layer using special text animator properties and selectors.

2 You can preview text animation presets by choosing Help > Animation Preset Gallery, or you can preview presets in Bridge by choosing Animation > Browse Presets. Bridge opens and displays the contents of the After Effects Presets folder. You can navigate to folders containing various types of text animation presets, such as Blurs or Paths, and watch samples in the Preview panel. Then, double-click a preset to add it to the currently selected layer in the After Effects Timeline panel.

3 You can use parenting relationships in After Effects to assign one layer's transformations to another layer (except opacity transformations). When a layer is made a parent to another layer, the other layer is called the *child layer*. Creating a parenting relationship between layers synchronizes the changes in the parent layer with corresponding transformation values of the child layers.

4 Text animator groups enable you to animate the properties of individual characters in a text layer over time. Text animator groups contain one or more *selectors*. Selectors are like masks: They let you specify which characters or section of a text layer that you want an animator property to affect. Using a selector, you can define a percentage of the text, specific characters in the text, or a specific range of text.

Illustration by Gordon Studer, www.gordonstuder.com

After Effects projects typically use a variety of imported footage, arranged in a composition, which is edited and animated using the Timeline panel. In this lesson, you'll get more familiar with animation fundamentals as you build a multimedia presentation.

4 Animating a Multimedia Presentation

Lesson overview

In this lesson you'll learn how to do the following:

- Create a complex animation with multiple layers.

- Adjust the duration of a layer.

- Clip live motion video into a vector mask.

- Animate with Position, Scale, and Rotation keyframes.

- Animate a precomposed layer.

- Apply the Radio Waves effect to a solid layer.

- Add audio to a project.

- Loop an audio track using Time Remapping.

In this lesson, you will work on a more complex animation project. Along the way, you'll learn to mix media, including motion video and Photoshop art; to work with audio; and to become more adept at using the Timeline panel to perform keyframe animations. The project in this lesson is an animated portfolio for a professional illustrator that can be delivered on a CD or on the web, and it is meant to be a useful, real-world self-promotion.

This lesson will take 1½ to 2 hours to complete.

Getting started

Make sure the following files are in the AE7_CIB > Lessons > Lesson04 folder on your hard disk, or copy them from the *Adobe After Effects 7.0 Classroom in a Book* DVD now.

• In the Start_Project_File folder: Lesson04_Start.aep

• In the Assets folder: CarRide.psd, GordonsHead.mov, HeadShape.ai, piano.wav, and several JPG images whose file names begin with "studer_"

• In the Sample_Movie folder: Lesson04.mov

1 Open and play the Lesson04.mov sample movie to see what you will create in this lesson. When you're done, quit the QuickTime player. You may delete the sample movie from your hard disk if you have limited storage space.

Setting up the project

For this project, professional illustrator Gordon Studer has created a Photoshop file of a city scene with several objects on separate layers that you will animate in After Effects. In fact, he has prepared an After Effects project that already contains this layered Photoshop file, as well as the video and audio clips that you will need later in the lesson.

When you begin this lesson, restore the default application settings for After Effects. See "Restoring default preferences," page 5.

1 Press Ctrl+Alt+Shift (Windows) or Command+Option+Shift (Mac OS) while starting After Effects. When asked whether you want to delete your preferences file, click OK.

2 Choose File > Open Project or press Ctrl+O (Windows) or Command+O (Mac OS).

3 Navigate to the AE7_CIB > Lessons > Lesson04 > Start_Project_File folder, select Lesson04_Start.aep, and click Open.

In this project, you will animate an illustration of the artist driving a car on a city street. The animation will end with an easel that displays a slide show of samples of the artist's work. This is a complex animation. You will start by animating the background and some objects in the scenery so that the virtual camera appears to moving from left to right across the scene. Then, you will animate the car driving down the road, including masking a photograph of the illustrator's face into the driver's seat. Next, you will animate some passing traffic and buildings to add interest to the background. Finally, you will animate the slide show of the artwork on the easel.

4 If necessary, double-click the CarRide composition in the Project panel to open it in the Composition and Timeline panels.

To see the contents of each layer of the Photoshop file, double-click each item in the CarRide Layers folder in the Project panel to view it in the Footage panel. Close the Footage panel when you're done.

5 Choose File > Save As.

6 In the Save As dialog box, navigate to the AE7_CIB > Lessons > Lesson04 > Finished_Project folder.

7 Name the project **Lesson04_Finished.aep**, and then click Save.

Animating the scenery using parenting

To animate to various elements of the scenery efficiently with the background, you're going to use parenting. As you learned in Lesson 3, "Animating Text," creating a parenting relationship between layers synchronizes the changes in the parent layer with the corresponding transformation values of the child layers. In Lesson 3, you used parenting to quickly apply one layer's scale transformation to another layer. Now, you will use it to synchronize the movement of the objects in three layers—the Leaves, Full Skyline, and the FG (foreground) layers—with the BG (background) layer of the animation.

Setting up parenting

First, set up the parent-child relationship between the relevant layers in the Timeline panel.

1 In the Timeline panel, Ctrl-click (Windows) or Command-click (Mac OS) to select the Leaves, FG, and Full Skyline layers.

2 In the Parent column for any one of the selected layers, choose 8.BG from the pop-up menu. This establishes all three selected layers as child layers to the parent layer, which is layer 8, BG (the background).

If you don't see the Parent column, choose Columns > Parent from the Timeline panel menu.

Animating the parent layer

Now, you'll animate the position of the background layer—the parent layer—so that it moves horizontally. This, in turn, will make the child layers animate in the same way.

1 Press the Home key to make sure the current-time indicator is at the beginning of the time ruler.

2 Select the BG layer in the Timeline panel and press the P key to reveal its Position property.

3 Set the BG layer's Position values to **1029.0, 120.0,** and click the stopwatch icon (⏱) to create a Position keyframe. This moves the background layer off to the left side of the scene, as if the camera had been moved.

4 Go to 10:15.

> *You will be moving all over the time ruler as you animate the elements of this project, so remember, a quick way to go to a frame is to press Ctrl+G (Windows) or Command+G (Mac OS) to open the Go To Time dialog box. Then, type the desired time without punctuation (as in **1015** for 10:15) and press Enter (Windows) or Return (Mac OS).*

5 Set the BG layer's Position values to **–626.0, 120.0**. After Effects automatically sets a second keyframe and shows you the motion path of the animation in the Composition panel. The background now moves across the composition, and because the Leaves, Full Skyline, and FG layers are child layers to the BG (parent) layer, they all move horizontally as well, from the same starting position.

6 Select the BG layer and press U to hide its properties and keep the Timeline panel neat.

Animating the bee's position

Another element of the composition that moves across the scene at the beginning of the animation is the bee. You will animate it next.

1 Press the Home key to go to 0:00.

2 Select the Bee layer in the Timeline panel and press the P key to reveal its Position property. (The bee is not visible at 0:00 in the Composition panel.)

3 Set the Position values of the Bee layer to **825.0, 120.0**, which puts the bee off-screen to the left at the beginning of the animation. Then, click the stopwatch icon (⏱) to create a Position keyframe.

4 Go to 1:00 and set the Bee layer's Position values to **1411.0, 120.0**, which puts the bee off-screen to the right. After Effects adds a keyframe.

💡 *You can also change the Bee layer's Position values by dragging the layer in the Composition panel, using the Selection tool (*➤*), until the layer is in the correct position.*

5 Select the Bee layer and press the U key to hide its Position property in the Timeline panel.

Trimming a layer

Since you don't want the bee to appear in the composition after 1:00, you need to *trim* the layer. Trimming (hiding) footage at the beginning or end of a layer lets you change which frames are first or last in the composition. The first frame to appear is called the In point, and the last frame is called the Out point. You can trim by changing the In and Out points in the Layer panel or the Timeline panel, depending on what you want to change. For this exercise, you'll change the Out point of the Bee layer in the Timeline panel.

1 With the current-time indicator at 1:00 and the Bee layer selected in the Timeline panel, press Alt+] (Windows) or Option+] (Mac OS) to set the Out point to the current time.

💡 *You can also drag the right side of the layer duration bar to change the Out point.*

Applying motion blur

To finish up with the bee's animation, you will apply a motion blur so that its movement is more realistic.

1 Click the Motion Blur switch (⬤) for the Bee layer to turn on motion blur.

2 Click the Enable Motion Blur button (⬤) at the top of the Timeline panel to view the motion blur in the Composition panel.

Previewing the animation

Perform a quick manual preview to see the various elements in the scenery animate.

1 Drag the current-time indicator from 0:00 to 10:15. The animation of the background, leaves, bee, foreground objects, and the objects in the skyline makes it appear as if a camera is panning across the scene.

2 After you preview, return the current-time indicator to 0:00 and then choose File > Save to save your work.

Adjusting an anchor point

The background is moving; now it's time to animate the artist in his red car as he drives across the composition. To begin that process, you must first move the anchor point of the layer that contains the red car, without moving the layer's relative position in the composition. The layer with the red car is called Artist. To edit the anchor point of the Artist layer, you need to work on the Artist layer in the Layer panel.

1 Double-click the Artist layer in the Timeline panel to open it in the Layer panel.

2 At the bottom of the Layer panel, choose View > Anchor Point Path to display the layer's anchor point, which by default is at the center of the layer.

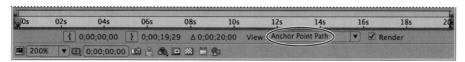

3 Select the Pan Behind tool (⌗) in the Tools panel (or press Y to select it).

4 Choose Fit Up To 100% from the Magnification Ratio pop-up menu if necessary to see the entire layer, and then drag the anchor point to the lower-left corner of the car.

5 Click the Composition panel name to view the CarRide composition.

6 Select the Artist layer in the Timeline panel and press P to reveal its Position property.

7 Set the Position values for the Artist layer to **50.0, 207.0** so that the car is in the center of the frame, and then click the stopwatch icon (⏱) to set a Position keyframe. This is a temporary position that lets you see the car on-screen while you mask the driver into place, which is your next task. Then, you will animate the car so that it drives across the composition.

8 Select the Artist layer and press U to hide its properties, and then choose File > Save to save your work.

Masking video into a vector shape

With the car positioned on-screen, you can give it a driver. To do this, you will mask a video head shot of the illustrator into a vector mask in the composition. This shape clips a frontal head shot into a side-view profile shape, which is a "Picasso-esque" signature style of the artist's work.

Creating a new composition

For this task, you will create a new composition for the vector shape and the video clip.

1 Ctrl-click (Windows) or Command-click (Mac OS) to select both GordonsHead.mov and HeadShape.ai in the Project panel, and drag them onto the Create A New Composition button (■) at the bottom of the panel.

2 In the New Composition From Selection dialog box, choose Use Dimensions From > GordonsHead.mov, and then click OK. After Effects creates a new composition named GordonsHead based on the settings of the movie, and it opens the new composition in the Timeline and Composition panels.

Unfortunately, the GordonsHead movie is a different resolution from the CarRide composition, so you need to fix that now.

3 Choose Composition > Composition Settings and set the Width to **360** pixels. After Effects automatically changes the Height to 240 pixels. Click OK.

Now, scale the layers to fit the composition.

4 Shift-click to select both the GordonsHead and HeadShape layers in the Timeline panel and choose Layer > Transform > Fit To Comp or press Ctrl+Alt+F (Windows) or Command+Option+F (Mac OS).

5 Make sure HeadShape is above GordonsHead in the layer stack. Drag to reposition the layers if necessary.

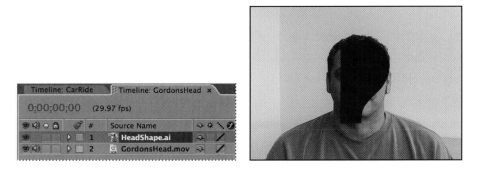

6 Drag the right side of the HeadShape layer duration bar to the end of the time ruler so that it is the same length as the GordonsHead layer (13:10).

Creating the mask

There are a few ways to make masks in After Effects. You can, for example, clip a video or artwork to a vector shape that is drawn in After Effects, or you can use a shape that is imported from Illustrator. To be true to this artist's style, you will use a vector profile for the head that Gordon Studer has created himself in Illustrator, which makes a nice, hard-edge mask for this stylized design.

1 Click the Transfer Controls button at the bottom of the Timeline panel to view the Mode column.

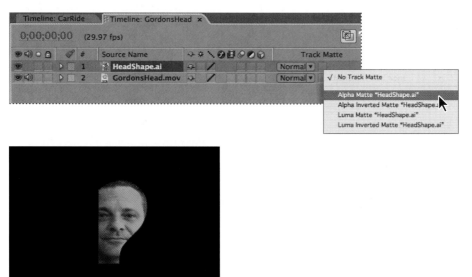

2 For the GordonsHead layer, choose TrkMat > Alpha Matte "HeadShape.ai." In the Composition panel, notice that the movie is now constrained by the Illustrator shape.

Swapping a composition into a layer

Now that Gordon Studer's mug is masked to the vector shape, you need to attach it to the car. To do that, you'll return to the main CarRide composition and swap the GordonsHead composition into the Head layer, which is currently a solid layer that serves as a placeholder.

1 Click the CarRide Timeline panel to bring it forward.

2 Select the Head layer in the Timeline panel and then do one of the following:

• Select the GordonsHead composition in the Project panel and press Ctrl+Alt+/ (Windows) or Command+Option+/ (Mac OS) .

• Option-drag (Mac) or Alt-drag (Windows) the GordonsHead composition from the Project panel to the Head layer in the Timeline panel.

3 Using the Selection tool (➤), drag the Head layer in the Composition panel so that Gordon Studer is sitting properly in the car.

Now, use parenting again so that Gordon Studer's head will animate with the car.

4 In the Head layer in the Timeline panel, choose Parent > 2. Artist.

5 Choose File > Save to save your work.

Keyframing a motion path

Finally, you're ready to animate the car so that it drives on-screen at the beginning of the composition, scales larger during the middle of the composition—as if it's approaching the camera—and then pops a wheelie and drives off-screen. You'll start by keyframing the car's position to get it on-screen.

1 Press the Home key to make sure the current-time indicator is at the beginning of the time ruler.

2 Click the Video switch in the Timeline panel to turn off visibility of Leaves layer so that you can clearly see the Artist layer below it.

3 Select the Artist layer in the Timeline panel and expand all of its Transform properties.

4 Position the Artist layer off-screen to the left (behind the leaves) by changing its Position values to **–162.0, 207.0**.

Note: There's already a keyframe at this time from the anchor-point exercise.

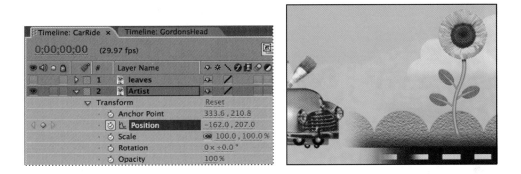

5 Go to 2:20 and change the Position values for the Artist layer to **54.5, 207.0**. After Effects adds a keyframe.

6 Go to 6:00 and click the Add/Remove Keyframe button (in the Switches column) for the Artist layer to add a Position keyframe for the Artist layer at the same values (54.5, 207.0).

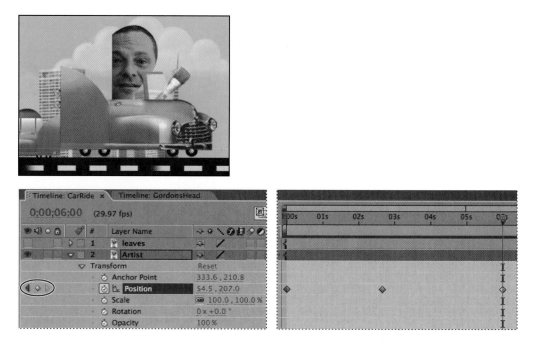

When you animate the Position property, After Effects displays the movement as a motion path. You can create a motion path for the position of the layer or for the anchor point of a layer. A position motion path appears in the Composition panel; an anchor-point motion path appears in the Layer panel. The motion path appears as a sequence of dots in which each dot marks the position of the layer at each frame. An *X* in the path marks the position of a keyframe. The density of dots between the *X*s in a motion path indicates the layer's relative speed. Dots close together indicate a slower speed; dots farther apart indicate a faster speed.

Keyframing scale and rotation transformations

The car is zooming on-screen; now, you'll make it appear as if the car is getting closer to the camera by scaling it larger. Then you'll make it pop a wheelie by keyframing the Rotation property.

1 Go to 7:15 and set the Scale values for the Artist layer to **80.0, 80.0%**. Then, click the stopwatch (⏱) to set a Scale keyframe.

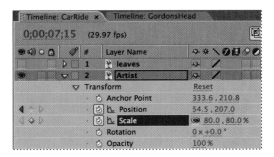

2 Go to 10:10 and set the Position values for the Artist layer to **28.0, 303.0**. After Effects adds a keyframe.

4 Still at 10:10, change the Scale values to **120.0, 120.0%**. After Effects adds a keyframe.

5 Still at 10:10, click the stopwatch icon (⏱) for the Rotation property to set a Rotation keyframe at the default value, 0.0˚.

6 Go to 10:13 and change the Rotation value to **−14.0**˚. After Effects adds a keyframe, and now the car pops a wheelie.

Now, animate the car driving off-screen.

7 Go to 10:24 and set the Position values for the Artist layer to **369.0, 258.0**. After Effects adds a keyframe.

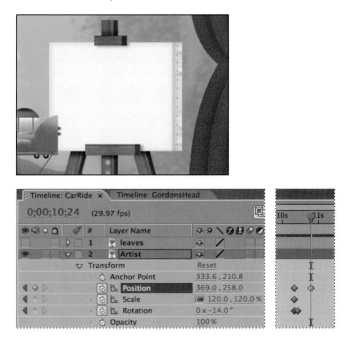

Adding motion blur

Finally, apply a motion blur to smooth out the driving sequence.

1 Turn on Motion Blur switch ( ) for the Artist and Head layers.

The blur will be visible as the car drives off-screen, and it will be visible for the flying bee as well, because you turned on motion blur for that layer earlier in the lesson. You'll see all of this in a minute.

2 Select the Artist layer in the Timeline panel and press UU to hide its Transform properties.

Previewing your work

Now that the keyframes are set for the moving car, preview the entire clip and make sure that the driver is framed to create a pleasant composition.

1 Turn on visibility of the Leaves layer in the Timeline panel by clicking the Video switch (👁), and then press 0 on the numeric keypad to watch a RAM preview the animation.

2 Choose File > Save to save your work so far.

Animating additional elements

To continue practicing creating keyframe animations, you will now animate the passing traffic and the buildings in the background.

Animating the passing traffic

Perhaps you noticed in the preview you just watched: The blue car is tailgating the artist in his red hot rod. The blue car is actually on a precomposed layer that also contains a yellow car. Next, make the scene more dynamic by animating the blue and yellow cars so that they drive past the artist's car in the background.

Note: Remember, a precomposed layer is simply a layer with nested layers in it. In this example, the precomposed Vehicles layer contains one nested layer with a blue car and one nested layer with a yellow car.

1 Select the Vehicles layer in the Timeline panel and click the Solo switch (◉) to isolate it as you work. Then, press the P key to reveal the layer's Position property.

2 Go to 3:00.

3 Using the Selection tool (▶), drag the Vehicles layer in the Composition panel so that both cars are off-screen to the right. Press Shift after you start to drag to constrain the movement vertically. Or, simply set the Vehicles layer's Position values to **684.0, 120.**).

4 Click the stopwatch icon (⏱) to create a Position keyframe for the Vehicles layer.

5 Go to 4:00 and drag the Vehicles layer in the Composition panel so that both cars are off-screen to the left. Or, simply set the layer's Position values to **93.0, 120.0**. After Effects adds a keyframe.

6 Turn on motion blur for the Vehicles layer.

7 Select the Vehicles layer in the Timeline panel and press U to hide its properties.

8 Unsolo the Vehicles layer, and then manually preview the passing traffic by dragging the current-time indicator from about 2:25 to 4:06.

Animating the buildings

Animated buildings? You bet. You'll animate a couple of buildings rising and "jumping" in the background as the artist cruises through downtown San Francisco. Once again, you'll be working with a precomposed layer (Full Skyline), but by opening it up, you can individually animate its nested layers.

1 Alt-double-click (Windows) or Option-double-click (Mac OS) the full Skyline layer in the Timeline panel to open it in its own Timeline and Composition panels. Notice that this composition has three layers: Skyline, Building, and Buildings. You'll start with the Buildings layer.

2 Go to 5:10, select the Buildings layer in the Full Skyline Timeline panel, and press P to reveal its Position property.

3 Click the stopwatch icon (⏱) to set a Position keyframe for the Buildings layer at the default values (160.0, 120.0).

4 Go to 4:20 and in the Composition panel, use the Selection tool (▶) to drag the Buildings layer off the bottom of the composition until its *y* Position value is 350.0. Press Shift after you start to drag to constrain the horizontal axis. After Effects adds a keyframe.

💡 *Dragging the layer into position is good practice, but you can also directly enter the* y *Position values in steps 4 and 5 if you don't want to drag the layer in the Composition panel.*

5 Go to 5:02 and drag the Buildings layer up in the Composition panel until its *y* Position value is 90.0. After Effects adds a keyframe.

Great. You've got your first animated building. Next, you'll finesse the movement at the high point of the jump to make it more natural. (Naturally jumping buildings? Aw, come on. This is fun.)

Adding Easy Ease

Finesse the movement at the high point of the jump by adding an easy ease.

1 Right-click (Windows) or Control-click (Mac OS) the keyframe at 5:02 and choose Keyframe Assistant > Easy Ease. This adjusts the speed of change as the motion approaches and retreats from the keyframe.

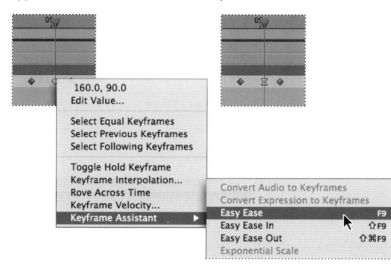

2 Drag the current-time indicator from 4:20 to 5:10 if you'd like to watch a manual preview of the jumping building.

Copying the building animation

To animate the other layers in the Full Skyline composition, you'll copy and paste the Buildings layer's keyframes to those other layers—but at different times—so that the elements jump in sequence.

1 Click the Position property name for the Buildings layer to select all of the property's keyframes, and then choose Edit > Copy or press Ctrl+C (Windows) or Command+C (Mac OS).

2 Go to 5:00 and select the Building layer in the Timeline panel. Choose Edit > Paste or press Ctrl+V (Windows) or Command+V (Mac OS) to paste the keyframes to this layer.

3 Go to 5:10 and select the Skyline layer. Choose Edit > Paste or press Ctrl+V (Windows) or Command+V (Mac OS) again to paste the keyframes to this layer, too.

4 Select the Building layer name and press the P key to see the copied keyframes. Repeat for the Skyline layer.

5 Turn on motion blur for all three layers, and then switch to the CarRide Timeline panel and turn on motion blur for the Full Skyline precomposed layer. This applies motion blur to all of the nested layers.

You've done a lot of work. Let's see how the animation looks from the beginning.

6 Press the 0 key on the numeric keypad to watch a RAM preview.

7 Choose File > Save to save your work.

Applying an effect

You've created several keyframed animations in this project. You'll switch gears now and apply an effect in this next exercise. The effect will animate some radio waves emitting from the Transamerica Pyramid building.

Adding a solid-color layer

You need to apply the radio wave effect on its own layer, which will be a solid-color layer.

About solid-color layers

You can create solid images of any color or size (up to 30,000 x 30,000 pixels) in After Effects. After Effects treats solids as it does any other footage item: You can modify the mask, transform properties, and apply effects to a solid layer. If you change settings for a solid that is used by more than one layer, you can apply the changes to all layers that use the solid or to only the single occurrence of the solid. Use solid layers to color a background or to create simple graphic images.

1 Make sure you're in the CarRide Timeline panel.

2 Choose Layer > New > Solid. In the Solid Settings dialog box that appears, name the new layer **radio waves**, and then click the Make Comp Size button. Then click OK to create the layer.

3 Drag the Radio Waves layer in the Timeline panel so that it sits above the BG layer.

By default, the Radio Waves layer lasts the duration of the composition. However, you need it to be only a few seconds long, to last the length of the effect. So you need to change the layer's duration.

4 Click the Expand Or Collapse The In/Out/Duration/Stretch Panes button (↕) in the lower-left corner of the Timeline panel to view those four columns.

5 Click the blue, underlined Duration value for the Radio Waves layer.

6 In the Time Stretch dialog box, set the New Duration to **8:00**. Then, click OK.

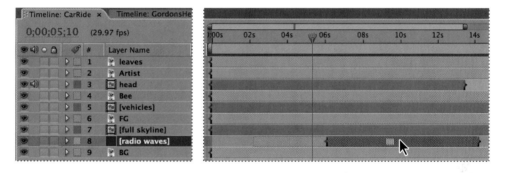

7 In the time ruler, drag the Radio Waves layer duration bar (from the center) so that it starts at 6:00. Watch the In value for the layer to see when it's at 6:00.

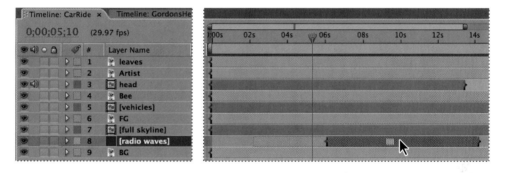

8 Go to 6:00, the first frame of the radio waves effect.

Applying the effect

Now, you're ready to apply the radio waves effect to the solid layer.

1 With the Radio Waves layer selected in the Timeline panel, choose Effect > Generate > Radio Waves. Nothing changes in the Composition panel, because the first wave hasn't emitted yet.

2 In the Effect Controls panel, expand the Wave Motion and Stroke properties. Then, do the following:

- Choose Parameters Are Set At > Each Frame.

- Set the Expansion rate to **0.40**.

- Set the Velocity to **1.00**.

- Set the Opacity to **0.500**.

- Set the Color to white (RGB=255, 255, 255).

- Set both the Start Width and End Width to **3.00**.

3 Still in the Effect Controls panel, click the cross-hair icon for the Producer Point setting near the top of the panel, and then in the Composition panel, click to set the producer point at the top of the pyramid.

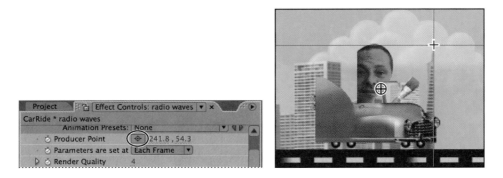

Radio waves with the settings you specified will now emit from the top of the pyramid building. You just need to parent the Radio Waves layer to the Full Skyline layer so that the waves travel with the building across the composition.

4 In the Parent column of the Radio Waves layer, choose 7. Full Skyline from the pop-up menu.

5 Go to 5:28, just before the radio waves effect begins, and in the Time Controls panel, check the From Current Time box. Then click the RAM Preview button to watch a RAM preview of just the radio waves effect.

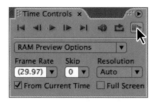

After watching the preview, tidy up the Timeline panel.

6 Click the Expand Or Collapse The In/Out/Duration/Stretch Panes button (↕) to hide those columns, and then press the Home key to go to the beginning of the time ruler.

7 Choose File > Save to save your work.

Creating an animated slide show

Now that you've completed this complex animation of the artist driving through a stylized cityscape, it's time to add samples of his work to the easel—this is, after all, the point: to show off the artist's work to potential new clients. However, this slide-show technique could easily be adapted to other uses, such as presenting family photos or making a business presentation.

Importing the slides

The artist has provided a folder of sample artwork, but you're not going to use all of the images. To help you choose, use Bridge to preview them.

1 Choose File > Browse to jump to Bridge.

2 In the Folders panel, navigate to the AE7_CIB > Lessons > Lesson04 > Assets folder on your hard disk.

3 Click the various "studer_" images and study them in the Preview panel.

4 Ctrl-click (Windows) or Command-click (Mac OS) to select your five favorite images, and then double-click to add them to the After Effects Project panel. We chose studer_Comcast.jpg, studer_map.jpg, studer_music.jpg, studer_Puzzle.jpg, and studer_Real_Guys.jpg.

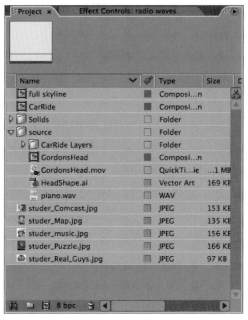

5 Leave Bridge open in the background.

Making a new composition

You'll put these images in their own composition, which will make it easier to turn them into a slide show complete with transition effects between slides.

1 In After Effects, Shift-click to select the five Studer images in the Project panel, and drag them onto the Create A New Composition button (▣) at the bottom of the panel.

2 In the New Composition From Selection dialog box, do the following:

• In the Create area, select Single Composition.

• In the Options area, set the Still Duration to **2:00**.

• Check the Sequence Layers and Overlap boxes.

• Set the Duration to **0:10**.

• Choose Transition > Cross Dissolve Front And Back Layers.

• Click OK.

The transition option creates a sequence of still images that dissolve one to the next. When you click OK, After Effects opens the new composition, named for the Studer image at the top of the list in the Project panel, in the Composition and Timeline panels. Before continuing, rename the composition something more intuitive.

3 Choose Composition > Composition Settings and rename the composition **Artwork**. Then, click OK.

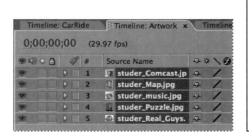
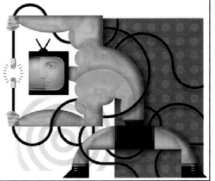

Positioning the slide show

Wasn't it easy to make the slide show? Now, you have to position the slide show on the canvas of the easel. The slides are actually larger than the canvas, but since they're in a composition, you can size them as a unit.

1 Switch to the CarRide Timeline panel and go to 11:00, which is when the canvas is centered in the composition.

2 Drag the Artwork composition from the Project panel into the CarRide Timeline panel, placing it at the top of the layer stack.

Currently, the Artwork layer is set to start at 0:00. You need to adjust the timing of the layer so that it appears at 11:00.

3 Drag the layer duration bar (from the center) for the Artwork layer in the time ruler so that its In point is at 11:00.

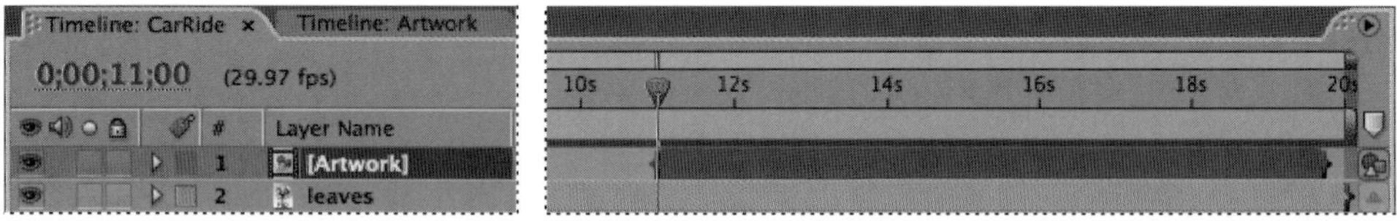

Now, scale the slides to fit the canvas.

4 With the Artwork layer selected in the Timeline panel, press S to reveal its Scale property.

5 Set the Scale values to **45.0, 45.0%**.

6 Select the Artwork layer in the Timeline panel and choose Layer > Blending Mode > Darken. This drops out the pure white in each image and replaces it with the softer white of the canvas.

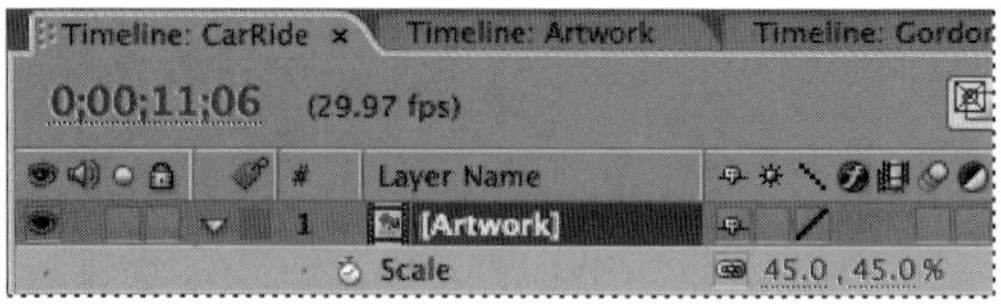

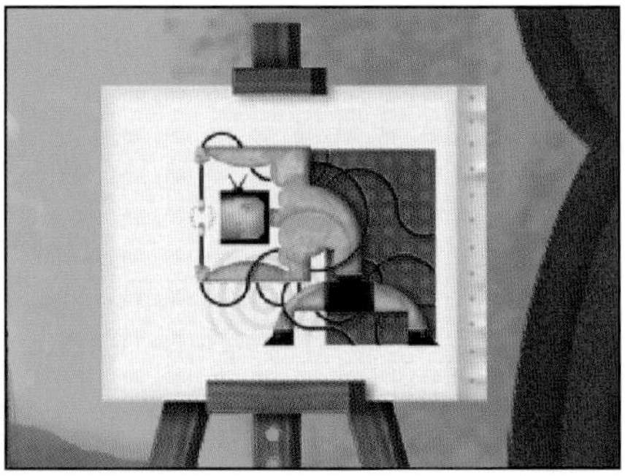

7 Click the RAM Preview button (▮▮▶) in the Time Controls panel to watch a RAM preview of the slide show. (Make sure the From Current Time box is checked to start the RAM preview at 11:00.)

Fading in the first slide

As it stands, the first slide instantly appears in the easel at 11:00. Let's animate the Artwork layer's opacity so that the first slide fades in.

1 Select the Artwork layer in the Timeline panel and press T to reveal its Opacity property.

2 Go to 11:00.

3 Set the Artwork layer's Opacity to **0%**, and click the stopwatch icon (⏱) to set an Opacity keyframe.

4 Go to 11:03 and set the Artwork layer's Opacity to **100%**. After Effects adds a keyframe. That should do the trick.

5 Manually preview the animation from 11:00 to 11:03 to see the first slide fade in.

6 Select the Artwork layer in the Timeline panel and press U to hide its Opacity property. Then, choose File > Save to save your work.

Adding an audio track

Give yourself a hand. You've done a lot of animating in this project. You're not done yet, though. Although Gordon Studer speaks to the viewer while he drives the car across the composition, you'll add some polish by dropping in a background audio track.

1 Choose File > Browse to jump to Bridge.

2 In the content area, click to select the piano.wav thumbnail preview. Bridge lets you preview audio.

3 Click the Play button (▶) in the Preview panel to hear the track. Click the Pause button (❚❚) to stop.

4 Double-click the piano.wav file to import it into the After Effects Project panel.

5 Drag piano.wav from the Project panel into the CarRide Timeline panel, placing it at the bottom of the layer stack.

6 Notice the duration bar for the Piano layer: It doesn't last for the entire length of the composition. You can have it play continuously for the entire composition, however, by *looping* it.

Supported audio file formats

You can import any of the following types of audio files into After Effects:

- Advanced Audio Coding (AAC)
- AU (Requires QuickTime)
- Audio Interchange File Format (AIFF; requires QuickTime)
- MP3 (Requires QuickTime)
- Video for Windows (AVI, WAV)
- WAVE (WAV)

Looping the audio track

Luckily, this music track has been composed to loop cleanly; you just have to know how to create a loop. You're going to do it using the Time Remapping feature. You'll learn to use Time Remapping in more depth in Lesson 5, "Animating Layers." For now, you're simply going to use it to loop the audio in this project.

1 Select the Piano layer in the Timeline panel.

2 Choose Layer > Time > Enable Time Remapping. A Time Remap property appears for the layer in the Timeline panel, and two Time Remap keyframes appear for the layer in the time ruler.

3 Alt-click (Windows) or Option-click (Mac OS) the stopwatch icon (⏱) for the layer's Time Remap property. This sets the default expression for time remapping; it has no immediate effect in the Composition panel.

4 In the Expression: Time Remap property for the Piano layer, click the Expression Language pop-up menu and choose Property > loopOut(type = "cycle", numKeyframes = 0).

The audio is now set to loop in a cycle, repeating the clip endlessly. All you need to do is extend the Out point of the layer to the end of the composition.

5 Select the Piano layer in the Timeline panel and press the End key to go to the end of the time ruler. Then, press Alt+] (Windows) or Option+] (Mac OS) to extend the layer to the end of the composition.

You'll preview the entire composition in a minute.

6 Select the Piano layer in the Timeline panel and press U to hide its properties, then choose File > Save to save your work.

Zooming in for a final close-up

Everything is looking good, but zooming in for a final close-up of the slide show will really focus the viewer's attention on the artwork.

1 In the Project panel, drag the CarRide composition onto the Create A New Composition button (▣) at the bottom of the panel. After Effects creates a new composition, named CarRide 2, and opens it in the Timeline and Composition panels. Rename the composition to avoid confusion.

2 With the CarRide 2 composition selected in the Project panel, press Enter (Windows) or Return (Mac OS), and type **Lesson04**. Then, press Enter or Return again to accept the new name.

3 In the Lesson04 Timeline panel, go to 10:24, the first frame where the car clears the right side of the composition.

4 Select the CarRide layer in the Lesson04 Timeline panel and press S to reveal its Scale property.

5 Click the stopwatch icon (⏱) to set a Scale keyframe at the default values, 100.0, 100.0%.

6 Go to 11:00 and change the Scale values to **110.0, 110.0%**. After Effects adds a keyframe, and for the rest of the composition, the slide show will be prominent and eye-catching.

7 Select the CarRide layer and press U to hide its Scale property.

Previewing the entire composition

It's time to watch the whole shebang.

1 In the Time Controls panel, uncheck the From Current Time box and then click the RAM Preview button (⫴▶) to watch a RAM preview of the entire composition.

2 Press the spacebar to stop playback when you're done.

3 Choose File > Save.

Congratulations. You've just created a complex animation, practicing all kinds of After Effects techniques and capabilities along the way, from parenting to audio looping. Although you're not going to render it out right now, this project is used for Lesson 12, "Rendering and Outputting." You can skip to that lesson now if you'd like to learn how to output this project for a few different media, or you can proceed sequentially through the book and render it later.

Review

▶ **Review questions**

1 How does After Effects display an animation of the Position property?

2 What is a solid-color layer and what can you do with it?

3 What types of audio can you import into an After Effects project?

▶ **Review answers**

1 When you animate the Position property, After Effects displays the movement as a motion path. You can create a motion path for the position of the layer or for the anchor point of a layer. A position motion path appears in the Composition panel; an anchor-point motion path appears in the Layer panel. The motion path appears as a sequence of dots, where each dot marks the position of the layer at each frame. An *X* in the path marks the position of a keyframe.

2 You can create solid images of any color or size (up to 30,000 x 30,000 pixels) in After Effects. After Effects treats solids as it does any other footage item: You can modify the mask, transform properties, and apply effects to the solid layer. If you change settings for a solid that is used by more than one layer, you can apply the changes to all layers that use the solid or to only the single occurrence of the solid. Use solid layers to color a background or create simple graphic images.

3 You can import any of the following types of audio files into After Effects: Advanced Audio Coding (AAC), AU (requires QuickTime), Audio Interchange File Format (AIFF; requires QuickTime), MP3 (also requires QuickTime), Video for Windows (AVI, WAV), and WAVE (WAV).

Animation is all about making changes over time—changes to an object or image's position, opacity, scale, and other properties. In this lesson, you will get more practice animating the layers of a Photoshop file, including dynamically remapping time.

5 Animating Layers

Lesson overview

In this lesson, you'll learn how to do the following:

- Animate a layered Photoshop file.

- Duplicate an animation using the pick whip.

- Apply a track matte to control the visibility of layers.

- Animate a layer using the Corner Pin effect.

- Apply the Lens Flare effect to a solid layer.

- Use time remapping and the Layer panel to dynamically retime footage.

- Edit Time Remap keyframes in the Graph Editor.

After Effects provides several tools and effects that allow you to simulate motion video using a layered Photoshop file. In this lesson, you will import a layered Photoshop file of the sun appearing through a window, and then you will animate it to simulate the motion of the sun rising through the panes of glass. This is a stylized animation in which the motion is first accelerated, and then slows down as clouds and birds move through the window's frame at the end.

This lesson will take approximately 1 hour to complete.

Getting started

Make sure the following files are in the AE7_CIB > Lessons > Lesson05 folder on your hard disk, or copy them from the *Adobe After Effects 7.0 Classroom in a Book* DVD now.

• In the Assets folder: clock.mov, sunrise.psd

• In the Sample_Movies folder: Lesson05_regular.mov, Lesson05_retimed.mov

1 Open and play the two sample movies to see what you will create in this lesson. The first sample movie, Lesson05_regular.mov, is the straightforward time-lapse animation that you will create in this lesson. The second sample movie, Lesson05_retime.mov, is the same animation after time has been remapped in it, which you will also do in this lesson. When you're done, quit the QuickTime player. You may delete the sample movies from your hard disk if you have limited storage space.

Setting up the project

When you begin the lesson, restore the default application settings for After Effects. See "Restoring default preferences," page 5.

1 Press Ctrl+Alt+Shift (Windows) or Command+Option+Shift (Mac OS) while starting After Effects. When asked whether you want to delete your preferences file, click OK.

After Effects opens to display an empty, untitled project.

2 Choose File > Save As.

3 In the Save Project As dialog box, navigate to the AE7_CIB > Lessons > Lesson05 > Finished_Project folder.

4 Name the project **Lesson05_Finished.aep**, and then click Save.

Importing the footage

You need to import one footage item for this lesson.

1 Double-click an empty area of the Project panel to open the Import File dialog box.

2 Navigate to the AE7_CIB > Lessons > Lesson05 > Assets folder on your hard disk and select the sunrise.psd file.

3 Choose Import As > Composition – Cropped Layers. This makes the dimensions of each layer match the layer's content.

4 Click Open.

Before continuing, take a moment to study the layers of the file you just imported.

5 In the Project panel, expand the Sunrise Layers folder to see the Photoshop layers. Resize the Name column to make it wider and easier to read, if necessary.

Each of the elements that will be animated in After Effects—the shadows, birds, clouds, and sun—is on a separate layer. In addition, there is one layer representing the initial, predawn lighting conditions in the room (Background), and a second layer that represents the final, bright daylight conditions in the room (Background Lit). Similarly, there are two layers for the two lighting conditions outside the window: Window and Window Lit.

After Effects preserves the layer order and transparency data from the source Photoshop document. It also preserves other features, such as adjustment layers and type, which you don't happen to be using in this project.

Preparing layered Photoshop files

Before you import a layered Photoshop file, prepare it carefully to reduce preview and rendering time. Avoid problems importing and updating Photoshop layers by naming them properly. Before you import them into After Effects, do the following:

• Organize and name layers. If you change a layer name in a Photoshop file after you have imported it into After Effects, After Effects retains the link to the original layer. However, if you delete a layer, After Effects will be unable to find the original layer and will list it as missing in the Project panel.

• Make sure that each layer has a unique name to avoid confusion.

Creating the composition

For this lesson, you'll use the imported Photoshop file as the basis of the composition.

1 Double-click the Sunrise composition in the Project panel to open it in the Composition panel and in the Timeline panel.

2 Choose Composition > Composition Settings.

3 In the Composition Settings dialog box, change the Duration to **10:00** to make the composition 10 seconds long, and then click OK.

Simulating changing lighting

The first part of the animation involves lightening the dark room. You'll animate this lighting condition by using Opacity keyframes.

1 In the Timeline panel, click the Solo boxes (⊙) in the Switches column for the Background Lit and Background layers. This isolates the layers to speed animating, previewing, and rendering.

Currently, the lit background is on top of the regular (darker) background, obscuring it and making the initial frame of the animation light. However, you want the animation to start dark, and then lighten. To accomplish this, you will make the Background Lit layer initially transparent, and have it "fade in" and appear to lighten the background over time.

2 Go to 5:00.

3 Select the Background Lit layer in the Timeline panel and press T to reveal its Opacity property.

4 Click the stopwatch icon (⏱) to set an Opacity keyframe. Note that the Opacity value is 100%.

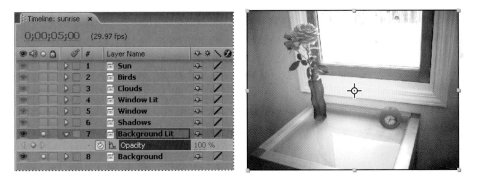

5 Press the Home key to go to 0:00, and then set the Opacity for the Background Lit layer to **0%**. After Effects adds a keyframe. Now, when the animation begins, the Background Lit layer is transparent, which allows the dark Background layer to show through.

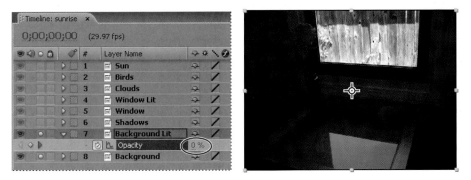

That's it. Watch a preview of the dark-to-light animation.

6 Click the Play/Pause button (▶) in the Time Controls panel, or press the spacebar. The interior of the room transitions gently from dimly to brightly lit.

7 Press the spacebar to stop playback anytime after 5:00.

8 Choose File > Save.

Duplicating an animation using the pick whip

Now, you need to lighten the view through the window. You'll do this by using the pick whip to duplicate the animation you just created. You can use the pick whip to create expressions that link the values of one property or effect to another. To use the pick whip, you simply drag it from one layer to another, and the property that you set or animated in the first layer is copied into the second layer.

About expressions

When you want to create and link complex animations, such as multiple car wheels spinning, but would like to avoid creating tens or hundreds of keyframes by hand, you can use expressions instead. With expressions, you can create relationships between layer properties and use one property's keyframes to dynamically animate another layer. For example, if you set rotation keyframes for a layer and then apply the Drop Shadow effect, you can use an expression to link the Rotation property's values with the Drop Shadow effect's Direction values; that way, the drop shadow changes accordingly as the layer rotates.

Expressions are based on the JavaScript language, but you do not need to know JavaScript to use them. You can create expressions by using simple examples and modifying them to suit your needs, or by chaining objects and methods together.

All of your work with expressions occurs in the Timeline panel. You can use the pick whip to create expressions, or you can enter and edit expressions manually in the expression field, a text field in the time graph under the property.

For more about expressions, see After Effects Help.

1 Press the Home key to go to the beginning of the time ruler.

2 Click the Solo icons (⬤) for the Background Lit and Background layers to restore the view of the other layers, including Window and Window Lit. Make sure to leave the Opacity property for the Background Lit layer visible.

3 Select the Window Lit layer and press T to reveal its Opacity property.

4 Alt-click (Windows) or Option-click (Mac OS) the Opacity stopwatch for the Window Lit layer to add an expression for the default Opacity value, 100%. The words *transform.opacity* appear in the time ruler for the Window Lit layer.

5 With the transform.opacity expression selected in the time ruler, click the pick whip icon (⦿) on the Window Lit Expression: Opacity line and drag to the Opacity property name in the Background Lit layer. When you release, the pick whip snaps, and the expression in the Window Lit layer time ruler now reads "thisComp.layer("Background Lit").transform.opacity." This means that the Opacity value for the Background Lit layer (0%) replaces the previous Opacity value (100%) for the Window Lit layer.

6 Drag the current-time indicator from 0:00 to 5:00, and notice that the Opacity values for the two layers match.

7 Press the Home key and then the spacebar to preview the animation again, and notice that the sky outside the window lightens as the room inside the window does.

8 Press spacebar to stop playback.

9 Select the Window Lit and Background Lit layers in turn, and press U to hide their properties and tidy up the Timeline panel for your next task.

10 Choose File > Save to save your project.

Now that the lighting is under control, it's time to animate the movement of the sun, the birds, and the clouds.

Animating movement in the scenery

The scenery outside the window is unrealistically static. For one thing, the sun needs to actually rise. In addition, the clouds need to shift and the birds need to fly to bring this scene to life. You'll start by making the sun rise in the sky by setting keyframes for its Position, Scale, and Opacity properties.

1 In the Timeline panel, select the Sun layer and click the triangle in the Label column to reveal the Transform property name, and then click the next triangle to see all of the Transform properties.

2 Go to 4:07 and click the stopwatch icons (⏱) to set keyframes for the Position, Scale, and Opacity properties at their default values.

3 Go to 3:13.

4 Still working with the Sun layer, set its Scale to **33.3, 33.3%** and its Opacity to **10%**. After Effects adds a keyframe for each property.

5 Press the End key to go to the end of the composition.

6 For the Position property of the Sun layer, set the *y* value to **18.0**, and then set the Scale values to **150.0, 150.0%**. After Effects adds two keyframes.

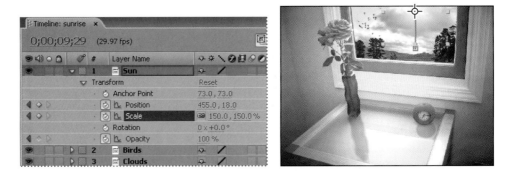

You've just set keyframes that instruct the sun to move up and across the sky, and become slightly larger and brighter as it rises. Next, animate the birds and the clouds, and then watch a preview of all the animations at once.

7 Select the Sun layer and then press UU to hide its Transform properties so that you have more space in the Timeline panel.

Animating the birds

Next, you'll animate the motion of the birds flying by.

1 Select the Birds layer in the Timeline panel and press P to reveal its Position property.

2 Go to 4:20 and set the Position values for the Birds layer to **200.0, 49.0**. Then, click the stopwatch (⏱) to add a Position keyframe.

3 Go to 4:25 and set the Position values of the Birds layer to **670.0, 49.0**. After Effects adds a keyframe.

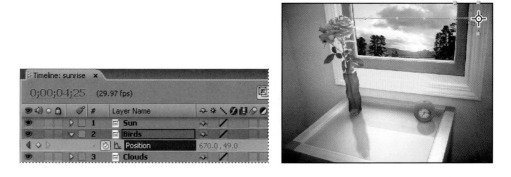

4 Select the Birds layer and press U to hide its Position property.

Animating the clouds

Next, animate the shifting and drifting of the clouds in the sky.

1 Select the Clouds layer in the Timeline panel and expand its Transform properties.

2 Go to 5:22 and click the stopwatch icon (⏱) for the Position property to set a Position keyframe at the current value (406.5, 58.5).

3 Still at 5:22, set the Opacity for the Clouds layer to **33%**, and click the stopwatch icon to set an Opacity keyframe.

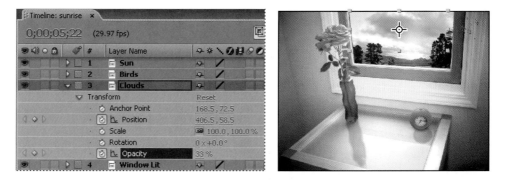

4 Go to 5:02 and set the Clouds layer Opacity value to **0%**. After Effects adds a keyframe.

5 Go to 9:07 and set the Clouds layer Opacity value to **50%**. After Effects adds a keyframe.

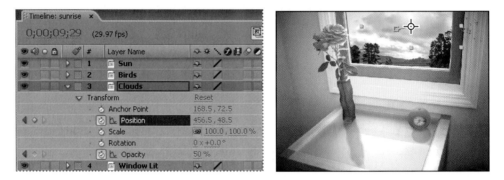

6 Go to the last frame of the composition by pressing the End key.

7 Set the Position of the Clouds layer to **456.5, 48.5**. After Effects adds a keyframe.

Now, preview the animation.

8 Press the Home key to go to 0:00, click on the pasteboard of the Composition panel to deselect the paths in the image, and then press the spacebar to preview the animation. The sun rises in the sky, the birds fly by (very quickly), and the clouds drift. However, there's a fundamental problem: These elements all overlap the window frame—the birds even appear to be flying inside the room. You'll solve this next.

9 Press the spacebar to stop playback, select the Clouds layer in the Timeline panel, click the triangle to hide its properties, and then choose File > Save.

Adjusting the layers and creating a track matte

To solve the problem of the sun, birds, and clouds overlapping the window frame, you must first adjust the hierarchy of the layers within the composition, and then you will use an alpha track matte to allow the outside scenery to show through the window, but not appear to be inside the room.

Precomposing layers

You'll start by precomposing the Sun, Birds, and Clouds layers into one composition.

1 Shift-click to select the Sun, Birds, and Clouds layers in the Timeline panel.

2 Choose Layer > Pre-Compose.

3 In the Pre-Compose dialog box, name the new composition **Window Contents**. Make sure the Move All Attributes Into The New Composition option is selected, and check the Open New Composition box. Then, click OK.

A new Timeline panel named Window Contents appears. It contains the Sun, Birds, and Clouds layers you selected in step 1 of this exercise.

4 Click the Sunrise Timeline panel to see the contents of the main composition. Notice that the Sun, Birds, and Clouds layers have been replaced by the layer Window Contents, which is actually a composition.

Creating the track matte

Now, you will create the track matte to hide the outside scenery behind all areas of the image except the window pane. To do that, you'll duplicate the Window Lit layer and use its alpha channel.

About track mattes and traveling mattes

When you want one layer to show through a hole in another layer, set up a *track matte*. You'll need two layers—one to act as a matte, and another to fill the hole in the matte. You can animate either the track matte layer or the fill layer. When you animate the track matte layer, you create a *traveling matte*. If you want to animate the track matte and fill layers using identical settings, you can precompose them.

You define transparency in a track matte using values from either its alpha channel or the luminance of its pixels. Using luminance is useful when you want to create a track matte using a layer without an alpha channel, or a layer imported from a program that can't create an alpha channel. In both alpha-channel mattes and luminance mattes, pixels with higher values are more transparent. In most cases, you use a high-contrast matte so that areas are either completely transparent or completely opaque. Intermediate shades should appear only where you want partial or gradual transparency, such as along a soft edge.

After Effects preserves the order of a layer and its track matte after you duplicate or split the layer. Within the duplicated or split layers, the track matte layer remains on top of the fill layer. For example, if your project contains Layers A and B, where A is the track matte and B the fill layer, duplicating or splitting both of these layers results in the layer order ABAB.

A   B   C

Traveling matte

A. *Track matte layer: a solid with a rectangular mask, set to Luma Matte. The mask is animated to travel across the screen.* **B.** *Fill layer: a solid with a pattern effect.* **C.** *Result: The pattern is seen in the track matte's shape and added to the image layer, which is below the track matte layer.*

Note: You'll learn more about track mattes in Lesson 8, "Performing Color Correction."

1 In the Sunrise Timeline panel, select the Window Lit layer.

2 Choose Edit > Duplicate.

3 Drag the duplicate layer, Window Lit 2, up in the layer stack so that it's above the Window Contents layer.

4 Choose Columns > Modes from the Timeline panel menu.

Now, you can apply the track matte.

5 Select the Window Contents layer and choose Alpha Matte "Window Lit 2" from the TrkMat pop-up menu. The alpha channel of the layer above (Window Lit 2) is used to set transparency for the Window Contents layer, allowing the scenery outside the window to show through the transparent areas of the window pane.

6 Press the Home key and then preview the animation by pressing the spacebar. Press the spacebar again when you're done.

7 Choose File > Save to save your project.

Adding motion blur

The birds will look more authentic if they include motion blur. You'll add that quickly before animating the shadows.

1 Switch to the Window Contents Timeline panel.

2 Go to 4:22—the middle of the birds animation—and, with the Birds layer selected, choose Layer > Switches > Motion Blur to turn on the motion blur for the Birds layer.

Now, enable motion blur previewing in the Composition panel.

3 Click the Enable Motion Blur button (⊘) at the top of the Timeline panel to display the motion blur for the Birds layer in the Composition panel.

Now you can set the shutter angle and phase, which control the intensity of the motion blur.

4 Choose Composition > Composition Settings.

5 In the Composition Settings dialog box, click the Advanced tab and reduce the Shutter Angle to **30˚**. This setting imitates the effect of adjusting a shutter angle on a real camera, which controls how long the camera aperture is open, gathering light.

6 Leave Shutter Phase at 0, and then click OK.

Animating the shadows

It's time to turn your attention to the shadows being cast on the table by the clock and the vase. In a realistic time-lapse image, they would shorten as the sun rises.

There are a few ways to create and animate shadows in After Effects. For example, you could use 3D layers and lights. In this project, however, you will use the Corner Pin effect to distort the Shadows layer of the imported Photoshop image. Using the Corner Pin effect is like animating with the Photoshop Free Transform tool. The effect distorts an image by repositioning each of its four corners. You can use it to stretch, shrink, skew, or twist an image, or to simulate perspective or movement that pivots from the edge of a layer, such as a door opening.

1 Switch to the Sunrise Timeline panel and press the Home key to make sure you're at the beginning of the time ruler.

2 Select the Shadows layer in the Timeline panel and then choose Effect > Distort > Corner Pin. Small circles appear around the corner points of the shadow layer in the Composition panel.

Note: If you don't see the controls, choose View Options from the Composition panel menu. In the View Options dialog box that opens, check the Handles and Effect Controls boxes and then click OK.

You'll start by setting the four corners of the Shadows layer to correspond to the four corners of the glass tabletop. You'll start about midway into the animation, when the sun is high enough to start affecting the shadow.

3 Go to 6:00 and then drag each of the four corner-pin handles to the respective corner of the glass table top. Notice that the *x, y* coordinates update in the Effect Controls panel.

> *The lower-right corner of the Shadows layer is off-screen. To adjust that corner, switch to the Hand tool (✋) and drag up in the Composition panel so that you can see some of the pasteboard below the image. Then, switch back to the Selection tool (▶) and drag the lower-right corner-pin handle to the approximate location of the lower-right corner of the glass tabletop.*

If you have trouble getting the shadows to look right, you can enter the values manually, as shown in the following figure.

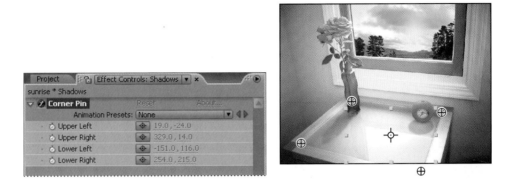

4 Set a keyframe for each corner at 6:00 by clicking the stopwatch icon (🕙) for each position in the Effect Controls panel.

Now, go to the end of the animation and adjust the position of the shadow.

5 Press the End key to go to the last frame of the composition.

6 Using the Selection tool (▸), drag the two lower corner-pin handles to shorten the shadows: Drag them about 25% closer to the back edge of the tabletop. You may also need to move the two upper corners in slightly so that the bases of the shadows still align properly with the vase and clock. Your corner-pin values should be similar to those in the following figure; you can enter the values directly if you prefer not to drag the corners. After Effects adds keyframes.

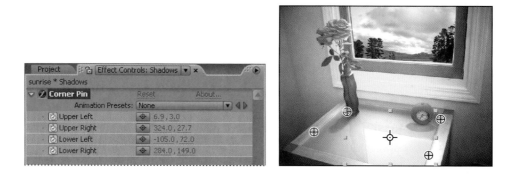

7 If necessary, select the Hand tool (✋) and drag the composition down to center it vertically in the Composition panel. Then, switch back to the Selection tool (▸) and click on the pasteboard of the Composition panel to deselect the layer.

8 Press the Home key to go to 0:00, and then press the spacebar to preview the entire animation, including the corner-pin effect. When you're done, press the spacebar again.

9 Choose File > Save to save your project.

Adding a lens flare effect

In photography, when bright light (such as sunlight) reflects off the lens of a camera, it causes a flare effect. Lens flares can be bright, colorful circles and halos, depending on the type of lens in the camera. After Effects offers a few lens flare effects. You'll add one now to enhance the realism of this time-lapse photography composition.

1 Go to 5:10, where the sun is brightly shining into the lens of the camera.

2 Choose Layer > New > Solid.

3 In the Solid Settings dialog box, name the layer **Lens Flare** and click the Make Comp Size button. Then, set the Color to black by clicking the swatch and setting the RGB values to 0 in the Color Picker dialog box. Click OK to close the Color Picker and return to the Solid Settings dialog box.

4 Click OK to create the Lens Flare layer.

5 With the Lens Flare layer selected in the Sunrise Timeline panel, choose Effect > Generate > Lens Flare. The Composition panel and the Effect Controls panel display the visual and numeric default Lens Flare settings, respectively; let's customize the effect for this composition.

6 Drag the Flare Center cross-hair icon (⊕) in the Composition panel to the center of the sun. You cannot see the sun in the Composition panel; the *x, y* coordinates, which you can read in the Effect Controls or Info panel, are approximately 455, 135.

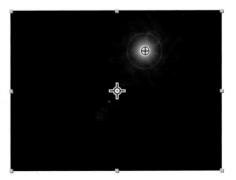

💡 *You can also enter the Flare Center values directly in the Effect Controls panel.*

7 In the Effect Controls panel, change the Lens Type to 35mm Prime, a more diffuse flare effect.

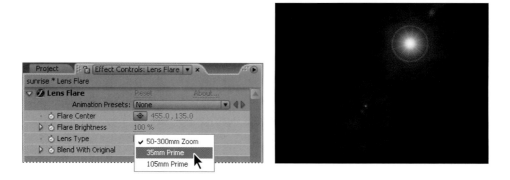

8 Make sure you're still at 5:10 and, in the Effect Controls panel, click the stopwatch icon (⏱) for the Flare Brightness property to set a keyframe at the default value of 100%.

9 Now, adjust the brightness of the lens flare to peak when the sun is highest.

• Go to 3:27 and set the Flare Brightness value to **0%**.

• Go to 6:27 and set the Flare Brightness value to **0%**, also.

• Go to 6:00 and set the Flare Brightness to **100%**.

10 Finally, with the Lens Flare layer selected in the Timeline panel, choose Layer > Blending Mode > Screen to change the blend mode to screen.

You can also choose Screen from the Mode pop-up menu in the Timeline panel.

11 Press the Home key and then the spacebar to preview the lens flare effect. When you're done, press the spacebar again.

12 Choose File > Save to save your project.

Animating the clock

The animation now looks very much like a time-lapse photo—except the clock isn't working yet! The hands of the clock should be spinning quickly to show the progress of time. To show this, you will add an animation that was created specifically for this scene. The animation was created in After Effects as a set of 3D layers that are lit, textured, and masked to blend into the scene.

Note: You'll learn more about 3D layers in Lessons 9 and 10, "Building and Animating a 3D Object" and "Using 3D Effects," respectively.

1 Bring the Project panel forward and double-click an empty area in it to open the Import File dialog box.

2 In the AE7_CIB > Lessons > Lesson05 > Assets folder, select the clock.mov file and click Open.

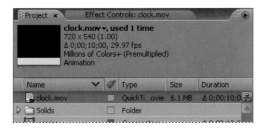

The QuickTime movie clock.mov appears at the top of the Project panel.

3 Click in the Sunrise Timeline panel to make it active and then press the Home key to go to the beginning of the time ruler. Then, drag the Clock movie from the Project panel to the top of the layer stack in the Timeline panel.

4 Preview the animation by pressing the spacebar. Press the spacebar to stop playback when you're done.

5 Choose File > Save to save the project.

Rendering the animation

To prepare for the next task, retiming the composition, you need to render the Sunrise composition.

1 Select the Sunrise composition in the Project panel and then choose Composition > Add to Render Queue.

The Render Queue panel opens. Resize it to make it larger, if necessary.

2 Accept the default Render Settings in the Render Queue panel, and then click the blue, underlined words *Not Yet Specified* next to the Output To pop-up menu.

3 Navigate to the AE7_CIB > Lessons > Lesson05 > Assets folder for your destination and name the file **Lesson05_retime.mov** (Mac OS) or **Lesson05_retime.avi** (Windows). Then, click Save.

4 Click the Render button in the Render Queue panel.

After Effects displays a progress bar as it renders the composition, and it plays an audio alert when it is finished.

5 When After Effects finishes rendering the composition, close the Render Queue panel.

Retiming the composition

So far, you have created a straightforward time-lapse simulation. That's fine, but After Effects offers more ways to play with time using the time-remapping feature. Time remapping allows you to dynamically speed up, slow down, stop, or reverse footage. You can also use it to do things like create a freeze-frame effect. The Graph Editor and the Layer panel are a big help when remapping time, as you'll see in the following exercise, when you retime the project so that the time-lapse speed changes dynamically.

For this exercise, you'll use the movie that you just rendered as the basis of a new composition, which will be easier to remap.

1 Double-click an empty area of the Project panel to open the Import File dialog box.

2 In the AE7_CIB > Lessons > Lesson05 > Assets folder, select the Lesson05_retime.mov (Mac OS) or Lesson05_retime.avi (Windows) file that you just rendered, and click Open.

3 Drag the Lesson05_retime movie onto the Create A New Composition button (⊞) at the bottom of the Project panel. After Effects creates a new composition named Lesson05_retime, and displays it in the Timeline and Composition panels.

Now, you can remap all of the elements of the project at once.

4 With the Lesson05_retime layer selected in the Timeline panel, choose Layer > Time > Enable Time Remapping. After Effects adds two keyframes, at the first and last frames of the layer. You can see the keyframes in the time ruler. A Time Remap property also appears under the layer name in the Timeline panel; this property lets you control which frame is displayed at a given point in time.

5 Double-click the Lesson05_retime layer name in the Timeline panel to open it in the Layer panel. The Layer panel provides a visual reference of the frames you change when you remap time. It displays two time rulers: The time ruler at the bottom of the panel displays the current time. The Source Time ruler above that has a remap-time marker, which indicates what frame is playing at the current time.

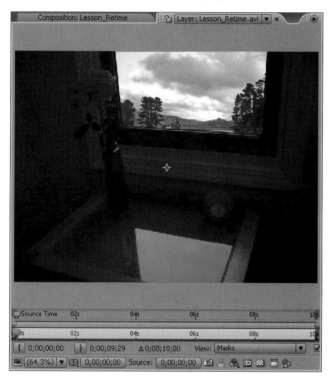

6 Drag the current-time indicator across the time ruler in the Timeline panel, and notice that the source-time and current-time markers in the two Layer panel rulers are synchronized. That will change as you remap time.

7 Go to 4:00 and change the Time Remap value to **2:00**. This remaps time so that frame 2:00 plays at 4:00. In other words, the composition now plays back at half-speed for the first 4 seconds of the composition.

8 Press the spacebar to preview the animation. The composition now runs at half-speed until 4:00, and at a regular speed thereafter.

Viewing time remapping in the Graph Editor

The Graph Editor lets you view and manipulate all aspects of effects and animations, including effect property values, keyframes, and interpolation. It represents changes in effects and animations as a two-dimensional graph, with playback time represented horizontally (from left to right). In layer bar mode, in contrast, the time ruler represents only the horizontal time element, without showing a visual representation of changing values. Let's see what the time-remap change looks like in the Graph Editor.

1 Make sure the Time Remap property is selected for the Lesson05_retime layer in the Timeline panel, and then click the Graph Editor button (⬚) to display the Graph Editor.

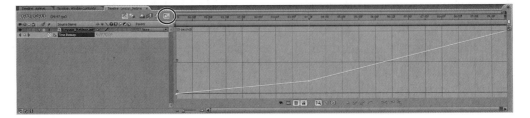

The Graph Editor displays a time-remap graph that shows a white line connecting the keyframes at 0:00, 4:00, and 10:00. The angle of the line is shallow up to 4:00, and then it becomes steeper. The steeper the line, the faster the playback time.

Using the Graph Editor to remap time

When remapping time, you can use the values in the time-remap graph to determine and control which frame of the movie plays at which point in time. Each Time Remap keyframe has a time value associated with it that corresponds to a specific frame in the layer; this value is represented vertically on the time-remap graph. When you enable time remapping for a layer, After Effects adds a Time Remap keyframe at the start and end points of the layer. These initial Time Remap keyframes have vertical time values equal to their horizontal position.

By setting additional Time Remap keyframes, you can create complex motion effects. Every time you add a Time Remap keyframe, you create another point at which you can change the playback speed or direction. As you move the keyframe up or down in the time-remap graph, you adjust which frame of the video is set to play at the current time.

Let's have some fun with the timing of this project.

1 In the time-remap graph, drag the middle keyframe from 4:00 up to 10 seconds.

Use the tooltips that appear as you drag to help you pinpoint the exact value of the keyframe.

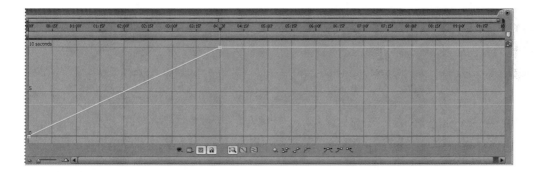

2 Drag the last keyframe down to 0 seconds.

Now the animation progresses rapidly over the first four seconds of the composition and then plays in reverse, and at a faster speed, for the rest of the composition.

3 Press the Home key to go to 0:00 and then press the spacebar to preview the results. Watch the time ruler and source time ruler in the Layer panel to see what frames are playing at any given point in time.

Having fun yet? Let's keep going.

4 Press the spacebar to stop the preview.

5 Command-click (Mac OS) or Ctrl-click (Windows) the last keyframe to delete it. The composition still is in fast-forward mode for the first four seconds, but now it holds on a single frame (the last frame) for the rest of the composition.

6 Press the Home key and then the spacebar to preview the animation. Press the spacebar again when you're done.

7 Command-click (Mac OS) or Ctrl-click (Windows) the dotted line at 6:00 to add a keyframe at 6:00 with the same value as the keyframe at 4:00.

8 Command-click (Mac OS) or Ctrl-click (Windows) at 10:00 to add another keyframe, and then drag it down to 0 seconds. Now the animation progresses rapidly, holds for two seconds on the last frame, and then runs in reverse.

9 Press the Home key and then the spacebar to preview the change. Press the spacebar again when you're done.

Adding an Easy Ease Out

Let's soften the shift in time that occurs six seconds into the animation by adding an Easy Ease Out.

1 Click to select the keyframe at 6:00 and then click the Easy Ease Out button (🔧) at the bottom of the Graph Editor. This slows the shift into reverse—the footage runs slowly in reverse at first, and then gradually speeds up.

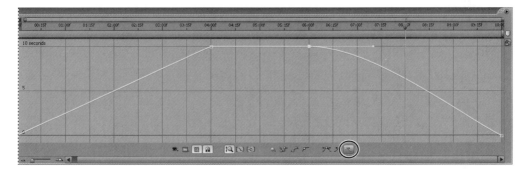

💡 *You can refine the amount of ease on this transition further by dragging the bezier handle that appears out of the right side of keyframe at 6:00. If you drag it to the right, the ease is more pronounced; if you drag it down or to the left, the ease is softer.*

Scaling the animation in time

Finally, use the Graph Editor to scale the entire animation in time.

1 Click the Time Remap property name in the Timeline panel to select all of the Time Remap keyframes.

2 Make sure the Show Transform Box button (▦) at the bottom of the Graph Editor is on; a free transform selection box should be visible around all of the keyframes.

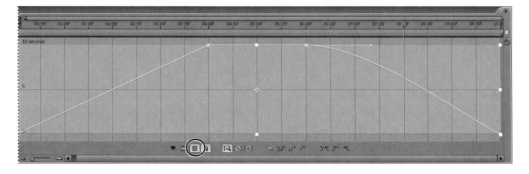

3 Drag one of the upper transform handles from 10 seconds to 5 seconds to reduce the top keyframe values and slow the playback.

If you press Command (Mac OS) or Ctrl (Windows) while you drag, the entire free transform box scales around the center point, which you can also drag to offset. If you press Option (Mac OS) or Alt (Windows) and drag one corner of the free transform box, the animation is skewed in that corner as you drag. You can also drag one of the right transform handles to the left to scale the entire animation so that it happens more quickly.

4 Press the Home key and then the spacebar to preview the change. Press the spacebar again when you're done.

5 Choose File > Save.

Congratulations. You've completed a complex animation, complete with shifts in time. You can render the time-remap project if you'd like. Follow the instructions on page 190 of this lesson, or see Lesson 12, "Rendering and Outputting," for detailed instructions on rendering.

Review

▶ Review questions

1 How does After Effects import Photoshop files?

2 What is the pick whip and how do you use it?

3 What is a track matte and how do you use it?

4 How do you remap time in After Effects?

▶ Review answers

1 When you import a layered Photoshop file into After Effects as a composition, After Effects preserves the layer order and transparency data from the source Photoshop document. It also preserves other features, such as adjustment layers and type.

2 The pick whip allows you to create expressions that link the values of one property or effect to another layer. To use the pick whip, you simply drag the pick whip icon (⊚) from one layer to another, and the property that you set or animated in the first layer is copied into the second layer.

3 When you want one layer to show through a hole in another layer, you can use a track matte. To create a track matte, you need two layers: one to act as a matte, and another to fill the hole in the matte. You can animate either the track matte layer or the fill layer. When you animate the track matte layer, you create a traveling matte.

4 Time remapping allows you to dynamically speed up, slow down, stop, or reverse footage. When remapping time, you can use the values in the time-remap graph in the Graph Editor to determine and control which frame of the movie plays at which point in time. When you enable time remapping for a layer, After Effects adds a Time Remap keyframe at the start and end points of the layer. By setting additional Time Remap keyframes, you can create complex motion effects. Every time you add a Time Remap keyframe, you create another point at which you can change the playback speed or direction.

When working in After Effects, there will be times when you won't need (or want) everything in the shot to be included in the final composite. This is when you can use masking, a technique that you will learn to use in this lesson.

6 | Working with Masks

Lesson overview

In this lesson, you'll learn how to do the following:

- Create a mask using the Pen tool.

- Change a mask's mode.

- Edit a mask shape by controlling vertices and direction handles.

- Feather a mask edge.

- Replace the contents of a mask shape.

- Adjust the position of a layer in 3D space to blend it with the rest of the shot.

- Create a reflection effect.

- Create a vignette.

- Use Auto Levels to correct the color of the shot.

In this lesson, you will create a mask for the screen of a desktop computer and replace the screen's original content with a TV news promo. Then, you will adjust the positioning of the new footage so that it fits the perspective of the shot. Finally, you will polish the scene by adding a reflection, creating a vignette effect, and adjusting the color.

This lesson will take approximately 1 hour to complete.

About masks

A mask in After Effects is a path, or outline, that is used to modify layer effects and properties. The most common use of masks is to modify a layer's alpha channel. A mask consists of segments and vertices. Segments are the lines or curves that connect vertices. Vertices define where each segment of a path starts and ends.

A mask can be either an open or a closed path. An open path has a beginning point that is not the same as its end point. For example, a straight line is an open path. A closed path is continuous and has no beginning or end. For example, a circle is a closed path. Closed-path masks can create transparent areas for a layer. Open paths cannot create transparent areas for a layer, but are useful as parameters for an effect. For example, you can create a visible line or shape from the mask using the Stroke effect.

A mask belongs to a specific layer. Each layer can contain multiple masks.

You can draw four types of masks:

Rectangular A rectangular mask can be square. This type of mask is previewed and rendered faster than any other kind of drawn mask.

Elliptical An elliptical mask can be circular.

Bezier Create any shape of bezier mask using the Pen tool.

RotoBezier The main difference between RotoBezier and Bezier is that tangent handles are calculated automatically with RotoBezier masks.

Getting started

Make sure the following files are in the AE7_CIB > Lessons > Lesson06 folder on your hard disk, or copy them from the *Adobe After Effects 7.0 Classroom in a Book* DVD now.

- In the Assets folder: news_promo.mov, office_mask.mov
- In the Sample_Movie folder: Lesson06.mov

1 Open and play the Lesson06.mov sample movie to see what you will create in this lesson. When you are done, quit the QuickTime player. You may delete the sample movie from your hard disk if you have limited storage space.

Setting up the project

When you begin the lesson, restore the default application settings for After Effects. See "Restoring default preferences," page 5.

1 Press Ctrl+Alt+Shift (Windows) or Option+Command+Shift (Mac OS) while starting After Effects 7.0 to restore default preferences settings. When asked whether you want to delete your preferences file, click OK.

After Effects opens to display a new, untitled project.

2 Choose File > Save As.

3 In the Save Project As dialog box, navigate to the AE7_CIB > Lessons > Lesson06 > Finished_Project folder.

4 Name the project **Lesson06_Finished.aep**, and then click Save.

Importing the footage

You need to import two footage items for this exercise.

1 Double-click an empty area of the Project panel to open the Import File dialog box.

2 Navigate to the AE7_CIB > Lessons > Lesson06 > Assets folder, Shift-click to select the news_promo.mov and office_mask.mov files, and then click Open.

Note: The news_promo.mov file represents the finished project that you will create in Lesson 7, "Keying," sized for this project.

3 In the Interpret Footage dialog box that appears, select Ignore, and then click OK. There is an alpha channel in the news_promo movie, but it isn't needed for this project.

About the Interpret Footage dialog box

After Effects uses a set of internal rules to automatically interpret footage that you import. Generally, you don't need to change these settings. However, if your footage isn't standard, After Effects may interpret it incorrectly. In this case, you can use the settings in the Interpret Footage dialog box to reinterpret your footage. The settings in the Interpret Footage dialog box should match your source footage settings; don't use it to specify settings for your final rendered output.

When you choose Ignore, you instruct After Effects to disregard all transparency data in the file.

For more information on the various settings in the Interpret Footage dialog box, see After Effects Help.

Start by organizing the files in the Project panel.

4 Choose File > New > New Folder to create a new folder in the Project panel, or click the Create A New Folder button (▢) at the bottom of the Project panel.

5 Type **mov_files** to name the folder, press Enter (Windows) or Return (Mac OS) to accept the name, and then drag the two movie files into the mov_files folder.

6 Click the triangle to expand the folder so that you can see the files inside.

Creating the composition

Now, create the composition based on the aspect ratio and duration of one of the source footage items.

1 Select the Office_mask.mov file in the Project panel and drag it to the Create A New Composition button (⊞) at the bottom of the panel.

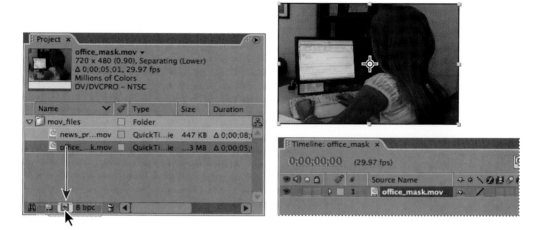

After Effects creates a composition named Office_mask and opens it in the Composition and Timeline panels.

2 Choose File > Save to save your work so far.

Creating a mask with the Pen tool

To replace the image on the computer screen, you need to mask the screen.

1 Press the Home key to make sure the current-time indicator is at the beginning of the time ruler.

2 Zoom into the Composition panel until the monitor screen fills the view. You may need to use the Hand tool (🖑) to reposition the view in the panel.

3 Select the Pen tool (✒) in the Tools panel. The Pen tool allows you to create straight lines or curved segments. Since the monitor appears to be square, you will try using straight lines first.

4 Click the upper-left corner of the monitor screen to place the first vertex.

5 Click the upper-right corner of the monitor to place the second vertex. After Effects connects the two points with a segment.

6 Click to place a third vertex in the lower-right corner of the monitor, and then click to place a fourth vertex in the lower-left corner of the monitor.

7 Move the Pen tool over the first vertex (in the upper-left corner). When you notice a circle appear next to the pointer (as in the middle image below), click to close the mask shape.

Editing a mask

The mask shape looks pretty good, but instead of masking the information *inside* the monitor, the mask has removed everything *outside* the monitor. So you need to change the mask mode, which is set to Add by default.

About mask modes

Blending modes for masks (mask modes) control how masks within a layer interact with one another. By default, all masks are set to Add, which combines the transparency values of any masks that overlap on the same layer. You can apply one mode to each mask, but you cannot change a mask's mode over time.

The first mask you create interacts with the layer's alpha channel. If that channel doesn't define the entire image as opaque, then the mask interacts with the layer frame. Each additional mask that you create interacts with masks located above it in the Timeline panel. The results of mask modes vary depending on the modes set for the masks higher up in the Timeline panel. You can use mask modes only between masks in the same layer. Using mask modes, you can create complex mask shapes with multiple transparent areas. For example, you can set a mask mode that combines two masks and sets the opaque area to the areas where the two masks intersect.

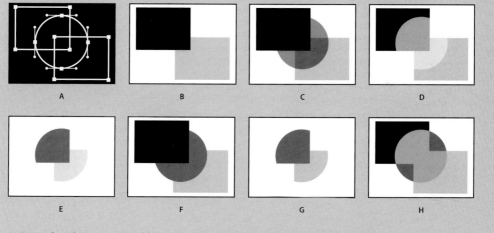

A. *Original masks* **B.** *None* **C.** *Add* **D.** *Subtract* **E.** *Intersect* **F.** *Lighten* **G.** *Darken* **H.** *Difference*

Changing the mask mode

For this project, you need everything inside the mask to be transparent and everything outside the mask to be opaque. So you'll change the mask mode now.

1 With the Office_mask layer selected in the Timeline panel, press the M key to see the Mask Shape property for the mask.

💡 *Pressing the M key twice in quick succession will display all mask properties for the selected layer.*

There are two ways you can change the mask mode: by choosing Subtract from the Mask Mode pop-up menu, or by checking the Inverted box.

2 Check the Inverted box for Mask 1.

The mask inverts.

3 Deselect the Office_mask layer by clicking in any empty area of the Timeline panel. If you look closely at the monitor, you will probably see portions of the screen still appearing around the edges of the mask.

These errors will certainly call attention to changes being made to the layer, and they need to be fixed. To fix them, you will change the straight lines to curves.

Creating curved masks

Curved or freeform masks use bezier curves to define the shape of the mask. Bezier curves give you the greatest control over the shape of the mask. With them, you can create straight lines with sharp angles, perfectly smooth curves, or a combination of the two.

1 In the Timeline panel, select Mask 1, the mask for the Office_mask layer. This makes the mask active and also selects all the vertices.

2 In the Tools panel, select the Convert Vertex tool (↖), which is hidden behind the Pen tool.

💡 *The keyboard shortcut for the Pen tool is G. Pressing the G key multiple times will cycle through the various Pen tools.*

3 In the Composition panel, click any of the vertices. The Convert Vertex tool changes the corner vertices to smooth points.

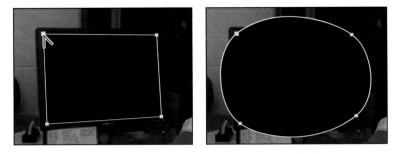

4 Switch to the Selection tool (▸) and click anywhere in the Composition panel to deselect the mask, and then click the first vertex that you created.

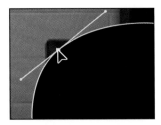

Two direction handles extend off the smooth point. The angle and length of these handles control the shape of the mask.

5 Drag the right handle of the first vertex around the screen. Notice how this changes this shape of the mask. Notice also that the closer you drag the handle to another vertex, the less the shape of the path is influenced by the direction handle of the first vertex, and the more it is influenced by the direction handle of the second vertex.

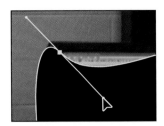

6 Once you are comfortable moving the handles, position the handle of the upper-left vertex as in the preceding figure. As you have seen, you can create very fluid shapes.

Press Ctrl+Z (Windows) or Command+Z to undo a change if you make a mistake. Also, change the zoom level of your view and use the Hand tool to reposition the image in the Composition panel if necessary as you work.

Breaking direction handles

By default, the direction handles of any smooth point are connected to one another. As you drag one handle, the opposite handle moves as well. However, you can break this connection to get greater control over the shape of the mask, and you can create sharp points or long, smooth curves.

1 With the Selection tool (➤) still active, press the Ctrl key (Windows) or the Command key (Mac OS) to temporarily switch to the Convert Vertex tool (ᐳ).

2 Still pressing the Ctrl or Command key, drag the right direction handle of the upper-left vertex. The left direction handle remains stationary.

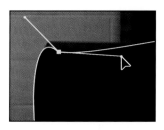

3 Adjust the right direction handle until the top segment of the mask shape more closely follows the curve of the monitor in that corner. It doesn't have to be perfect.

4 Drag the left direction handle of the same vertex until the left segment of the shape more closely follows the curve of the monitor in that corner.

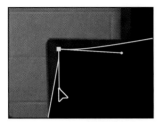

5 Repeat steps 1–4 for the other three corner points of the mask until the shape of the mask more closely matches the curvature of the monitor.

Again, you may need to adjust your view in the Composition panel as you work. You can use the Zoom tool or the Magnification Ratio pop-up menu at the bottom of the Composition panel to zoom in and out, and you can reposition the image in the Composition panel by dragging it with the Hand tool. You can temporarily switch to the Hand tool by pressing and holding the spacebar.

6 When you're done, deselect the Office_mask layer in the Timeline panel to check the edge of your mask. You should not see any of the monitor screen.

7 Choose File > Save to save your work.

Creating a bezier mask

Although you can use the Convert Vertex tool (◥) to change a corner vertex to a smooth point with bezier handles, you can also create a bezier mask from the start. To do so, click in the Composition panel with the Pen tool (◊) where you want to place the first vertex. Then, click where you want to place the next vertex, and drag in the direction you want to create a curve. When satisfied with the curve, release the mouse button. Continue to add points until you've created the shape you want. Close the mask by either clicking on the first vertex or double-clicking the last vertex. Then, switch to the Selection tool to refine the mask.

Feathering the edges of a mask

The mask shape looks good, but you need to soften the edges a bit.

1 Choose Composition > Background Color or press Ctrl+Shift+B (Windows) or Command+Shift+B (Mac OS).

2 Click the color swatch and choose white for the background color (RGB=255, 255, 255). Then click OK to close the Color Picker, and OK again to close the Background Color dialog box.

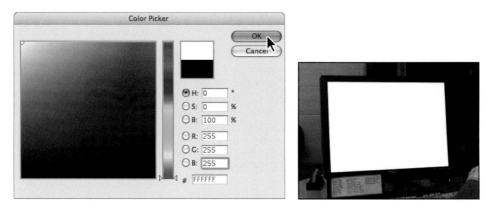

The white background allows you to see that the edge of the monitor screen looks a little too sharp and unrealistic. So next you will feather, or soften, the edges.

3 Select the Office_mask layer in the Timeline panel and press the F key to display the Mask Feather property for the mask.

4 Increase the Mask Feather amount to **1.5, 1.5** pixels.

5 Choose File > Save to save your work.

Replacing the content of the mask

You are now ready to replace the background with the TV news promo movie and blend it with the overall shot.

1 In the Project panel, select the News_promo.mov file and drag it to the Timeline panel, placing it below the Office_mask layer.

2 If necessary, choose Fit Up To 100% from the Magnification Ratio pop-up menu at the bottom of the Composition panel.

3 Using the Selection tool (◄), drag the News_promo layer in the Composition panel until the anchor point is centered in the monitor screen.

Repositioning and resizing the news clip

The news promo clip is too big for the monitor screen, so you'll resize it as a 3D layer, which will give you more control over its shape and size in this shot.

1 With the News_promo layer selected in the Timeline panel, turn on the 3D switch for the layer.

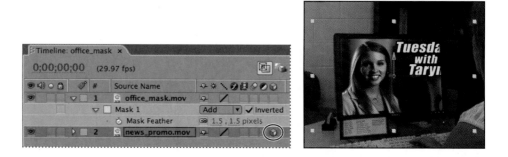

2 Press the P key to show the Position property for the News_promo layer.

The Position property for a 3D layer has three values: From left to right they represent the *x*, *y*, and *z* axes of the image. The *z* axis controls the distance of depth of the layer from viewer. You can see these axes represented in the Composition panel.

Note: You will learn more about 3D layers in Lessons 9 and 10, "Building and Animating a 3D Object" and "Using 3D Effects."

3 Position the pointer in the Composition panel over the red arrow so that a small *x* appears. This lets you control the *x* (horizontal) axis of the layer.

4 Drag left or right as necessary to center the clip horizontally in the monitor screen.

5 Position the pointer in the Composition panel over the green arrow so that a small *y* appears. Then, drag up and down as necessary to position the clip vertically in the monitor screen.

6 Position the pointer in the Composition panel over the blue cube where the red and green arrows meet so that a small *z* appears. Then, drag to increase the depth of field.

7 Continue to drag to the *x*, *y*, and *z* axes until the entire clip fits into the monitor screen as shown in the following image. The final *x*, *y*, and *z* values should be approximately 114, 219, 365.

💡 *You can also enter the Position values directly in the Timeline panel instead of dragging in the Composition panel.*

Rotating the clip

The news clip fits better, but you need to rotate it slightly to improve the perspective.

1 Select the News_promo layer in the Timeline panel and press the R key to reveal its Rotation property. Again, since this is a 3D layer, you can control rotation on the *x*, *y*, and *z* axes.

2 Change the Y Rotation value to **–10.0°**. This swivels the layer to match the perspective of the monitor.

3 Change the Z Rotation value to **–2.0°**. This aligns the layer with the monitor.

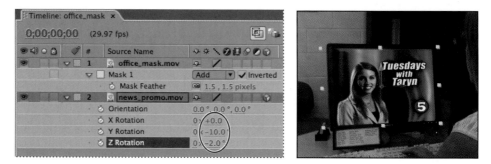

Your composition should now resemble the preceding image.

4 Choose File > Save to save your work.

Adding a reflection

The masked image looks convincing, but you can make it look even more realistic by adding a reflection to the monitor.

1 Choose Layer > New > Solid or press Ctrl+Y (Windows) or Command+Y (Mac OS).

2 In the Solid Settings dialog box, name the layer **Reflection**, click the Make Comp Size button, change the Color to white, and then click OK.

Instead of trying to exactly re-create the shape of the Office_mask layer's mask, it is easier to copy it to the Reflection layer.

3 Select the Office_mask layer in the Timeline panel and press the M key to display the Mask Shape property for the mask.

4 Select Mask 1, and then choose Edit > Copy or press Ctrl+C (Windows) or Command+C (Mac OS).

5 Select the Reflection layer in the Timeline panel, and then choose Edit > Paste or press Ctrl+V (Windows) or Command+V (Mac OS).

This time, you want to keep the area inside the mask opaque and make the area outside the mask transparent.

6 Select the Reflection layer in the Timeline panel and press the M key to reveal the Mask 1 Mask Shape property for the layer.

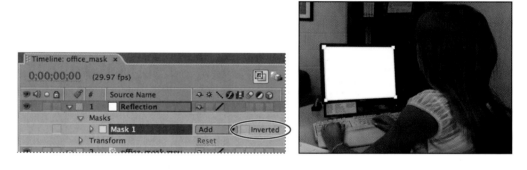

7 Deselect the Inverted check box. The Reflection layer now obscures the News_promo layer.

8 Zoom in if desired, and then, in the Composition panel, select the lower-right vertex of the Reflection layer's mask and drag it to the upper-left corner of the mask.

9 Adjust the other vertices and direction handles until your shape resembles the following figure.

10 With the Reflection layer selected in the Timeline panel, press the F key to display the Mask Feather property for the mask.

11 Increase the Feather amount to **90.0, 90.0** pixels.

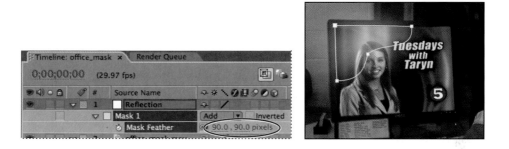

This creates an apparent reflection on the monitor, but because of the layers' stacking order, the reflection spills onto the whole shot.

12 Select the Reflection layer in the Timeline panel and drag it below the Office_mask layer.

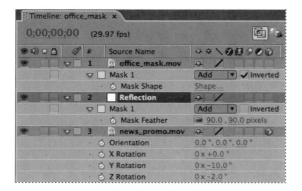

13 Select the Reflection layer in the Timeline panel and press T to reveal its Opacity property.

14 Reduce the Opacity value to **65%** to reduce the intensity of the reflection.

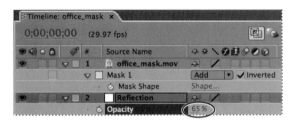

15 Close all of the properties for all of the layers in the Timeline panel and deselect all layers.

Applying a blending mode

To create unique interactions between layers, you may want to experiment with blending modes. Blending modes control how each layer blends with, or reacts to, layers beneath it. Blending modes for layers in After Effects are identical to blending modes in Photoshop.

1 In the Timeline panel menu, choose Columns > Modes to display the Mode pop-up menu.

2 Choose Add from the Reflection layer's Mode pop-up menu.

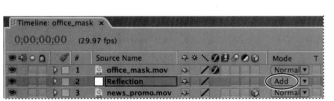

This creates a hard glare on the monitor screen image and boosts the colors underneath.

3 Choose File > Save to save your work.

Adding a 3D light layer

Instead of creating the reflection using a solid layer and a feathered mask, you could also use a 3D light layer to create realistic surface reflection. As noted earlier, you'll learn more about 3D layers, including using 3D light layers, in Lessons 9 and 10. If you're ambitious, however, you can follow these steps to create a 3D light layer now with this project. This exercise is optional.

1 *Turn off visibility of the Reflection layer by clicking its Video switch (👁).*

2 *Choose Layer > New > Light.*

3 *Click OK to accept the default values in the Light Settings dialog box.*

4 *With the Light 1 layer selected in the Timeline panel, press the P key to display its Position property. The Position property affects the placement of the light in the scene.*

5 *Set the Position values for the Light 1 layer to **260.0, –10.0, –350.0**, which moves the light above the monitor and off the image.*

6 *Select the Light 1 layer in the Timeline panel and press the A key to reveal its Point Of Interest property. The Point of Interest determines where the light is "looking."*

7 *Set the Point Of Interest values to **135, 200, 0**.*

8 *Select the News_promo layer in the Timeline panel and press AA to reveal the layer's Material Options properties. Material Options determine how a 3D layer interacts with light and shadow, both of which are important components of realism and perspective in 3D animation.*

9 *Increase the Specular value to **75%** and the Shininess value to **50%**.*

10 *Lower the Metal value to **50%**. The Metal value determines how much of the layer's color reflects the light. Because there are dark blues in the layer, little light is being reflected. Because you are simulating glass in front of the layer, lowering this value causes the reflection to take on the same color as the light.*

That's it. You can continue with the "Creating a vignette" exercise.

Creating a vignette

A popular effect in motion graphic design is to apply a vignette to the composition. This is often done to simulate light variations of a glass lens. It creates an interesting look that focuses the attention on the subject and sets the shot apart.

1 Choose Layer > New > Solid or press Ctrl+Y (Windows) or Command+Y (Mac OS).

2 In the Solid Settings dialog box, name this layer **Vignette**, click the Make Comp Size button, change the Color to black (RGB=0, 0, 0), and then click OK.

In addition to the Pen tool, After Effects has tools that let you easily create square and elliptical masks.

3 In the Tools panel, click and hold the Rectangular Mask tool (▣) so that you can see the Elliptical Mask tool (⬤) hidden behind it. Select the Elliptical Mask tool.

4 In the Composition panel, position the cross-hair pointer in the upper-left corner of the image. Drag to the opposite corner to create an elliptical shape that fills the image. Adjust the shape and position using the Selection tool, if necessary.

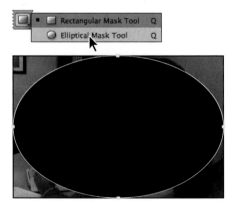

Using the Rectangular Mask and Elliptical Mask tools

The Rectangular Mask tool, as the name suggests, creates a rectangular or square mask. The Elliptical Mask tool creates an elliptical or circular mask. You create mask shapes with these tools by dragging them in the Composition or Layer panel. A mask created with the Rectangular Mask tool or the Elliptical Mask tool renders and updates faster than a mask created with the Pen tool.

Often, you will want to the mask to be a perfect square or circle. To do this, press the Shift key as you drag with the Rectangular Mask tool or the Elliptical Mask tool (to create a square or circle, respectively). To create your mask from the center, press Ctrl (Windows) or Command (Mac OS) after you start to drag. Press Ctrl+Shift or Command+Shift after you start to drag to create a perfect square or circle mask from a center anchor point.

5 With the Vignette layer selected in the Timeline panel, press the M key twice (MM) to display all of the mask properties for the layer.

6 Choose Subtract from the Mask 1 Mode pop-up menu.

7 Increase the Mask Feather amount to **200.0, 200.0** pixels.

Your composition should now resemble the following figure.

Even with this large feather amount, the vignette is a bit intense and constricting. You can give the composition more breathing room by adjusting the Mask Expansion property. The Mask Expansion property represents, in pixels, how far from the original mask edge you are expanding or contracting the adjusted edge.

8 Increase Mask Expansion to **90.0** pixels.

That's better.

9 Close the properties for the Vignette layer and then choose File > Save.

Tip for creating masks

If you have worked with other programs such as Illustrator or Photoshop, then masks and bezier curves are probably familiar to you. If not, here are a few additional tips to help you create them effectively.

- Use as few as vertices as possible.

- As you saw in this lesson, you can close a mask by clicking the starting vertex. You can also open a closed mask. To do so, click one of the mask segments, choose Layer > Mask, and deselect the Closed option.

- If you have an open path and want to continue to add additional points to it, simply press Ctrl (Windows) or Command (Mac OS) and click the last point on the path. This will select that point, and you can continue adding points in the normal manner.

Adjusting the color

The shot is looking quite polished, but there's just one more thing you have to fix: The color of the Office_mask layer is rather dull. Warm it up and make the image really pop.

1 Select the Office_mask layer in the Timeline panel.

2 Choose Effect > Color Correction > Auto Levels. The Auto Levels effect sets highlights and shadows by defining the lightest and darkest pixels in each color channel as white and black, and then it redistributes intermediate pixel values proportionately. Because Auto Levels adjusts each color channel individually, it may remove or introduce color casts.

Why apply this effect? Sometimes video cameras favor a certain color channel that makes the image cooler (bluer) or warmer (redder). The Auto Levels effect sets the black and white pixels for each channel, with the end result looking much more natural.

The color of the Office_mask layer should look much better now.

3 Choose File > Save to save the finished project.

In this lesson you have worked with the various mask tools to hide, reveal, and adjust portions of a composition to create a stylized inset shot. Next to keyframes, masks are probably the most-used feature of After Effects.

You can preview the clip now if you'd like, or render it according to the process outlined in Lesson 12, "Rendering and Outputting."

Review

▶ Review questions

1 What is the difference between a smooth point and a corner point?

2 Name two ways to adjust the shape of a mask.

3 What is a direction handle used for?

4 What is the difference between an open mask and a closed mask?

▶ Review answers

1 A smooth point is used to control the bezier curves of a mask. A corner point creates straight segments in a mask.

2 You can adjust the shape of a mask by dragging individual vertices, or by dragging a segment.

3 A direction handle is used to control the shape and angle of a bezier curve.

4 An open mask can be used to control effects or the placement of text; it does not define a region of transparency. A closed mask defines a region that will affect the alpha channel of a layer.

The word keying *might conjure up images of a weather person on the evening news, or a shooting technique used in major motion pictures, but with After Effects, even the simplest, least-expensive project can take advantage of this technique.*

7 | Keying

Lesson overview

In this lesson, you'll learn how to do the following:

- Create a garbage mask.
- Use the Color Difference Key effect to key an image.
- Check an image's alpha channel for errors in a key.
- Use the Spill Suppressor effect to remove unwanted light spill.
- Pull a key using the Keylight effect.
- Adjust the contrast of an image using the Levels effect.

In this lesson, you will build a promotional spot for a weekly news segment on a fictional television station. You'll begin by working with live-action footage of an actor captured on a green-screen stage. You will learn how to use keying effects to remove the green background and clean up the edge of the key to remove any lingering green spill. Then you will add a title to the promo, and place the station ID that was created in Lesson 2 into the composition to complete the project.

This lesson will take approximately 1 hour to complete.

About keying

Keying is defining transparency by a particular color value (with a color key or chroma key) or brightness value (with a luminance key) in an image. When you *key out* a value, all pixels that have similar colors or luminance values become transparent.

Keying makes it easy to replace a background of a consistent color or brightness with another image, which is especially useful when working with objects that are too complex to mask easily. The technique of keying out a background of a consistent color is often called *bluescreening* or *greenscreening*, although you do not have to use blue or green; you can use any solid color for a background.

Difference keying defines transparency with respect to a particular baseline background image. Instead of keying out a single-color screen, you can key out an arbitrary background.

Why might you use keying? There are a variety of reasons, but some of them include:

- A stunt may be too dangerous for an actor to perform on location.
- The location may be too hazardous for cast and crew.
- In the case of science-fiction movies, the location may not exist at all.
- You are working with a limited budget and cannot shoot any other way.

The best way to ensure a good key is to know what format works best. MiniDV is a popular format, and we'll use it in this lesson, but compression can cause MiniDV footage to have artifacts such as blocky regions or aliasing along the curves and diagonals of your subject. The greater the digital compression, the harder it is to pull a clean key. Enter After Effects, which you can use to solve these and other keying problems.

You will have greater success when pulling a key in MiniDV format if your backdrop is green instead of blue. Luminance information, which comprises 60% of the video signal, is encoded into the green channel. The green channel is also the least compressed of the RGB color channels. Blue, meanwhile, tends to be the noisiest of the channels.

Getting started

Make sure the following files are in the AE7_CIB > Lessons > Lesson07 folder on your hard disk, or copy them from the *Adobe After Effects 7.0 Classroom in a Book* DVD now.

- In the Assets folder: 5.ai, Channel5_logo.aep, L7BG.mov, rotatedtype.ai, talent_DV.mov

- In the Sample_Movie folder: Lesson07.mov

1 Open and play the Lesson07.mov sample movie to see what you will create in Lesson 7. When you are done, quit the QuickTime player. You may delete this sample movie from your hard disk if you have limited storage space.

Setting up the project

When you begin the lesson, restore the default application settings for After Effects. See "Restoring default preferences," page 5.

1 Press Ctrl+Alt+Shift (Windows) or Command+Option+Shift (Mac OS) while starting After Effects 7.0 to restore default preferences settings. When asked whether you want to delete your preferences file, click OK.

After Effects opens to display a new, untitled project.

2 Choose File > Save As.

3 In the Save Project As dialog box, navigate to the AE7_CIB > Lessons > Lesson07 > Finished_Project folder.

4 Name the project **Lesson07_Finished.aep**, and then click Save.

Importing the footage

You need to import two footage items for this lesson.

1 Choose File > Import > File.

2 Navigate to the AE7_CIB > Lessons > Lesson07 > Assets folder. Select the talent_DV.mov file, and then Ctrl-click (Windows) or Command-click (Mac OS) to also select the L7BG.mov file, and then click Open. The footage items appear in the Project panel. You will organize them before getting underway.

3 Choose File > New > New Folder to create a new folder in the Project panel, or click the Create A New Folder button (⬛) at the bottom of the panel.

4 Type **mov_files** to name the folder, press Enter (Windows) or Return (Mac OS) to accept the name, and then drag the two footage items into the mov_files folder.

5 Click the triangle to expand the folder so that you can see the files inside.

Creating the composition

To begin building your promotional spot, you need to create a new composition.

1 Choose Composition > New Composition or press Ctrl+N (Windows) or Command+N (Mac OS).

2 In the Composition Settings dialog box, type **Color Difference Key** in the Composition Name field.

3 Make sure the Preset pop-up menu is set to NTSC DV. This automatically sets the width, height, pixel aspect ratio, and frame rate for the composition.

4 In the Duration field, type **800** to specify 8 seconds, which matches the length of the talent_DV.mov file, and then click OK.

After Effects opens the new composition in the Timeline and Composition panels.

Changing the background color

The default background in After Effects is black, which makes it hard to see holes or other errors when pulling a key. So you'll start by changing the background to something other than black or white. In this lesson, you will use orange.

1 Choose Composition > Background Color or press Ctrl+Shift+B (Windows) or Command+Shift+B (Mac OS).

2 Click the color swatch and select a bright orange hue, such as RGB 255, 200, 0. Then click OK to close the Color Picker, and OK again to close the Background Color dialog box.

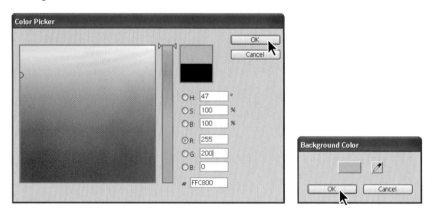

 Instead of changing the background color, you can also click the Toggle Transparency Grid button ( ) at the bottom of the Composition panel. This turns on a checkerboard background that reveals transparency, which is another good way to spot errors in a key.

Adding the foreground subject

Now, you will add the talent_DV.mov footage item to the composition.

1 Press the Home key to make sure that the current-time indicator is at the beginning of the time ruler.

2 Drag the Talent_DV.mov file from the Project panel to the Timeline panel. The Talent_DV image appears in the foreground of the Composition panel.

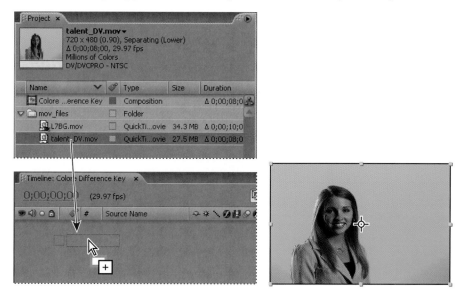

This is a simple green-screen shot. If you manually preview the shot by dragging the current-time indicator across the time ruler, you will notice that the actor doesn't move very much, which will aid in your keying. However, notice that the backdrop is not lit evenly. The upper portion is much brighter than the lower portion. This might cause some problems.

When After Effects pulls a key, it looks at the entire frame. The larger the area that must be analyzed and the larger the variation in color, the greater risk that you won't be able to remove all of the background color. You can reduce this risk by using a *garbage mask*.

A garbage mask (or matte) is so named because it is used to mask out the bad, or unnecessary, parts of the image. When you create a garbage mask for a layer, it's a good idea to keep it fairly loose. If the foreground subject is moving, you need to leave enough room in the garbage mask to accommodate the motion. If you make it too tight, you will have to animate the mask over time—and that isn't much fun. Remember, a garbage mask is used to help solve problems, not create new ones.

Creating a garbage mask

There is no limit to the number of garbage masks you can have in a composition. In fact, on some complex shots it is not uncommon to have multiple garbage masks isolate limbs, faces, hair, or different subjects in the scene.

1 Press the Home key to make sure that the current-time indicator is at the beginning of the time ruler.

2 Select the Pen tool (✆) in the Tools panel.

4 Using the Pen tool, click to place vertices around the actor until you have enclosed her completely.

5 To make sure that your garbage mask isn't too tight, drag the current-time indicator across the time ruler and make sure the actor does not move out of the masked area. If she does, switch to the Selection tool (➤) and adjust the vertices.

6 Choose File > Save to save your work.

Applying the Color Difference Key effect

There are many keying effects in After Effects. The Color Difference Key effect creates transparency from opposite starting points by dividing an image into two mattes, Matte Partial A and Matte Partial B. Matte Partial B bases the transparency on the specified key color, and Matte Partial A bases transparency on areas of the image that do not contain a second, different color. By combining the two mattes into a third matte, called the *alpha matte*, the Color Difference Key creates well-defined transparency values.

Confused yet? Most people who come across the Color Difference Key usually stop right there and run away in terror. But the Color Difference Key doesn't have to be feared, as you'll see in this exercise.

1 Select the Talent_DV layer in the Timeline panel, and choose Effect > Keying > Color Difference Key.

2 In the Effect Controls panel click the eyedropper for the Key Color setting. Then, click the green background color in the left thumbnail preview at the top of the panel.

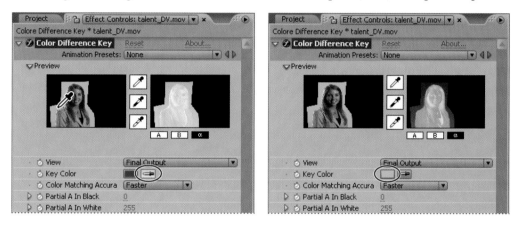

3 Click the A button under the right thumbnail preview to view the Matte Partial A.

Portions of the background are still visible in the Matte Partial A preview. This is actually a good thing, because it allows you to refine your key, which you'll do now.

4 Using the Black eyedropper (the middle one between the two thumbnail previews), click the brightest portion of background that did not key out in the Matte Partial A thumbnail preview. This will be near the top of the actor's head.

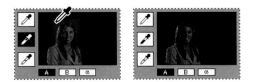

5 Click the B button under the right thumbnail preview to see the Matte Partial B, which is the inverse of Matte Partial A.

6 Using the Black eyedropper again, click the brightest portion of the remaining background in the Matte Partial B thumbnail preview (near the bottom). This should remove any remaining traces of the background.

7 Click the Alpha button under the right thumbnail preview. If this were a clean matte, the actor would be completely white. She's not, so you need to make some adjustments to the effect.

8 In the Effect Controls panel, increase the Matte In Black amount to **50** and decrease the Matte In White amount to **109**. You can think of the Matte In Black and Matte In White as being similar to the Levels effects.

Adjusting these two controls cleans up the alpha channel of the image. The result is a clean key accomplished with just a few clicks of the mouse.

Checking the alpha channel for errors

The orange (or transparent) background of the composition makes it easy to see any lingering bits of the green screen, but it may still be difficult to see any holes that may have been created with the actor. To double-check your key, switch to the alpha-channel view to see the resulting matte.

1 At the bottom of the Composition panel, click the Show Channel button (⬤) and choose Alpha from the pop-up menu.

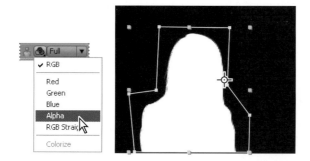

You can now see the black-and-white matte of your key. The black portion of the image represents the area that is transparent. The white portion represents the area that is opaque. Gray areas of the alpha channel (the feathered edge around the actor) are semi-transparent.

2 Make sure no portion of the actor is black or gray. If you have followed the steps so far, you should be in good shape.

3 Choose Show Channel > RGB to return to RGB view.

4 Choose File > Save to save your work.

Choking the matte

Because the Color Difference Key only removes color from the clip, the edge of the actor still has an unwanted fringe. To refine the edge of your matte, you need to choke, or tighten, it.

1 Select the Talent_DV layer in the Timeline panel and choose Effect > Matte > Matte Choker. This effect gives you more control over the edge of the matte than the Simple Choker effect. The main difference between the two is that the Simple Choker only allows you to tighten up the matte, while the Matte Choker also allows you to smooth, or feather, the edges.

In the Effect Controls panel, the top three Matte Choke controls—Geometric Softness 1, Choke 1, and Gray Level Softness 1—can be used to spread the matte out as far as possible without changing its shape. The next three controls can be used to choke the matte.

In this lesson, most of the default settings work well. Consider yourself fortunate if this is the case on all your future keying projects. The only setting that needs adjusting is the Geometric Softness 2 setting, which you'll use to create a slight blur along the edge of the matte.

2 Increase the Geometric Softness 2 amount to **4.00**.

3 Check the matte by clicking the Show Channel button at the bottom of the Composition panel and choosing Alpha from the pop-up menu.

The matte looks great!

4 Switch back to the RGB view to get ready to remove some green spill.

Removing spill

If you look closely at the actor's hair, you will see green highlights. This is the result of green light bouncing off the background and onto the subject. You can remove this and any unwanted green fringes around the actor with the Spill Suppressor effect. Typically, the Spill Suppressor is used to remove key color spills from the edges of a matte. It is essentially a simple desaturation filter.

1 Select the Talent_DV layer in the Timeline panel and choose Effect > Keying > Spill Suppressor.

You may find it easier to select the spill color if you temporarily turn off the Color Difference Key effect.

2 At the top of the Effect Controls panel, click the effect icon (⊘) next to the Color Difference Key effect to turn it off.

3 In the Spill Suppressor area at the bottom of the Effect Controls panel, select the Color To Suppress eyedropper and click a green region near the actor's hair.

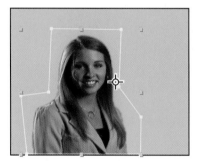

4 Turn the Color Difference Key effect back on. The subject is now keyed out and the unwanted green in and around her hair is gone.

Pulling a key with the Keylight effect

There are many ways to pull a key in After Effects. In addition to using the Color Difference keyer, another good alternative is to use the Keylight effect. Keylight is a plug-in effect, licensed from The Foundry, that comes with After Effects 7.0 Professional. It is a powerful keyer with numerous controls, and it is also one of the few effects that can pull a clean key in just one click.

If you'd like to try the Keylight effect, install it from the After Effects 7.0 install disc if you haven't done so yet, and then start this lesson over and complete the following exercise instead of the "Applying the Color Difference Key effect," "Choking the matte," and "Removing spill" exercises.

1 With the Talent_DV layer selected in the Timeline panel, choose Effect > Keying> Keylight.

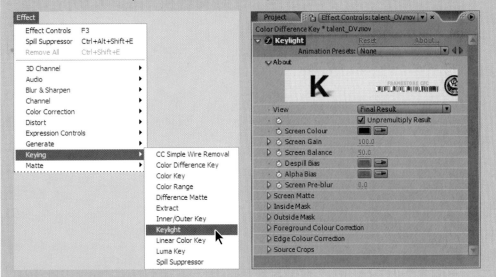

As with the Color Difference Key, the first thing is to select the key color.

2 In the Effect Controls panel, select the Screen Colour eyedropper.

3 In the Composition panel, click a green area of the background near the actor's right shoulder.

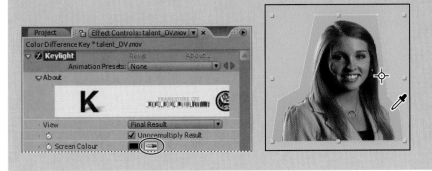

The results are instantaneous, and for many keying projects, one click will produce the desired result. Still, you need to check for possible errors or holes. The effect's View pop-up menu will help you find and correct errors.

4 In the Effect Controls panel, choose View > Status.

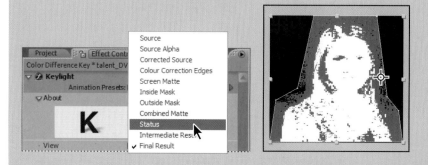

This shows an exaggerated view of the matte that is generated by the key color selection. Areas that are white will be opaque, black regions will be transparent, and gray pixels will be semi-transparent. You can see that large areas of the image are not keyed correctly.

5 In the Effect Controls panel, expand the Screen Matte property. Increase the Clip Black amount to **20.0,** and decrease the Clip White amount to **90.0**.

This tightens up the matte. There are still gray pixels in and around the subject, but that's OK because they blend with the background.

6 Choose View > Final Result. The key looks good, but there are artifacts around the edge of the actor.

7 Choose View > Colour Correction Edges. This shows you the edge of the matte.

8 In the Effect Controls panel, increase the Screen Pre-Blur amount to **5.0**, and increase the Clip Rollback amount to **0.5**.

9 Choose View > Final Result.

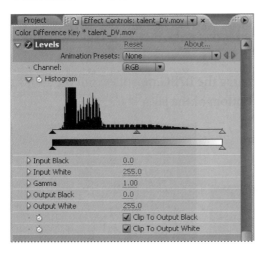

That's all. Now you can continue with the rest of the lesson

Adjusting contrast

You can make the image stand out more by adjusting the levels.

1 Select the Talent_DV layer in the Timeline panel, and then choose Effect > Color Correction > Levels.

6 In the Paragraph panel, click the Center Text button (≣).

There's a good chance that centering the text caused it to jump on-screen, so adjust its position.

7 Using the Selection tool (↖), drag to reposition the text layer in the Composition panel so that it is in the upper-right corner of the image.

8 In the Effect Controls panel, increase the Screen Pre-Blur amount to **5.0**, and increase the Clip Rollback amount to **0.5**.

9 Choose View > Final Result.

That's all. Now you can continue with the rest of the lesson

Adjusting contrast

You can make the image stand out more by adjusting the levels.

1 Select the Talent_DV layer in the Timeline panel, and then choose Effect > Color Correction > Levels.

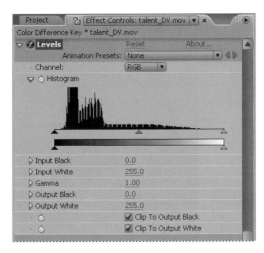

2 In the Levels area of the Effect Controls panel, increase the Input Black amount to **13.0**.

3 Decrease the Input White amount to **225.0**.

The Levels effect remaps the range of input color levels onto a new range of output color levels and changes the gamma correction curve. The Levels effect is useful for basic image-quality adjustment. It works the same way as the Levels adjustment in Photoshop.

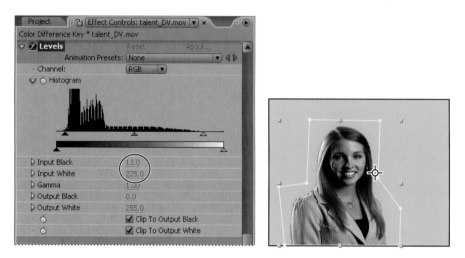

Adding the background animation

With a clean key, you are now ready to add the background to the composition.

1 Press the Home key to make sure the current-time indicator is at the beginning of the time ruler.

2 Bring the Project panel forward and drag the L7BG.mov file from the Project panel to the Timeline panel, placing it at the bottom of the layer stack.

Let's see how the keyed actor looks against the animated background.

3 Press the 0 key on the numeric keypad to watch a RAM preview of the composition. If you have a sharp eye, you may still notice a few aliasing artifacts here and there around the actor. Remember, you are working with footage that originated in MiniDV, so some aliasing is going to occur. Also, keep in mind that the computer monitor has a better resolution than a television set. To accurately judge the results of your key, you need to connect your system to a video monitor and view the results there.

4 When you are done watching the RAM preview, press the spacebar to stop playback.

5 Choose File > Save to save your work.

Adding the title

Now, you'll add a text layer and create the title of the promo.

1 Press the Home key to go to the beginning of the time ruler.

2 Select the Horizontal Type tool (T) in the Tools panel and then choose Window > Character or press Ctrl+6 (Windows) or Command+6 (Mac OS) to open the Character panel.

3 In the Character panel, do the following:

- Choose a bold sans serif font, such as Impact or Helvetica Bold.

- Increase the Font Size to **60** pixels.

- Click the Fill Color swatch and choose a light yellow hue, such as RGB 255, 242, 158.

4 Click in the Composition panel to the right of the actor and type **Tuesdays with Taryn**, pressing Enter (Windows) or Return (Mac OS) after each word.

Stylizing the title

The text is OK, but a little boring. Spiff it up with a few adjustments.

1 In the Timeline panel, double-click the text layer name to select all of the text in the Composition panel.

2 In the Character panel, do the following:

• Double-click the Stroke Color swatch. Set the color to black (RGB=0, 0, 0), and then click OK.

• Change the Stroke Width to **6** pixels, and then choose Fill Over Stroke from the Stroke Option pop-up menu.

• Change the Leading amount to **50** pixels.

• Change the Tracking amount to **25** pixels.

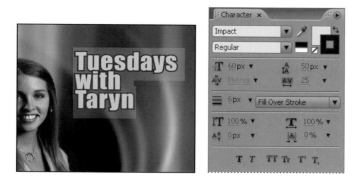

It's getting better, but you're not done yet. The word *with* is not an important word in the title, so make it smaller to de-emphasize it.

3 Highlight the word *with* in the Composition panel and change the Font Size to **48** pixels, the Leading amount to **48** pixels, and the Tracking amount to **50**.

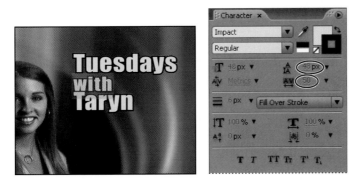

4 Double-click the text layer name in the Timeline panel to select all of the words again, and then click the Faux Italic button (*T*) near the bottom of the Character panel.

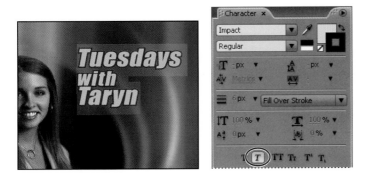

5 Open the Paragraph panel by choosing Window > Paragraph or by pressing Ctrl+7 (Windows) or Command+7 (Mac OS).

6 In the Paragraph panel, click the Center Text button (≣).

There's a good chance that centering the text caused it to jump on-screen, so adjust its position.

7 Using the Selection tool (➤), drag to reposition the text layer in the Composition panel so that it is in the upper-right corner of the image.

Checking placement

When positioning text, you should always make sure it falls within the title-safe area of the screen. This is the area that will be visible to viewers watching the final movie at home on TV. To check your title's position, turn on the title-safe guide.

1 Click the Choose Grid And Guide Options button (⊞) at the bottom of the Composition panel and choose Title/Action Safe from the pop-up menu.

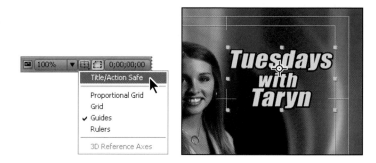

2 Drag with the Selection tool if necessary to reposition the title within the title-safe zone.

You can leave the guides visible for the remainder of this lesson, or turn them off, whichever you prefer.

Adding a drop shadow

The text looks pretty good, but you can make it even better by adding a drop shadow.

1 With the Tuesdays with Taryn text layer selected in the Timeline panel, choose Effect > Perspective > Drop Shadow.

2 In the Effect Controls panel, increase Opacity to **100%**.

3 Reduce the Distance (the distance of the shadow from the text) amount to **0.0**, and increase the Softness amount to **80.0**.

Now, the title looks dramatic.

4 Choose File > Save to save your work.

Adding the animated logo

In Lesson 2, you created an ID for the fictional Channel 5 newscast. Next, you'll import that project into this one and add it to the composition.

1 Bring the Project panel forward and double-click an empty area in it to open the Import File dialog box.

2 Navigate to the AE7_CIB > Lessons > Lesson07 > Assets folder. Select the Channel5_logo.aep file, and then click Open.

This project file is the same as the one you created in Lesson 2, except that it doesn't include the Golden Gate Bridge image and it has been resized to match the aspect ratio of this project.

When you import a project, After Effects creates a folder for it in the Project panel that contains the composition and its associated media files.

3 Expand the Channel5_logo.aep folder in the Project panel to see its contents.

4 Press the Home key to make sure the current-time indicator is at the beginning of the time ruler. If necessary, close the Render Queue panel so that you can see the Color Difference Key Timeline panel.

5 Drag the Logo/Channel 5 news composition file from the Project panel to the Timeline panel, and place it at the top of the layer stack.

Copying effects across two layers

The Channel 5 news logo could use some pizazz similar to the improvements we made to the title *Tuesdays with Taryn*. The easiest way to make the same changes is to copy and paste them onto the logo.

1 Select the Tuesdays with Taryn text layer in the Timeline panel and press E to display all of the effects properties for the layer.

2 Select the Drop Shadow property name for the Tuesdays with Taryn layer, and then choose Edit > Copy or press Ctrl+C (Windows) or Command+C (Mac OS).

3 Select the Logo/Channel 5 news layer in the Timeline panel, and then choose Edit > Paste or press Ctrl+V (Windows) or Command+V (Mac OS).

After Effects copies the drop shadow effect to the Channel 5 news logo, with the same settings you applied to the title text layer.

4 Save your project, and then press the 0 key on the numeric keypad to create and watch a RAM preview of the final spot. You might want to drag the work area end bar to about 4:20 to just preview the first half, which is where most of the animation occurs.

5 Press the spacebar when you want to stop playback.

Congratulations. You have just successfully keyed a composition. If you'd like to render it, see Lesson 12, "Rendering and Outputting," for instructions.

Review

▶ **Review questions**

1 What is *keying* and when do you use it?

2 What is the purpose of using a garbage mask?

3 How can you check for errors in a color key?

4 What is *spill* and how can you fix it in After Effects?

▶ **Review answers**

1 *Keying* is defining transparency by a particular color value (with a color key or chroma key) or brightness value (with a luminance key) in an image. When you *key out* a value, all pixels that have similar colors or luminance values become transparent. Keying makes it easy to replace a background of a consistent color or brightness with another image, which is especially useful when working with objects that are too complex to mask easily.

2 A garbage mask is used to remove unwanted portions of the image. This limits the region After Effects must search when keying, thus speeding up the keying calculations and increasing the chances for a cleaner key.

3 Use the alpha channel to check for errors in a color key. Make sure the background is a contrasting color, or toggle on the transparency grid, and then click the Show Channel button (◉) at the bottom of the Composition panel and choose Alpha from the pop-up menu. This displays a black-and-white matte of your key. The black portion of the image represents the area that is transparent; the white portion of the image represents the area that is opaque; and gray areas are semi-transparent.

4 Light spill occurs when light illuminating the background reflects onto the subject and colors the shadows and highlights. You can remove spill in After Effects using the Spill Suppressor effect, which is essentially a simple desaturation filter. To apply it, select the keyed layer in the Timeline panel and choose Effect > Keying > Spill Suppressor.

Before

After

*Not every shot you receive will be
a pristine masterpiece. Most shots
will require some degree of color
correction. With After Effects, you can
transform a dull, lifeless shot into a
bright, sharp clip in no time.*

8 Performing Color Correction

Lesson overview

In this lesson, you'll learn how to do the following:

- Use masks to isolate areas of an image for color correction.

- Use the Color Balance effect to enhance areas of a shot.

- Use the Auto Levels effect to introduce a color shift.

- Use a track matte to isolate an area of an image.

- Apply the Hue/Saturation and Brightness & Contrast effects to convert a color image to a high-contrast, black-and-white image.

- Correct a range of colors using Synthetic Aperture Color Finesse.

- Apply the Photo Filter effect to warm portions of an image.

- Remove unwanted elements of a scene with the Clone Stamp tool.

As the name implies, color correction is a way of altering or adapting the color of the captured image. Color correction is performed to optimize source material, to focus attention on a key element in a shot, to correct errors in white balance and exposure, to ensure color consistency from one shot to another, or to create a color palette for a specific visual look desired by a director.

In this lesson, you will improve the color and saturation of a video clip that was shot on a partly cloudy day. You will begin by using masks to isolate sections of the shot. Then, you'll apply a variety of color-correction effects to clean up and enhance the image. Finally, you will remove an unwanted portion of the shot with the Clone Stamp tool.

This lesson will take approximately 1 hour to complete.

Getting started

Make sure the following files are in the AE7_CIB > Lessons > Lesson08 folder on your hard disk, or copy them from the *Adobe After Effects 7.0 Classroom in a Book* DVD now.

- In the Assets folder: campus_before.mov, storm_clouds.jpg
- In the Sample_Movie folder: Lesson08.mov

1 Open and play the Lesson08.mov file to see what you will create in this lesson. When you're done, quit the QuickTime player. You may delete the sample movie from your hard disk if you have limited storage space.

Setting up the project

When you begin this lesson, restore the default application settings for After Effects. See "Restoring default preferences," page 5.

1 Press Ctrl+Alt+Shift (Windows) or Command+Option+Shift (Mac OS) while starting After Effects. When asked whether you want to delete your preferences file, click OK.

After Effects opens to display an empty, untitled project.

2 Choose File > Save As.

3 In the Save Project As dialog box, navigate to the AE7_CIB > Lessons > Lesson08 > Finished_Project folder.

4 Name the project **Lesson08_Finished.aep**, and then click Save.

Importing the footage

You need to import two footage items for this lesson.

1 Choose File > Import > File.

2 Navigate to the AE7_CIB > Lessons > Lesson08 > Assets folder, Shift-click to select the campus_before.mov and storm_clouds.jpg files, and then click Open. Organize the footage items before continuing.

3 Choose File > New > New Folder to create a new folder in the Project panel, or click the Create A New Folder button (⬛) at the bottom of the panel.

4 Type **Movies** to name the folder, press Enter (Windows) or Return (Mac OS) to accept the name, and then drag the Campus_before.mov file into the Movies folder.

5 Create another new folder and name it **Images**. Then, drag the Storm_clouds.jpg file into the Images folder.

6 Click the triangles to open the folders so that you can see their contents.

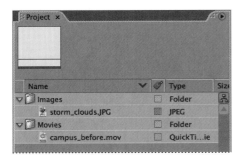

Creating the composition

Now, you will create a new composition based on the Campus_before.mov movie.

1 Drag the Campus_before.mov file onto the Create A New Composition button (⬛) at the bottom of the Project panel. After Effects creates a new composition named for the source file and displays it in the Composition and Timeline panels.

2 (Optional) Check the composition's aspect ratio and duration by choosing Composition > Composition Settings. This is a NTSC DV composition that is 5 seconds long. Click Cancel to close the Composition Settings dialog box.

3 Drag the Campus_before composition to an empty area of the Project panel to move it out of the Movies folder.

4 Choose File > Save to save your work.

Viewing After Effects on a video monitor

If possible, perform color correction on a video monitor instead of a computer monitor. The gamma differences between a computer monitor and a broadcast monitor vary greatly. What may look good on a computer screen may be too bright and washed out on a broadcast monitor.

After Effects allows you to view compositions on a broadcast monitor via the IEEE 1394 (FireWire) port on your computer. One way to accomplish this is to use a video tape recorder that accepts FireWire. You can loop the signal from your computer to the video tape recorder and then run a cable to your video monitor via the monitor/video output on the video tape recorder.

1 With a video monitor connected to your computer system, start After Effects 7.0.

2 Do one of the following, depending on your platform:

• On Windows, choose Edit > Preferences > Video Preview. Then, choose IEEE 1394 (OHCI Compliant) from the Output Device pop-up menu.

• On the Mac OS, choose After Effects > Preferences > Video Preview. Then, choose FireWire from the Output Device pop-up menu.

3 For Output Mode (Windows and Mac OS), choose the appropriate format for your system, which is NTSC in North America.

4 To view the composition you are working on, check the Previews, Mirror On Computer Monitor, Interactions, and Renders boxes. By selecting all of these options, you will be able to see every update and change you make to the composition on the video monitor.

5 Click OK to close the Preferences dialog box.

Always be sure your video or computer monitor is properly calibrated before performing color correction. For instructions on calibrating a computer monitor, see After Effects Help.

Adjusting color balance

Now, you're ready to get down to business. Start by previewing the source footage to see what you need to do.

1 Drag current-time indicator across the time ruler to manually preview the shot. Notice that the grass, shrubs, and trees are dark and underexposed. They look almost dead. You can bring these elements back to life back by increasing their saturation and brightness. You'll start with the grass.

Masking the grass

First, isolate the grass so that you don't brighten the whole image and blow out other, well-exposed areas, such as the sky.

1 Press the Home key to make sure the current-time indicator is at the beginning of the time ruler.

2 Select the Campus_before layer in the Timeline panel.

3 Rename the layer by pressing the Enter (Windows) or Return (Mac OS), typing **Grass**, and pressing Enter or Return again.

As you learned in Lesson 6, "Working with Masks," it helps to change the background color of the layer when you're creating or editing masks.

4 Choose Composition > Background Color and select a color of your choice. For this exercise, we selected red (RGB=255, 0, 0). Click OK to close the Background Color dialog box.

💡 *Alternately, you can click the Toggle Transparency Grid button (▒) to see transparent areas of the composition.*

Now, you will isolate the grass on this layer by creating a mask with the Pen tool.

5 Using the Pen tool (✎), isolate the triangular area of grass between the sidewalk and the building: Set the three vertices, and then click the first vertex again to close the mask.

💡 *Refer to Lesson 6, "Working with Masks," if you need a refresher on using the Pen tool to create a mask.*

When you close the mask, the rest of the image disappears—that's not good. You want the rest of the image to be part of the scene. You could reveal it by changing the mask mode from Add to None, but then you'd have to do this for every mask you create on this layer—and you're going to create additional masks to isolate other areas of grass. A better alternative is to add a reference layer.

6 Drag another instance of the Campus_before.mov movie from the Project panel to the Timeline panel, placing it below the Grass layer.

7 Rename this layer **Background**.

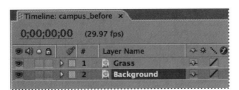

8 Select the Grass layer again in the Timeline panel and continue to use the Pen tool to mask all of the grassy areas of the shot.

You may use as many masks as you like to isolate the grass, but you should be able to get everything with three masks. You can click the Pen tool on the pasteboard of the Composition panel to be sure you include all the grass at the bottom of the image, right up to the edge.

9 With the Grass layer selected in the Timeline panel, press the F key to reveal the Mask Feather property for each mask in the layer.

10 Increase the Mask Feather amount to **10.0, 10.0** pixels for all three masks in the Grass layer. This will soften the edges of the masks and prevent noticeable artifacts when you apply the Color Balance effect in the next exercise.

Brightening the dark grass

As discussed earlier, the highlights, or bright areas, of the grass need to be pumped up. You'll do that now using the Color Balance effect. The Color Balance effect allows you to increase or decrease the saturation of one of the red, green, or blue channels over the three different intensity ranges (shadows, midtones, and highlights). Instead of affecting all colors in the shot, you will focus on just the greens.

1 With the Grass layer selected in the Timeline panel, choose Effect > Color Correction > Color Balance.

2 In the Effect Controls panel, increase the Hilight Green Balance value to **50.0**. The masked green areas of the image brighten considerably.

3 Unless you want the grass to look like mature bluegrass, decrease the Hilight Blue Balance to **–30.0**. This reduces the overall blue cast of the grass.

4 Check the Preserve Luminosity box. This preserves the average brightness of the image, which helps maintains the overall tonal balance and keeps the colors from getting too out of control. In other words, it keeps the colors from becoming unnaturally green while keeping shading consistent.

5 Select the Grass layer in the Timeline panel and press U to hide its properties and keep the Timeline panel neat.

6 Choose File > Save to save your work.

Replacing an element of the shot

You're going to change gears now and add some dramatic clouds to the sky.

1 Press the Home key to make sure the current-time indicator is at the beginning of the time ruler.

2 Bring the Project panel forward. Then, drag another instance of the Campus_before.mov movie from the Project panel to the Timeline panel, placing it at the top of the layer stack.

3 Rename the Campus_before layer **Sky**.

Adding the clouds

Now, add the clouds to the scene.

1 Drag the Storm_clouds.jpg file from the Project panel to the Timeline panel, placing it between the Sky and the Grass layers.

2 Turn off the visibility for the Sky layer by clicking the Video switch (👁). Now, you can fully see the storm clouds layer. You need to scale and reposition the clouds to fit the sky area of the image.

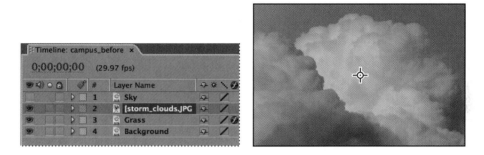

3 With the Storm_clouds layer selected in the Timeline panel, press the S key to display its Scale property.

4 Decrease the Scale values to **60.0, 60.0%**.

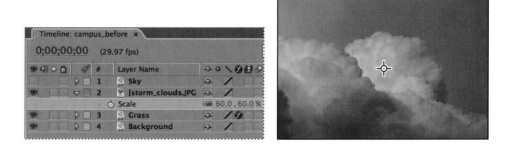

💡 *If you're typing in the values, press Tab to jump between the fields.*

5 Make sure the Storm_clouds layer is selected in the Timeline panel and press the P key to display its Position property.

6 Change the Position values to **425.0, 150.0**.

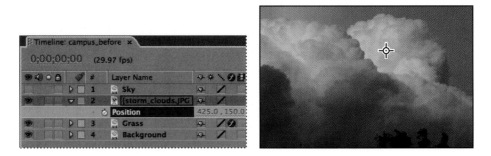

7 Make sure the Storm_clouds layer is selected in the Timeline panel and press U to hide its properties.

Color-correcting the clouds

Although the storm clouds are dramatic, the contrast of the image is limited. You don't want the clouds to look so dark and flat.

1 With the Storm_clouds layer selected in the Timeline panel, choose Effect > Color Correction > Auto Levels.

The Auto Levels effect automatically sets highlights and shadows by defining the lightest and darkest pixels in each color channel as white and black, and then it redistributes intermediate pixel values proportionately. Because Auto Levels adjusts each color channel individually, it may remove or introduce a color cast. In this case, with the default settings applied, Auto Levels introduces a blue color cast that makes the clouds more intense.

Masking the sky

Next, you need to remove the original sky from the image so that the storm clouds are visible. There are different ways to accomplish this, including drawing a detailed mask or using a track matte. You'll do the latter.

1 Choose Columns > Modes from the Timeline panel menu.

2 Change the TrkMat pop-up menu for the Storm_clouds layer to Luma Matte "Sky." This removes the bright part of the sky and creates a hole for the underlying storm clouds to show through.

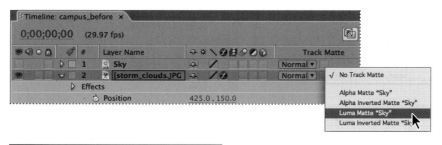

Cleaning up the mask

The Luma track matte did a good job, but there are some holes in the brighter portions of the layer, such as the windows of the building. The best way to fix these holes is to convert the Sky layer into a high-contrast, black-and-white image. But what effect or effects should you use to accomplish that? First you will use the Hue/Saturation effect, and then the Brightness & Contrast effect.

1 Temporarily turn on the Sky layer by clicking the Video switch (👁) for the layer in the Timeline panel.

2 Select the Sky layer in the Timeline panel and choose Effect > Color Correction > Hue/Saturation.

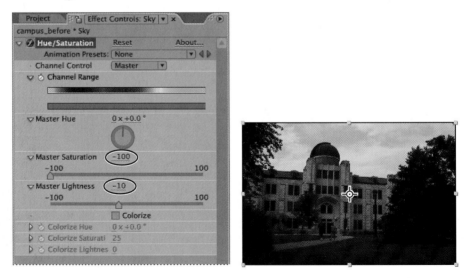

3 In the Effect Controls panel, decrease the Master Saturation to **−100** and decrease the Master Lightness to **−10**.

4 Choose Effect > Color Correction > Brightness & Contrast.

5 Close the properties for the Hue/Saturation effect in the Effect Controls panel so that you can more easily see the Brightness & Contrast effect properties.

6 Reduce the Brightness to **−52.0** and increase the Contrast to **100.0**.

Much better. However, there are a few stray pixels around the white light fixture by the door of the building. You can correct this with a simple mask.

7 With the Sky layer still selected in the Timeline panel, use the Rectangular Mask tool (■) to draw a selection around the two most pronounced white pixels on the building near the middle of the Composition panel.

As you drag with the Rectangle Mask tool, the full-color image appears outside of the selected area. This is because the default mask mode is Add, which keeps the information inside the mask intact and removes (or masks) the area outside the region. Because you still have the Background layer visible, you see that layer. In order to keep everything visible outside of the mask but remove the content inside the mask, you need to invert it.

8 Select the Sky layer in the Timeline panel and press the M key to reveal its Mask property. Then, check the Inverted box to invert the mask.

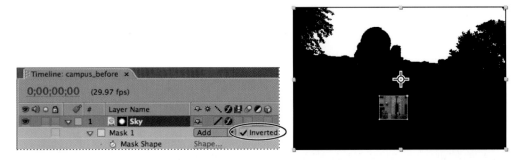

9 Now, turn off the visibility for the Sky layer by clicking on the Video switch (👁). Then, switch to the Selection tool (➤) and click the pasteboard of the Composition panel.

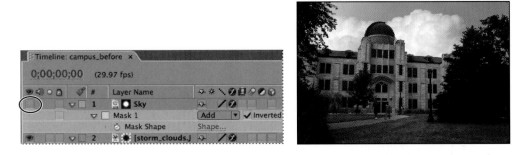

Ta da. That was certainly much easier than manually drawing a mask around the building and the trees.

10 Select the Sky layer in the Timeline panel and press U to close its properties click an empty area of the Timeline panel to deselect all layers; and then choose File > Save to save your work.

Lightening other dark areas

The image is looking better, and while the neighbors would certainly compliment you on the quality of the lawn, the foreground shrub and the large evergreen tree are still dark and underexposed. You'll fix that next.

Masking the shrub and tree

As you did for the grass, you will first isolate the shrub and tree, and then you will correct the color.

1 Press the Home key to make sure the current-time indicator is at the beginning of the time ruler.

2 Bring the Project panel forward and then drag another instance of the Campus_before.mov movie from the Project panel to the Timeline panel, placing it at the top of the layer stack.

3 Rename the Campus_before layer **Tree and Shrub**.

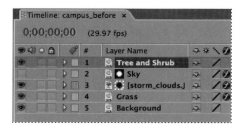

4 Using the Pen tool (✒), isolate the foreground shrub on the left side of the image and the evergreen tree on the right side of the image.

5 With the Tree and Shrub layer selected in the Timeline panel, press the F key to display the Mask Feather property for the two masks on the layer.

6 Increase the Mask Feather value for each mask to **10.0, 10.0** pixels.

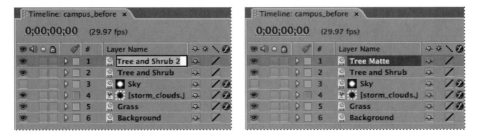

7 Select the Tree and Shrub layer in the Timeline panel and press U to hide its properties.

Removing stray sky elements and copying effects

Once again, the sky is your nemesis when trying to correct the color in this shot. In order to completely remove the original sky, you need to mask it from behind the tree. You also need to lighten the tree and shrub. But instead of doing the work all over again, you can speed the process by copying effects, and then apply the track matte.

1 Select the Tree and Shrub layer in the Timeline panel, press Ctrl+D (Windows) or Command+D (Mac OS) to duplicate it, and then rename the duplicated layer (Tree and Shrub 2) **Tree Matte**.

The Hue/Saturation and Brightness & Contrast effects that you applied to the Sky layer would be a good first step to lightening the shrub and the tree.

2 Select the Sky layer in the Timeline panel and press the E key to display the layer's Effects properties: Hue/Saturation and Brightness & Contrast.

3 Shift-click to select both the Hue/Saturation and Brightness & Contrast effect names in the Sky layer and then choose Edit > Copy or press Ctrl+C (Windows) or Command+C (Mac OS).

4 Select the Tree Matte layer in the Timeline panel and then choose Edit > Paste or press Ctrl+V (Windows) or Command+V (Mac OS).

Now that you've copied the effects, create the matte.

5 Select the Tree and Shrub layer in the Timeline and choose TrkMat > Luma Inverted Matte "Tree Matte."

Excellent. You can now correct the color in the Tree and Shrub layer.

6 Close the properties for the Sky layer in the Timeline panel and then choose File > Save to save your work.

Correcting a range of colors

Even though you isolated the tree and shrub from the shot, simply applying a levels effect would quickly reveal the edges of the mask. What you need is a way to select a specific color range, and correct just that area as a type of secondary color correction. For this, you will use the Synthetic Aperture Color Finesse effect, a third-party effect that comes bundled with After Effects and offers the capability to isolate a color range and adjust only those colors.

Note: The following exercise requires Synthetic Aperture's Color Finesse plug-in to be installed on your system. The installation files can be found on your After Effects disc.

1 With the Tree and Shrub layer selected in the Timeline panel, choose Effect > Synthetic Aperture > SA Color Finesse.

2 In the SA Color Finesse area of the Effect Controls panel, click the Setup button.

SA Color Finesse opens in a floating window.

3 Check the box in the Secondary tab to activate secondary color correction, and then click the tab to open the Secondary color-correction controls.

SA Color Finesse allows you perform up to six different secondary color-correction operations. You'll just perform one, however.

4 Check the box in the A tab to perform your color-correction operation.

5 Using the four Sample eyedroppers, make four color selections in the evergreen tree. Try to sample various shades of green from light to dark; zoom in if necessary to help you select a range of hues.

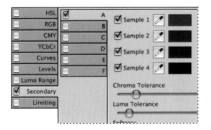

Even though four samples don't encompass the entire contrast range of the tree, SA Color Finesse has controls to refine the color selection.

6 Still in the A tab, choose Preview > Mask. Now you can see the areas that are selected and those that are masked (shaded in red).

7 Adjust the Chroma Tolerance, Luma Tolerance, and Softness sliders until everything but the tree and shrub and most of the grass is selected. There are no set values here, as the adjustments will depend on your sampled colors. However, our values are shown in the following image, and the selection should resemble the following image.

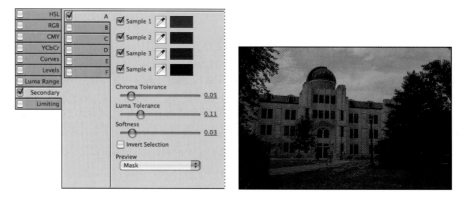

8 Increase the Gain amount to **1.33**.

9 Choose Preview > Off, then click OK to apply the correction and to close the SA Color Finesse window.

Thanks to the Gain adjustment you just performed, the tree and the shrub are much brighter in the image.

10 Choose File > Save to save your work.

Note: *To learn more about SA Color Finesse, read the manual that is included on the After Effects installation disc.*

Warming colors with the Photo Filter effect

Finally, warm up the building and make it more inviting with the Photo Filter effect.

The Photo Filter effect mimics the technique of using a colored filter on a camera lens to adjust the color balance and color temperature of the light transmitted through the lens and exposing the film. You can choose a color preset to apply a hue adjustment to an image, or you can specify a custom color using the Color Picker or the eyedropper.

1 With the Background layer selected in the Timeline panel, choose Effect > Color Correction > Photo Filter.

2 In the Effect Controls panel, choose Filter > Warming Filter (81).

There, that's better.

3 Choose File > Save.

Removing unwanted elements

The color is looking great, but you're not quite done. The director wants you to remove the student in the red shirt walking in the background, because he is visually distracting. You'll use the Clone Stamp tool to paint out this unwanted element of the scene on a frame-by-frame basis. This type of hand painting is not a glamorous job, but sometimes it has to be done.

Note: The following exercise is good practice, but it is quite time-consuming. Therefore, it is optional.

1 Select the Clone Stamp tool (⬤) in the Tools panel.

The Clone Stamp tool samples the pixels on a source layer and applies the sampled pixels to a target layer; the target layer can be the same layer or a different layer in the same composition.

Preparing the workspace

Now, configure the workspace with the panels you need for painting.

1 Choose Window > Workspace > Paint. After Effects opens the Layer panel, which is where you'll do the painting, and also displays the Paint and Brush Tips panels.

2 Double-click the Background layer in the Timeline panel to open it in the Layer panel. This is the layer on which you'll paint.

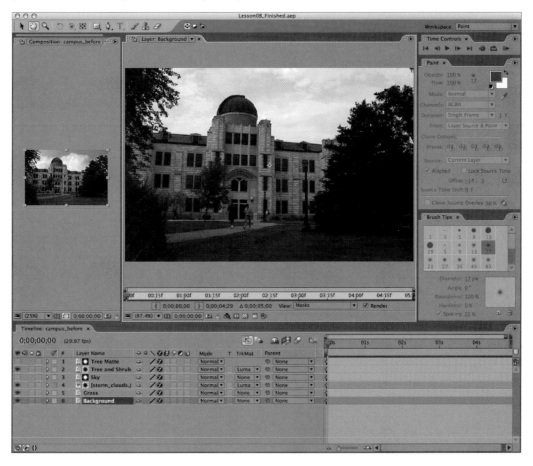

3 In the Brush Tips panel, choose a soft, round 17-pixel brush.

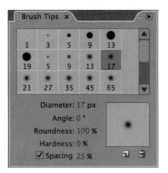

Note: As you work, you may need to increase or decrease the size of the brush, but 17 pixels is a good starting point.

Painting across time

If you've done any work in Photoshop, the concept of cloning is probably familiar to you. However, in After Effects you can clone across time, not just clone a static location in a 2D image.

1 Press the Home key to make sure the current-time indicator is at the beginning of the time ruler.

2 Zoom in to the student walking in the background on the left side of the image, and then choose the Clone Stamp tool again if necessary.

By default, any paint or clone procedure remains constant for the entire length of the composition. However, this will cause problems later in this scene when the student moves into the painted space, so you need to change the duration of the clone operation.

3 In the Paint panel, choose Duration > Single Frame. This will only keep the cloned area on-screen for a single frame.

Now, you need to instruct the Clone Stamp tool to take information from a future point in time—a point when the two subjects in the foreground are off-screen.

4 Slowly drag the Source Time Shift value in the Paint panel to 30 frames. As you drag the Source Time Shift value, you will see a ghost overlay of the frames being shifted. The Source Shift Time setting allows you to sample the layer from a different point in time.

5 In the Layer panel, paint out the student in the background using the Clone Stamp tool. The key here is to use small, essential strokes. Make sure your clone area is not too big, or you may pick up traces of the subject from the shifted time frame.

💡 *Although you can certainly use a mouse to paint in After Effects, doing so can be quite cumbersome. If you use the paint tools on a regular basis, you might want to invest in and use a graphics tablet instead.*

Now that you've painted out the student in the first frame, you need to advance to the next frame and repeat the procedure.

6 Press the Page Down key to advance one frame.

💡 *Use Page Down to advance in the Timeline panel by one frame. Use Page Up to move back one frame. Use Shift+Page Down or Shift+Page Up to move forward or backward, respectively, by 10 frames.*

7 Repeat steps 5 and 6 for each frame of the shot until the end. As the student gets closer to the two men in the foreground—around 2:15—you will need to reduce the size of your brush. You will also need to change the Source Time Shift value either forward or backward as you progress. For example, at 2:00, change the Time Shift to **–54** for a clear area to continue cloning. At other points in time ruler you will need to make your own determination as to the Time Shift value. The key is to find a frame where the foreground subjects do not interfere with the area you are cloning.

Checking your work

When you are finished, make a RAM preview and make sure the student doesn't "ghost" in and out of the shot.

1 Click the RAM Preview button (▶) in the Time Controls panel.

2 If you notice an arm or a leg appearing in the shot, go to the offending frame and touch up the area. If you have removed the subject completely, there should be no trace of him in any frame.

3 When you're done, choose File > Save to save the finished project.

If you'd like to render the composition, see Lesson 12, "Rendering and Outputting," for details.

Congratulations. You've done an excellent job of color-correcting this fine composition. And as you learned, painting out an unwanted subject from a shot is tedious work, but it's an important skill, and now you know how to do it.

Review

1 Why do you need to color correct a shot?

2 What does the Color Balance effect do, and what is the Preserve Luminosity option?

3 What effect can you use to warm up the colors in an image?

4 In order to paint out an object in a scene yet preserve the background behind the object, what setting should you adjust in the Paint panel?

▶ **Review answers**

1 Color correction is performed to optimize the source material, to focus attention on a key element in the shot, to correct errors in white balance and exposure, ensure color consistency from one shot to another, or to create a color palette to match the visual look of the director.

2 The Color Balance effect allows you to increase or decrease the saturation of one of the red, green, or blue channels over the three different intensity ranges (shadows, midtones, and highlights). Checking the Preserve Luminosity option preserves the average brightness of the image, which helps to maintain the overall tonal balance.

3 You can use the Photo Filter color-correction effect to warm up the color of an image. The Photo Filter effect mimics the technique of using a colored filter over the lens of a camera to adjust the color balance and color temperature of light transmitted through the lens and exposing the film. Choose the Warming Filter in the Photo Filter Effect Controls panel to warm up the color of an image.

4 You use the Source Time Shift setting, which specifies the number of seconds between the sample and the clone stroke, when painting out an object in a scene.

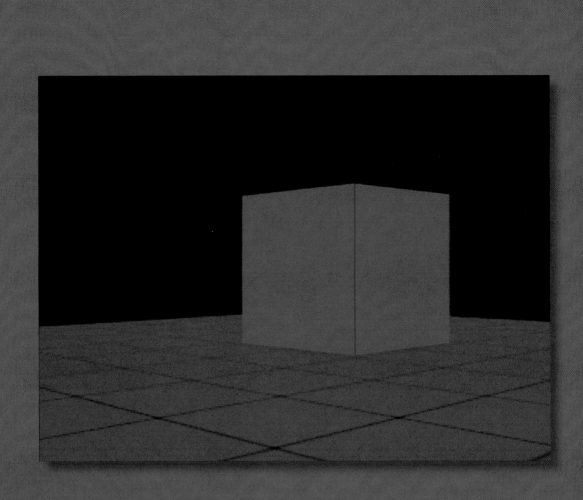

By clicking a single switch in the Timeline panel in After Effects, you can turn a 2D layer into a 3D layer, opening up a whole new world of creative possibilities.

9 Building and Animating a 3D Object

Lesson overview

In this lesson, you'll learn how to do the following:

- Create a 3D shape from a solid layer.

- Animate shapes in three dimensions.

- Look at a 3D scene from multiple views.

- Apply the Grid effect to add depth perspective.

- Control the way a layer animates by moving its anchor point.

- Rotate and position layers along *x, y,* and *z* axes.

After Effects can work with layers in two dimensions (*x, y*) or three dimensions (*x, y, z*). So far in this book, you've worked almost exclusively in two dimensions. When you specify a layer as three-dimensional (3D), After Effects adds the *z* axis, which provides control over the layer's depth. By combining this depth with a variety of lights and camera angles, you can create animated 3D projects that take advantage of the full range of natural motion, lighting and shadows, perspective, and focusing effects.

In this lesson, you'll explore how to control and animate basic 3D layers. Then, in Lesson 10, "Using 3D Effects," you'll continue working with this project, adding lights, effects, and other elements to complete the composition, which is a web animation for a fictional company called Orange Dot, Inc.

This lesson will take approximately 1½ hours to complete.

Getting started

Make sure the following file is in the AE7_CIB > Lessons > Lesson09 folder on your hard disk, or copy it from the *Adobe After Effects 7.0 Classroom in a Book* DVD now:

• In the Sample_Movie folder: Lesson09.mov

Note: There are no assets for this lesson. You will create the entire composition in After Effects.

1 Open and play the Lesson09.mov file to see what you will create in this lesson. When you are done, quit the QuickTime player. You may delete this sample movie from your hard disk if you have limited storage space.

Setting up the project

When you begin this lesson, restore the default application settings for After Effects. See "Restoring default preferences," page 5.

1 Press Ctrl+Alt+Shift (Windows) or Command+Option+Shift (Mac OS) while starting After Effects. When asked whether you want to delete your preferences file, click OK.

After Effects opens to display an empty, untitled project.

2 Choose File > Save As.

3 In the Save Project As dialog box, navigate to the AE7_CIB > Lessons > Lesson09 > Finished_Project folder.

4 Name the project **Lesson09_Finished.aep**, and then click Save.

Creating the composition

The animation you will create in this lesson is for the fictional Orange Dot, Inc., company website. You will set up the composition so that it's optimized for the web.

1 Click the Create A New Composition button (▦) at the bottom of the Project panel.

2 In the Composition Settings dialog box, name the composition **Orange_Dot**, choose the Web Video 320 x 240 preset, set the Duration to **10:00**, and click OK.

Animating a square in 3D space

The beginning of the animation features a blue square that zooms into space. Then it's followed by some other squares, which come together to form a cube. Start by creating and animating the first blue square.

Creating the square

Since the Orange Dot spot is destined for the web, you'll give the square a web-safe color so that the animation looks as consistent as possible on different systems.

1 With the Composition or Timeline panel active, choose Layer > New > Solid.

2 In the Solid Settings dialog box, do the following:

- Name the solid layer **Cube Bottom**.

- Set the Height to **320** pixels.

- Click the Color swatch, and in the Color Picker, set the color to **3333CC** in the # field. Then, click OK to set the color and return to the Solid Settings dialog box.

- Click OK.

Turning on the 3D Layer switch

Currently, this layer is flat, with only x (width) and y (height) dimensions. It can be moved only along those axes. But all you have to do is turn on the 3D Layer switch to move the layer in three dimensions, including z (depth).

1 Right-click (Windows) or Ctrl-click (Mac OS) the Parent column heading in the Timeline panel and choose Hide This. Repeat for the # (layer number) column heading. Hiding these columns will give you more room to work in the time ruler.

2 Ctrl-click (Windows) or Command-click the triangle in the Label column for the Cube Bottom layer in the Timeline panel to display all of the layer's Transform properties.

3 Click the right-most box in the Switches/Modes column for the Cube Bottom layer to turn on the 3D Layer switch. Three 3D Rotation properties appear in the Transform group for the layer, and properties that previously supported only two dimensions now display a third value for the *z* axis. In addition, a new property group named Material Options also appears.

Note: Material Options specify how the layer interacts with light. You'll work with the Material Options property group in Lesson 10, "Using 3D Effects."

Animating the square in space

Now, you can animate the layer's position in three dimensions.

1 With the Cube Bottom layer selected in the Timeline panel, press the P key to display just the layer's Position property.

2 Press the Home key to make sure the current-time indicator is at the beginning of the time ruler.

3 Click the Position stopwatch (⏱) to add a keyframe at the default values, 160, 120, 0 (*x, y,* and *z,* respectively).

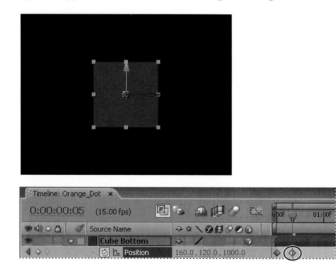

4 Go to 0:05.

5 Set the *z* (right) Position value to **1000.0**. After Effects adds a keyframe, and the square appears smaller in the Composition panel.

6 Drag the work area end marker to 0:10.

7 Press the spacebar to preview the frames in the work area. The square appears to scale down to a smaller size, but it is actually receding in 3D space.

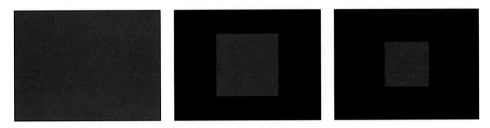

8 Press the spacebar again to end the preview, press the Home key to go to the beginning of the time ruler, and then choose File > Save to save your work.

Using 3D views

Sometimes the appearance of 3D layers can be deceptive. For example, a layer might appear to be scaling smaller along its *x* and *y* axes when it's actually moving along the *z* axis. You can't always tell from the default view in the Composition panel. The Select View Layout pop-up menu at the bottom of the Composition panel lets you divide the panel into different views of a single frame, so you can see your work from multiple angles. You specify the different views using the 3D View pop-up menu.

1 If you don't already have the After Effects application maximized to fill your entire screen, click the Maximize button in the upper-right corner (Windows), or click the green Maximize button in the upper-left corner (Mac OS).

2 With the pointer anywhere in the Composition panel, press the tilde key (~) to make the Composition panel fill the entire After Effects application window and hide all other panels. (Do not press Shift when you press the tilde key.)

3 At the bottom of the Composition panel, click the Select View Layout pop-up menu and choose 2 Views – Horizontal. The left side of the Composition panel displays the Top view of the frame, and the right side displays the Active Camera view, which you've been viewing.

4 Click in the left side of the Composition panel to make the Top view active, and then choose Left from the 3D View pop-up menu at the bottom of the panel.

After Effects identifies the active view with yellow corner tabs.

5 Click to select the Cube Bottom layer on the right side of the Composition panel (in the Active Camera view). A color-coded 3D axis appears over the layer's anchor point in both views. The red arrow controls the x axis, the green arrow controls the y axis, and the blue arrow controls the z axis. At the moment, the z axis appears at the intersection of the x and y axes. The letters x, y, and z appear when you position the pointer over the associated axis. When you move or rotate the layer while the pointer is over a particular axis, the layer's movement is restricted to that axis.

Note: These arrows also appeared when you first turned on the 3D Layer switch.

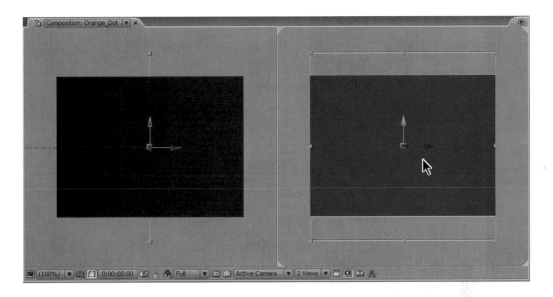

6 With the Cube Bottom layer still selected, press the Page Down key a few times to advance a few frames. The Cube Bottom layer's new position appears in both views; on the left side, you can see the *z* axis extending from the center of the layer off to the left side. (Temporarily zoom out for a better view, if desired.) As you press Page Down, you can see the shape receding in space, not scaling smaller in 2D space.

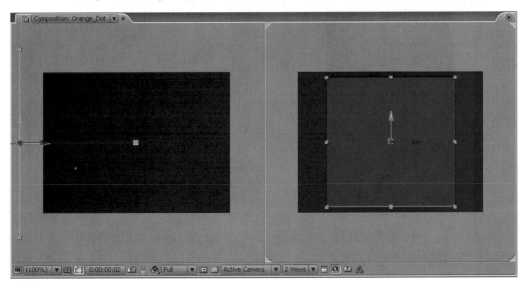

7 Press the ~ key to return to the Standard workspace.

Flipping the cube bottom

After the square zooms away from the viewer, you want it to fall backward. To accomplish this, you must rotate the square from its bottom edge, which means you have to move to layer's anchor point from the middle to the bottom of the shape.

Moving the layer's anchor point

You could move the anchor point by changing the layer's Anchor Point value in the Timeline panel, but that would cause the square to move relative to the composition, which you don't want. So instead, you'll drag the anchor point into position using the Pan Behind tool. As you may recall from Lesson 4, "Animating a Multimedia Presentation," when you use the Pan Behind tool to move a layer's anchor point, the layer's Position values automatically adjust in the Timeline panel to ensure the layer remains in its current position relative to the composition.

1 Press the Home key to return to the beginning of the time ruler.

2 Select the Cube Bottom layer in the Timeline panel and then press Shift+A to display the Anchor Point property above the Position property.

3 Select the Pan Behind tool (▦) in the Tools panel. In the Composition panel, a cross-hair icon (✛) marks the layer's anchor point. In the Active Camera view, it's at the intersection of the x and y axes.

4 In the Active Camera view, drag the anchor point to the bottom edge of the layer. Press Shift after you start dragging to horizontally constrain the movement. Stop dragging when the anchor point lies on the bottom edge of the layer, which is actually outside of the camera's view. The Anchor Point and Position values update in the Timeline panel as you drag. The Anchor Point values should be 160.0, 320.0, 0.0; the Position values should be 160.0, 280.0, 0.0. Enter the values manually if necessary to adjust your panning operation.

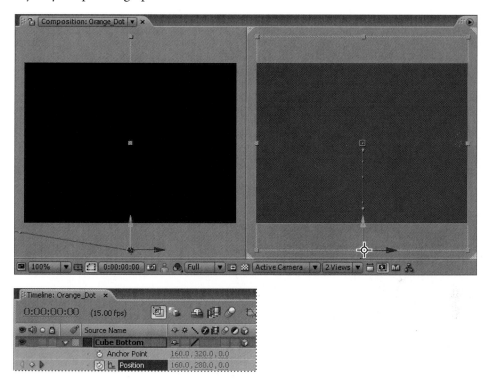

5 Press the K key to go to the next keyframe, 0:05.

6 Using the Selection tool (◥), position the pointer over the Cube Bottom layer's *y* axis (the green arrow) in the Active Camera View of the Composition panel and drag downward until the *y* Position value is 280.0. Now, the square is back in the middle of the composition.

7 Watch a spacebar preview of the work area in the Active Camera View of the Composition panel. The preview should look the same as the last time, but your work will pay off when you flip the square.

Flipping the square on its back

With the anchor point in its new position, the square will rotate around its lower edge.

1 Press the Home key to go to the beginning of the time ruler.

2 With the Cube Bottom layer selected in the Timeline panel, press Shift+R to display the layer's Orientation and Rotation properties under the Anchor Point and Position properties.

3 Click the stopwatch icon (⊘) for the X Rotation property to set a keyframe at the default angle, 0.0°.

4 Go to 0:10, which is five frames after the square has stopped receding in space.

5 Change the X Rotation angle value to **–45.0**°. After Effects adds a keyframe at the current time, and in the Active Camera View of the Composition panel, you can see how the square rotates by 45° along its bottom edge. This helps you see the rotation, but you really want the bottom to fall completely flat.

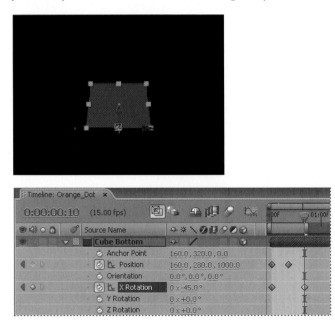

6 Change the X Rotation angle value to **–90.0°** so that the square falls flat in the Active Camera view of the Composition panel.

7 Drag the work area end marker to 2:00, which gives you some room to work and to watch the preview.

8 Press the spacebar to preview the animation you've created so far. The square recedes and falls back in space. Press the spacebar again when you're ready to stop playback.

About 3D rotation

You can adjust 3D rotation two ways: by changing a layer's Orientation values, or changing its X, Y, and Z Rotation values. You can use the Rotation tool to change Orientation or X, Y, or Z Rotation values.

When you animate any of a 3D layer's Orientation values, the layer moves along the shortest possible rotational path in 3D space, creating natural and predictable rotations. You can smooth this path by changing the spatial keyframe interpolation to Auto Bezier.

When you animate any of a 3D layer's X, Y, or Z Rotation values, the layer rotates along each individual axis. You can adjust the number of rotations as well as the angle of rotation. You can also add keyframes to the layer's rotation on each axis individually. Animating using these properties allows for more alternatives for fine control with keyframes and expressions than does animating with the Orientation property, but also may result in motion that is less predictable. The individual Rotation properties are useful for creating rotations with multiple revolutions along a single axis.

Rotating the square

Now, you want the square to rotate 45° clockwise so that you have a better perspective when the cube comes together.

1 Click anywhere in the Active Camera view on the right side of the Composition panel to make sure it's active.

2 Choose Select View Layout > 1 View at the bottom of the Composition panel. Make sure the 3D View pop-up menu is set to Active Camera.

3 Select the Rotation tool (↺) in the Tools panel and choose Set > Rotation from the panel pop-up menu.

4 Go to 0:10, the location of the last X Rotation keyframe.

5 Click the Z Rotation stopwatch icon (⌚) to add a keyframe to the property at the default angle, 0.0°.

6 Go to 1:10.

7 In the Composition panel, drag the *z* axis (the blue arrow) to the left. Press the Shift key after you start dragging to constrain the rotation to a 45-degree angle. Release the mouse when the Z Rotation value is +45.0. (Enter the value manually if necessary to adjust your rotation operation.) After Effects adds a keyframe.

8 Press the Home key to go to the beginning of the time ruler and then watch a spacebar preview of the animation. After the square recedes and falls flat, it rotates 45° clockwise.

Adding pauses

Now, tweak the keyframes to add a pause between each stage of the square's animation.

1 Go to 0:08, which is three frames after the last Position keyframe.

2 Click the X Rotation property name to select all of that property's keyframes.

3 Drag the first (left) X Rotation keyframe to the right; the other keyframe will move with it. Press Shift after you start dragging to snap the first keyframe to the current-time indicator, at 0:08, and then release.

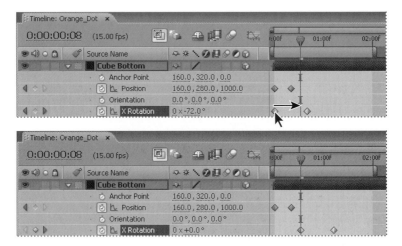

4 Go to 1:06, which is three frames after the last X Rotation keyframe.

5 Click the Z Rotation property name to select its keyframes.

6 Drag the first Z Rotation keyframe to the right, press Shift to snap it to the location of the current-time indicator (at 1:06), and then release.

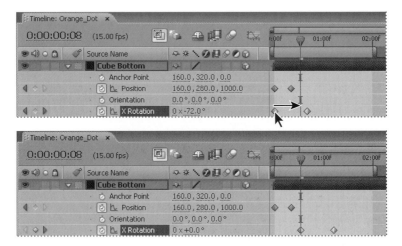

7 Drag the work area end marker to 2:10 so that the work area includes all of the keyframes plus a cushion of time after the last keyframe, and then watch another spacebar preview. The square recedes in space, pauses briefly, falls flat, pauses again, and then rotates.

8 Clean up the Timeline panel in preparation for the next exercise by closing all of the Cube Bottom layer's properties and pressing the Home key to go to 0:00.

9 Choose File > Save to save your work.

Creating the 3D floor

After the blue square falls and rotates, you want a purple floor to spread out beneath it. You'll make this floor from another solid layer.

Creating the floor layer

In fact, you can build the floor from a copy of the Cube Bottom layer.

1 Select the Cube Bottom layer in the Timeline panel and choose Edit > Duplicate.

2 Select the Cube Bottom layer at the bottom of the stack and rename it **Floor**.

3 Go to 2:09, which is three frames after the last keyframe in the Cube Bottom layer.

4 With the Floor layer selected in the Timeline panel, press Alt+[(Windows) or Option+[(Mac OS) to move the layer's In point to the current time.

5 With the Floor layer still selected in the Timeline panel, choose Layer > Solid Settings.

6 In the Solid Settings dialog box, change the solid's name to **Floor**, and then click the Color swatch to open the Color Picker.

Animating the floor

Now, you'll animate the floor so that it spreads outward from under the blue square.

1 Choose Active Camera from the 3D View pop-up menu in the Composition panel.

2 With the Floor layer selected in the Timeline panel, press the S key to display its Scale property.

3 Still at 2:09, click the Scale stopwatch (⏱) to add a keyframe.

4 Go to 3:00.

5 Drag any of the Floor layer's Scale values in the Timeline panel to the right until the Floor layer extends beyond the sides and the bottom of viewable composition, as shown in the following image. Your final Scale values don't have to be exact, but they should be somewhere between 575% and 600%. After Effects adds a Scale keyframe.

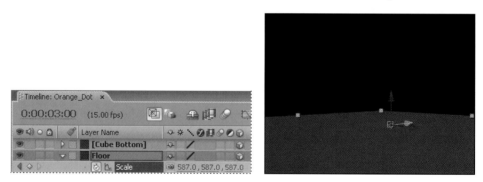

7 Drag the work area end marker to 2:10 so that the work area includes all of the keyframes plus a cushion of time after the last keyframe, and then watch another spacebar preview. The square recedes in space, pauses briefly, falls flat, pauses again, and then rotates.

8 Clean up the Timeline panel in preparation for the next exercise by closing all of the Cube Bottom layer's properties and pressing the Home key to go to 0:00.

9 Choose File > Save to save your work.

Creating the 3D floor

After the blue square falls and rotates, you want a purple floor to spread out beneath it. You'll make this floor from another solid layer.

Creating the floor layer

In fact, you can build the floor from a copy of the Cube Bottom layer.

1 Select the Cube Bottom layer in the Timeline panel and choose Edit > Duplicate.

2 Select the Cube Bottom layer at the bottom of the stack and rename it **Floor**.

3 Go to 2:09, which is three frames after the last keyframe in the Cube Bottom layer.

4 With the Floor layer selected in the Timeline panel, press Alt+[(Windows) or Option+[(Mac OS) to move the layer's In point to the current time.

5 With the Floor layer still selected in the Timeline panel, choose Layer > Solid Settings.

6 In the Solid Settings dialog box, change the solid's name to **Floor**, and then click the Color swatch to open the Color Picker.

7 Type **990099** in the # field to choose a web-friendly purple, and then click OK to close the Color Picker.

8 Back in the Solid Settings dialog box, click New.

Positioning the floor

You want the floor to spread out from all four sides of the blue square, so you have to return the Floor layer's anchor point to its default position in the center of the layer.

1 With the Floor layer selected in the Timeline panel, press the A key to display its Anchor Point property.

2 Right-click (Windows) or Control-click (Mac OS) the Anchor Point property name and choose Reset from the contextual menu. The Anchor Point returns to its default values (160.0, 160.0, 0.0) in the middle of the layer, and the layer moves accordingly in the Composition panel.

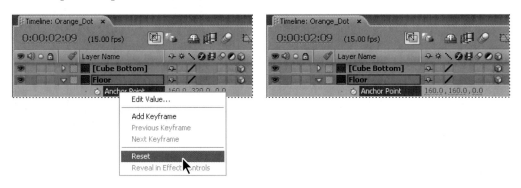

3 With the Floor layer selected in the Timeline panel, press the P key to display its Position property and hide its Anchor Point property.

4 Choose Top from the 3D View pop-up menu at the bottom of the Composition panel. The composition appears to be empty, because the layers are out of the default Top view.

5 With the Floor layer selected in the Timeline panel, choose View > Look At Selected Layers. After Effects adjusts the point of view and direction of view to include the selected layers. As a result, the Floor layer appears in the Composition panel, and you can see where the Cube Bottom layer overlaps it.

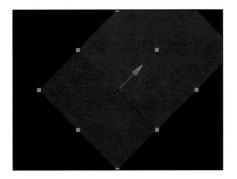

6 Using the Selection tool (➤), drag the Floor layer's y axis (the green arrow) toward the upper-right corner of the composition until it is hidden beneath the Cube Bottom layer. The resulting Position values should be 273.0, 280.0, 1111.0; enter them manually if necessary to adjust your move operation.

Note: After Effects adds a Position keyframe, because two other Position keyframes were copied to the Floor layer from the Cube Bottom layer. This doesn't affect the animation.

Animating the floor

Now, you'll animate the floor so that it spreads outward from under the blue square.

1 Choose Active Camera from the 3D View pop-up menu in the Composition panel.

2 With the Floor layer selected in the Timeline panel, press the S key to display its Scale property.

3 Still at 2:09, click the Scale stopwatch (⏱) to add a keyframe.

4 Go to 3:00.

5 Drag any of the Floor layer's Scale values in the Timeline panel to the right until the Floor layer extends beyond the sides and the bottom of viewable composition, as shown in the following image. Your final Scale values don't have to be exact, but they should be somewhere between 575% and 600%. After Effects adds a Scale keyframe.

6 Drag the work area end marker to 4:00, and then watch a spacebar preview of the sequence. After the cube bottom animates, the purple floor expands out from underneath it.

Adding the grid to the floor

Because the floor is currently a solid color, it doesn't offer a good sense of perspective with respect to the box. You'll apply the Grid effect to fix that.

1 Go to 3:10, where you can see the scaled floor in the Composition panel.

2 With the Floor layer selected in the Timeline panel, choose Effect > Generate > Grid. After Effects applies a grid to the layer.

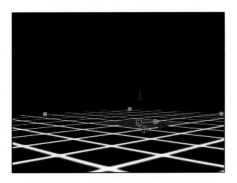

3 In the Effect Controls panel, check the Invert Grid box. The grid lines become transparent, and the grid squares become opaque, filled with white.

4 Click the eyedropper next to the Color property in the Effect Controls panel.

5 Move the eyedropper to the Timeline panel and click to select the purple square next to the Floor layer name. The squares of the grid in the composition fill with purple.

6 In the Effect Controls panel, change the Border value to **1.0** to create thinner lines in the grid.

7 Watch a spacebar preview of the results. Then, clean up the Timeline panel by closing all of the Floor layer's properties.

8 Choose File > Save to save your work.

Building the cube sides

The composition is coming along nicely. You've created the bottom of the cube and the floor. Now, you need to assemble the sides of the cube.

Creating the first side

Start by creating and positioning a new solid layer.

1 Go to 3:00.

2 Deselect all layers in the Timeline panel, and choose Layer > New > Solid.

3 In the Solid Settings dialog box, do the following:

• Name the solid **Cube Side**.

• Make sure the Width and Height are both set to 320 pixels.

• Use the Color eyedropper to choose the blue next to the Cube Bottom layer name in the Timeline panel.

• Click OK to create the layer.

4 Make sure the Cube Side layer is at the top of the layer stack in the Timeline panel. If it is not, drag it there.

5 Turn on the Cube Side layer's 3D switch.

6 With the Cube Side layer selected in the Timeline panel, press the A key to reveal its Anchor Point property.

7 Set the Cube Side layer's Anchor Point values to **160.0, 320.0, 0.0**. This sets the anchor point to the bottom of the layer, so you can flip the layer along that edge.

8 With the Cube Side layer selected in the Timeline panel, press Shift+R to also display its Rotation and Orientation properties. Then, set the Y Rotation to **+45.0°**.

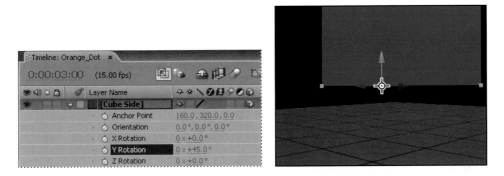

9 With the Cube Side layer selected in the Timeline panel, press Shift+P to also display the layer's Position property. Then, set the Position values to **388.0, 280.0, 1224.0**. This positions the Cube Side layer perpendicular to Cube Bottom layer and along its far right side.

10 Close all of the properties for the Cube Side layer to give yourself more room in the Timeline panel for the next exercise.

Creating the other sides

You can quickly create the other three sides of the cube by duplicating the side you just created.

1 Select the Cube Side layer in the Timeline panel and press Ctrl+D (Windows) or Command+D three times to create three copies of it.

2 Select each layer in turn and rename them **Cube Side 1**, **Cube Side 2**, **Cube Side 3**, and **Cube Side 4**. Cube Side 1 should be at the bottom of the stack; Cube Side 4 should be at the top, as in the following figure.

3 Shift-click to select all four Cube Side layers in the Timeline panel.

4 Press Alt+[(Windows) or Option+[(Mac OS) to move the In points for all four layers to the current time, 3:00.

Positioning the cube sides

In the real world, you would use the Selection tool to position and rotate all of the remaining three sides of the cube in the Composition panel. Luckily, this is an *Adobe Classroom in a Book*, so we'll speed things along for you by providing the Position and Rotation values you need to align the sides along the cube's bottom edges. If you'd like to drag to position the sides manually in the Composition panel, however, feel free to do so. It's good practice. Use the Selection tool and choose 3D View > Top at the bottom of the Composition panel.

1 Select just the Cube Side 2 layer in the Timeline panel. Press the P key and then press Shift+R to display the layer's Position, Rotation, and Orientation properties.

2 Set the Y Rotation to **135.0**° and set the Position values to **162.0, 280.0, 1226.0** for the Cube Side 2 layer. Then, hide the Cube Side 2 layer's properties to keep the Timeline panel neat.

3 Select the Cube Side 3 layer. Press the P key and then press Shift+R to display the layer's Position, Rotation, and Orientation properties.

4 Set the Y Rotation to **135.0**° and the Position values to **388.0, 280.0, 1000.0** for the Cube Side 3 layer. Then, hide the Cube Side 3 layer's properties.

5 Select the Cube Side 4 layer. Press P to display the layer's Position property.

6 Set the Position values to **162.0, 280.0, 1000.0** for the Cube Side 4 layer. Then, hide the Cube Side 4 layer's properties.

7 To help you visualize the cube, choose 2 Views – Horizontal from the Select View Layout pop-up menu at the bottom of the Composition panel. Set one view to Active Camera and one to Top (using the 3D View pop-up menu). The cube sides should sit along the four bottom edges and should stand perpendicular to them.

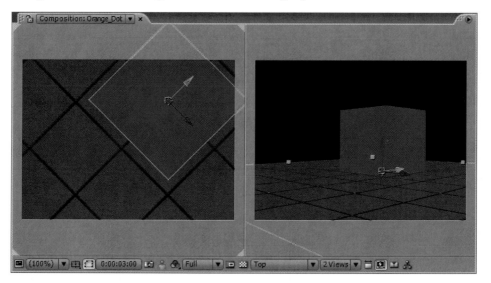

8 Return to 1 View, Active Camera when you're done.

Animating the cube sides

The cube sides are currently in their final, upright positions—that's a bit premature. They have to flip up first. To animate the sides, you'll first go forward in time to establish this result for each side, and then you'll go back in time and flip each side up. Once again, we're providing you with the correct values, but you can also manually rotate each layer along its *z* axis using the Rotation tool, set to Orientation in the Tools panel.

1 Go to 5:05, which is after the Floor layer finishes animating and gives each cube side enough time to animate into position.

2 Select the Cube Side 4 layer in the Timeline panel, press the R key to reveal its Orientation and Rotation properties, and click the stopwatch (⏱) to add an Orientation keyframe at the upright position (0.0°, 0.0°, 0.0°).

3 Go to 5:00 and change the Cube Side 4 layer Orientation values to **305.3°, 330.0°, 54.7°**. After Effects adds a keyframe.

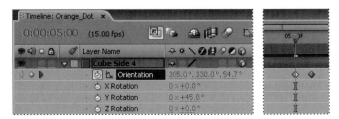

4 Close the Cube Side 4 layer's properties and then go to 4:10.

5 Select the Cube Side 3 layer in the Timeline panel, press the R key to reveal its Orientation and Rotation properties, and click the stopwatch (⏱) to add an Orientation keyframe.

6 Go to 4:05 and change the Cube Side 3 layer Orientation values to **305.3°, 30.0°, 305.3°**. After Effects adds a keyframe.

7 Close the Cube Side 3 layer's properties and then go to 4:00.

8 Select the Cube Side 2 layer in the Timeline panel, press the R key to reveal its Orientation and Rotation properties, and click the stopwatch (⏱) to add an Orientation keyframe.

9 Go to 3:10 and change the Cube Side 2 layer Orientation values to **54.7˚**, **30.0˚**, **54.7˚**. After Effects adds a keyframe.

10 Close the Cube Side 2 layer's properties and then go to 3:05.

11 Select the Cube Side 1 layer in the Timeline panel, press the R key to reveal its Orientation and Rotation properties, and click the stopwatch (⏱) to add an Orientation keyframe.

12 Go to 3:00 and change the Cube Side 1 Orientation values to **54.7˚**, **330.0˚**, **305.3˚**. After Effects adds a keyframe—and you're done.

Preview the entire animation and see your excellent work.

13 Extend the work area end marker to 5:10. Then, press the Home key to go to the beginning of the time ruler, deselect all layers in the Timeline panel, and watch a spacebar preview. The cube sides should flip up one at a time just after the floor has scaled to its final size.

14 After watching the preview, close the Cube Side 1 layer's properties in the Timeline panel, press the Home key to go to 0:00, and then choose File > Save.

Congratulations. You've assembled a 3D shape and animated it in space. In Lesson 10, "Using 3D Effects," you will continue working on this project. You will add visual interest to the scene by introducing a 3D light and a 3D camera, you'll create an animated orange sphere, and you'll add an animated text logo.

Review

▶ **Review questions**

1 What happens to a layer when you turn on its 3D Layer switch?

2 Why is it important to look at multiple views of a composition that contains 3D layers?

3 What happens when you move a layer's Anchor Point values in the Timeline panel compared to when you move a layer's anchor point using the Pan Behind tool in the Composition panel?

▶ **Review answers**

1 When you turn on a layer's 3D Layer switch in the Timeline panel, the layer can then be moved and rotated along its z axis in addition to its x and y axes. In addition, the layer takes on new properties and that are unique to 3D layers, such as the Material Options property group.

2 The appearance of 3D layers can be deceptive, depending on the view in the Composition panel. By enabling 3D views, you can see the true position of a layer relative to other layers in the composition.

3 When you adjust the Anchor Point values for a layer in the Timeline panel, the layer moves in the Composition panel even though its Position values remain the same. When you move an anchor point by using the Pan Behind tool, however, the Position values automatically change in the Timeline panel as needed to keep the layer in its current position relative to the composition and to other layers.

In Lesson 9, you created an animated 3D cube. In this lesson, you'll add 3D effects such as lights and cameras, as well as other animated elements, to complete the composition.

10 | Using 3D Effects

Lesson overview

In this lesson, you'll learn how to do the following:

- Create and position a light layer.

- Cast realistic shadows.

- Create and animate a camera layer.

- Use the CC Sphere and Warp effects.

- Apply the Spiral Long text animation preset.

This lesson picks up where the previous lesson left off. In Lesson 9, "Building and Animating a 3D Object," you created the first half of an animation for a fictional company called Orange Dot, Inc. So far, the animation features a cube unfolding in 3D space. In this lesson, you will complete the project by adding lights, shadows, effects, and other elements to the composition. In doing so, you'll learn how to use additional 3D features available in After Effects.

This lesson will take approximately 1½ hours to complete.

Getting started

Make sure the following files are in the AE7_CIB > Lessons > Lesson10 folder on your hard disk, or copy them from the *Adobe After Effects 7.0 Classroom in a Book* DVD now:

- In the Sample_Movie folder: Lesson10.mov
- In the Start_Project_File folder: Lesson10_Start.aep

1 Open and play the Lesson10.mov file to see what you will create in this lesson. When you are done, quit the QuickTime player. You may delete this sample movie from your hard disk if you have limited storage space.

Note: *Before starting this lesson, make sure you have installed the Cycore Effects plug-ins. The Cycore installer is available on the After Effects installation disc.*

Setting up the project

You don't need to create a new project for this lesson. You can start with the Lesson10_Start.aep project file provided with this book, or you can use the Lesson 9 project file that you saved at the end of that lesson, if you completed it. The two files should be equivalent. If you had difficulty with Lesson 9 or did not complete that lesson, use the Lesson10_Start.aep file that we have provided for you.

When you begin this lesson, restore the default application settings for After Effects. See "Restoring default preferences," page 5.

1 Press Ctrl+Alt+Shift (Windows) or Command+Option+Shift (Mac OS) while starting After Effects. When asked whether you want to delete your preferences file, click OK.

2 Choose File > Open Project.

3 Do one of the following:

• Navigate to AE7_CIB > Lessons > Lesson10 > Start_Project_File folder, select the Lesson10_Start.aep file, and click Open.

• Navigate to the AE7_CIB > Lessons > Lesson09 > Finished_Project folder, select the Lesson09_Finished.aep file, and click Open.

4 Choose File > Save As.

5 Navigate to the AE7_CIB > Lessons > Lesson10 > Finished_Project folder on your hard disk. Name the project **Lesson10_Finished.aep**, and then click Save.

Using 3D lights

So far, you've created the floor and the box for the Orange Dot spot. Before you add the bouncing orange sphere, you will apply some lighting effects to the scene.

Creating a light layer

In After Effects, a light is a type of layer that shines light on other layers. You can choose from among four different types of lights—Parallel, Spot, Point, and Ambient—and modify them with various settings. Lights, by default, point to a *point of interest*. The point of interest is a property that specifies the point in the composition at which the light points.

You will now add a light layer to the Orange_Dot composition.

1 Select the Orange_Dot composition in the Project panel, and then make either the Timeline or Composition panel active.

2 Press the Home key to make sure the current-time indicator is at the beginning of the time ruler.

3 Choose Layer > New > Light.

4 In the Light Settings dialog box, do the following:

- Name the layer **Spotlight 1**.

- Choose Light Type > Spot.

- Set Intensity to **225%** and Cone Angle to **117˚**.

- Make sure Cone Feather is set to 50%, and the Color is white.

- Check the Casts Shadows box.

- Make sure Shadow Darkness is set to 100%, and set Shadow Diffusion to **100** pixels.

- Click OK to create the light layer.

The light layer is represented by a light bulb icon (💡) in the Timeline panel, and the point of interest appears in the Composition panel as a cross-hair icon (✛).

Adjusting the point of interest

By default, the point of interest of a light layer is at the center of the composition, and the light's view is automatically oriented toward it. You will position the spotlight to point at the cube from above.

1 Choose 2 Views – Horizontal from the Select View Layout pop-up menu at the bottom of the Composition panel.

2 Click to make the left view active, and make sure the 3D View pop-up menu is set to Top. (The right view should be Active Camera.)

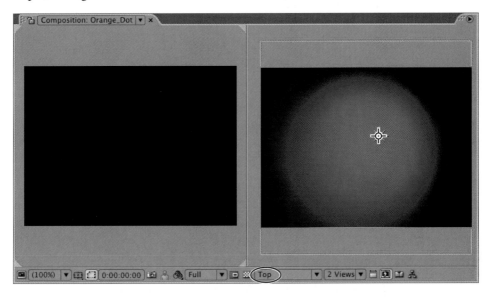

3 Go to 5:05, at which time all four cube sides have flipped up.

Note: The light will appear throughout the composition, but by working at 5:05, you can clearly see how the light interacts with the cube.

4 Select the Cube Bottom layer in the Timeline panel and then Ctrl-click (Windows) or Command-click (Mac OS) the Spotlight 1 layer to also select it.

5 Choose View > Look At Selected Layers. You should be able to see both layers in both views in the Composition panel.

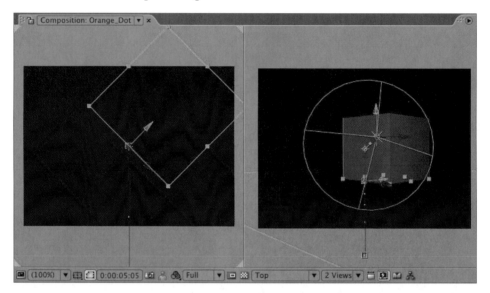

6 Select just the Spotlight 1 layer in the Timeline panel and expand all of its Transform properties.

7 With the Spotlight 1 layer selected in the Timeline panel, drag the *x*- and *z*-axis values of the Point Of Interest property until the point of interest icon (⬦) appears in the center of the cube in the Top view in the Composition panel. When you're done, the Point Of Interest values should be 270.0, 120.0, 1103.0; enter them manually if necessary.

You can also drag the point of interest icon in the Top view of the Composition panel to reposition it.

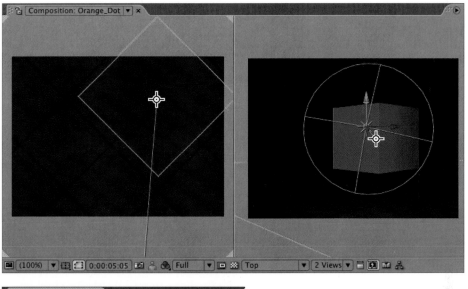

8 Choose 4 Views – Left from the Select View Layout pop-up menu at the bottom of the Composition panel. Four 3D views appear: three stacked at the left side of the Composition panel, and a fourth, larger, view at right. The views at left are (from top to bottom) Top, Front, and Right. The Active Camera view appears on the right side of the Composition panel.

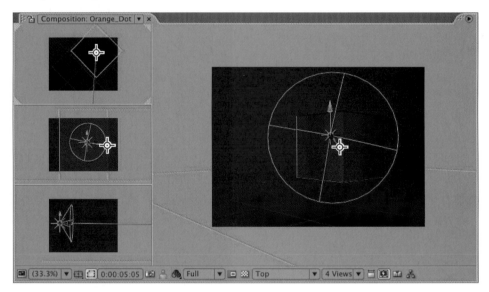

9 Select the Right view (at the bottom of the stack at left). Then, if necessary, zoom out and use the Hand tool (🖐) so that you can see the cone of the spotlight as well as the point of interest in the view. Switch back to the Selection tool (▸) after adjusting the view.

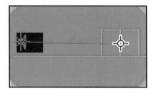

*Right view with the Spotlight 1
layer selected and the light cone
and the point of interest visible.*

10 While watching the point of interest icon (✥) in the various views in the Composition panel, drag the Point Of Interest *y*-axis value (the middle value) to the right in the Timeline panel until it is positioned just above the floor grid. When you're done, the Point Of Interest values should be 270.0, 264.0, 1103.0; enter them manually if necessary.

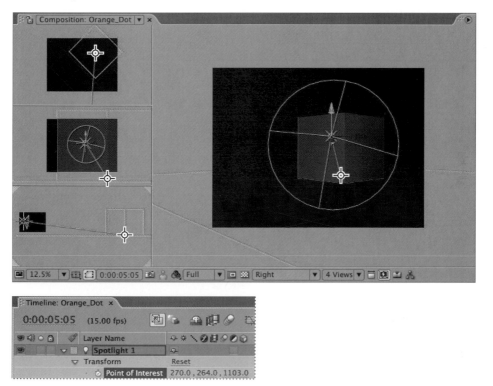

Positioning the spotlight

Now, you can adjust the position of the spotlight. Dragging it in the Composition panel would cause the light's point of interest to move, however, so you'll change the light layer's position in the Timeline panel instead.

1 Select the Spotlight 1 layer in the Timeline panel and press P to see its Position property.

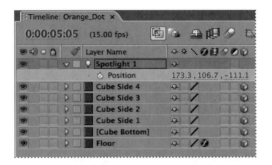

2 While watching the Right and Active Camera views in the Composition panel, drag the Position property *y*-axis value (the middle value) to the left in the Timeline panel until the light cone is far above the top of the composition. The final *y*-axis value should be –700.0; enter the value manually if necessary.

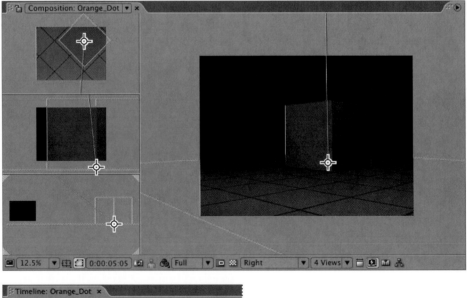

To speed things along, you'll adjust the Position property *z*-axis value more quickly.

3 Change the Position property's *z*-axis value in the Timeline panel to **–430.0**. This moves the light back in 3D space.

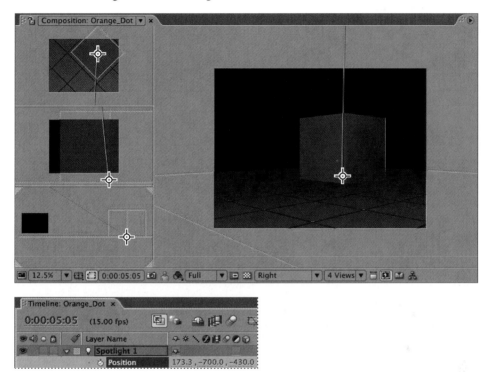

4 Select the Spotlight 1 layer in the Timeline panel and press the U key to hide its properties.

5 Deselect all layers in the Timeline panel, press the Home key, and watch a spacebar preview of the lighted animation. Then, choose File > Save to save your work.

Turning on shadows

When you turn on a layer's 3D Layer switch, the layer responds to light layers and shadows according to the settings in the layer's Material Options properties group. The Material Options properties are important components of realism and perspective in 3D animation.

1 Go to 5:05 to continue to view the four upright sides of the cube as you work.

2 Choose Select View Layout > 1 View at the bottom of the Composition panel, and make sure the 3D View pop-up menu is set to Active Camera.

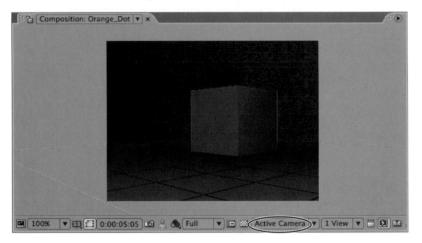

3 Shift-click to select all four cube side layers in the Timeline panel.

4 Press AA to expand the Material Options property group for the four selected cube side layers.

5 With all four cube side layers still selected, turn on the Casts Shadows property in the Material Options property group for the Cube Side 4 layer. Because all four sides are selected, this turns on the property on for all four layers.

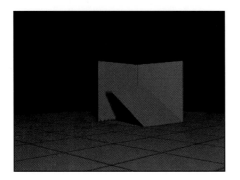

6 Close the properties for the four cube side layers and deselect all layers in the Timeline panel.

7 Press the Home key to go to the beginning of the time ruler, and then press the spacebar to preview the results. The cube sides cast shadows as they flip into position.

8 Press the spacebar to stop the preview when you're ready, and then choose File > Save to save your work.

Adding a camera

You can view 3D layers from any number of angles and distances using layers called *cameras*. When you set a camera view for your composition, you look at the layers as though you were looking through that camera. You can choose between viewing a composition through the active camera or through a named, custom camera. If you have not created a custom camera, then the active camera is the same as the default composition view.

So far, the Orange_Dot composition unfolds in front of the default active camera. But the next sequence in the animation requires a perspective that looks down into the cube from above. For that, you'll create a camera layer and animate the virtual camera.

1 Go to 5:05 and deselect all layers in the Timeline panel.

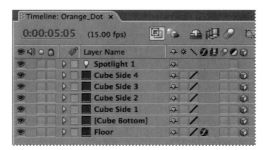

2 Choose Layer > New > Camera.

3 In the Camera Settings dialog box, accept all of the defaults, including the name, Camera 1, and the 50mm preset, and then click OK.

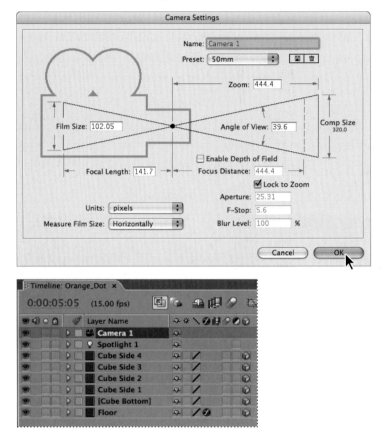

The Camera 1 layer appears at the top of the layer stack in the Timeline panel (with a camera icon next to the layer name), and Composition panel updates to reflect the new camera layer's perspective. The view doesn't appear to change, however, because the 50mm camera preset uses the same settings as the default Active Camera view.

4 Choose 2 Views – Horizontal from the 3D View pop-up menu at the bottom of the Composition panel. The Top view appears on the left; the Active Camera view remains on the right.

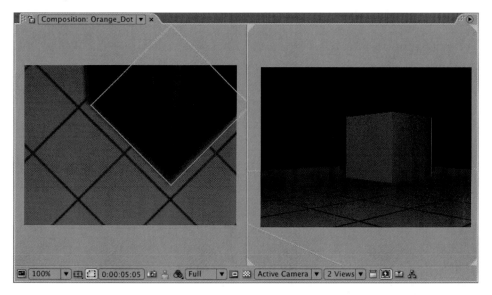

Setting the camera's point of interest

As with light layers, camera layers have a point of interest that determines what the camera looks at. You'll set this camera layer to look at the cube and stay focused on it as you animate the camera's position.

1 Expand the Camera 1 layer Transform property group in the Timeline panel.

2 While watching the Top view in the Composition panel, drag the Point Of Interest property *z*-axis value to the right in the Timeline panel until the point of interest icon (✦) in the Composition panel is inside the cube. The final value should be 1117.0; enter it manually if necessary.

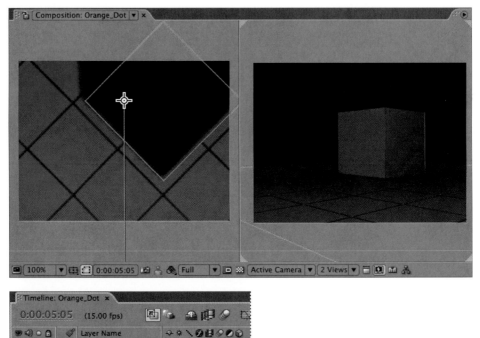

Animating the camera

If you move the camera layer by dragging it in the Composition panel, the layer's point of interest property moves, too, so you'll reposition the camera using the Timeline panel instead.

1 Go to 5:07, which is two frames after the sides have formed the cube.

2 Click the Camera 1 layer's Position stopwatch (⏱) to add a keyframe to the property at the default values (160.0, 120.0, −444.4).

3 Expand the Camera Options property group for the Camera 1 layer in the Timeline panel.

4 Click the Zoom stopwatch (⏱) to add a keyframe to the property at the default value, 444.4 pixels.

5 Go to 6:04, and then extend the work area end marker to 6:10.

6 Change the *y*-axis value of the Camera 1 layer's Position property to **–1000.0** to move the camera up. After Effects adds a keyframe.

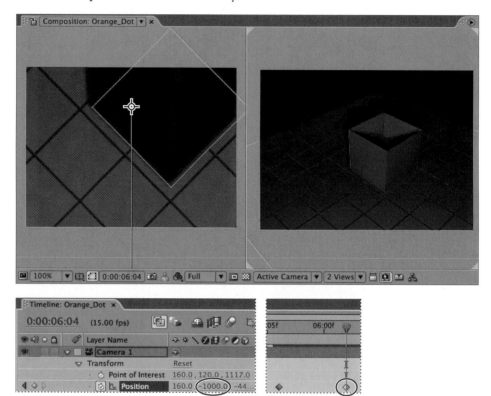

7 Change the Zoom value to **500.0** pixels. After Effects adds a keyframe.

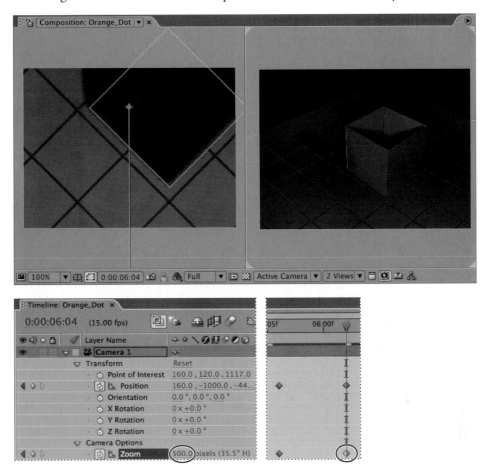

8 Return to one view in the Composition panel, set to Active Camera.

9 Press the Home key to go to 0:00, and then press the spacebar to watch a preview of the animation.

10 Press the spacebar to stop the playback when you're done.

11 Close the properties for the Camera 1 layer, and then choose File > Save to save your work.

Adding an animated sphere

Now that you have added some lights, shadows, and a camera to the animation, you can create another animated element: the orange dot (actually, a sphere) that emerges from the cube.

Creating the sphere

As with the sides of the cubes, you'll create the orange sphere from a solid layer. Then you'll apply the Cycore CC Sphere effect. Make sure you have installed the plug-in from the After Effects installation disc before continuing.

1 Go to 6:04.

2 Deselect all layers in the Timeline panel, and then choose Layer > New > Solid.

3 In the Solid Settings dialog box, do the following:

• Name the layer **Orange Dot**.

• Set the Height to **320** pixels.

• Click the Color swatch, and in the Color Picker, set the color to **FF9900** in the # field. Then, click OK to set the color and return to the Solid Settings dialog box.

• Click OK.

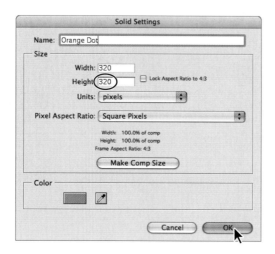

The new layer appears at the top of the layer stack in the Timeline panel and in the center of the Composition panel, as well.

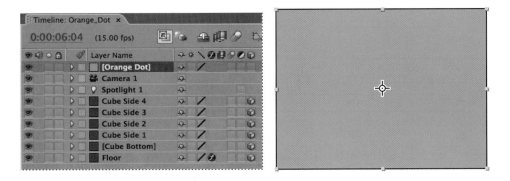

Now, turn this square into a sphere.

4 With the Orange Dot layer selected in the Timeline panel, choose Effect > Perspective > CC Sphere.

5 In the Effect Controls panel, set the Radius to **160.0**.

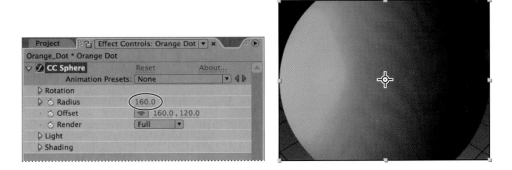

Congratulations. You've just created a bouncing baby sphere.

Positioning the sphere

Although the sphere appears to have depth, you can only move it along the x and y axes in the composition. You'll turn on the layer's 3D Layer switch so that you can animate the sphere alongside the other elements of the scene in 3D space.

1 Still at 6:04, turn on the Orange Dot layer's 3D Layer switch (⊙). The Orange Dot layer disappears from view in the Composition panel because its starting z-axis Position value is 0.0, which is out of the camera's view.

2 Select the Orange Dot layer in the Timeline panel and then press the P key to display its Position property.

3 Change the layer's Position values to **270.0, 138.0, 1115.0**. This puts the layer in the camera view and inside the cube.

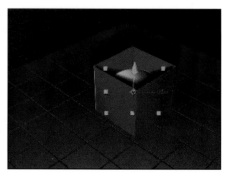

4 Select the Orange Dot layer in the Timeline panel and press AA to reveal its Material Options property group.

5 Turn off the Accepts Shadows and Accepts Lights properties. Now, the Orange Dot layer will not show shadows that are cast on it by other layers (the sides of the cube), and its color will not be affected by the light that reaches it.

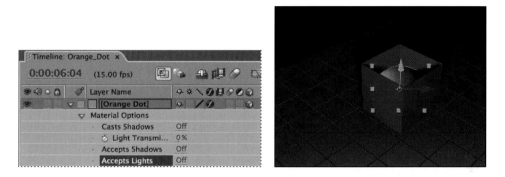

6 Click the triangle in the Label column of the Orange Dot layer to close all of the layer's properties.

Deflating the orange dot

To make the sphere gradually emerge from the cube, you'll apply the Warp effect to the layer, and then animate the effect.

1 Go to 6:09.

2 With the Orange Dot layer selected in the Timeline panel, press Alt+[(Windows) or Option+[(Mac OS) to move its In point to the current time.

3 With the Orange Dot layer still selected in the Timeline panel, choose Effect > Distort > Warp. The default settings for the effect distort the sphere into an egg—an egg that's oozing out of the corners of the cube. Time to customize the effect's properties.

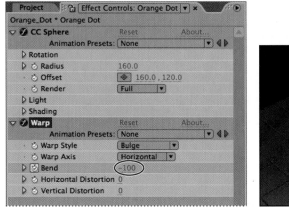 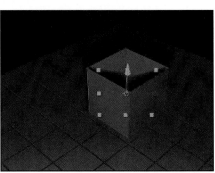

4 In the Warp area of the Effect Controls panel, choose Warp Style > Bulge.

5 Change the Bend value to **–100.** The sphere disappears from view. Then click the Bend stopwatch (⏱) to add a keyframe to the property.

Inflating the sphere

Now, it's time to make the sphere gently rise and fall a few times until it's fully inflated and bursting out of the cube. To do so, you'll animate the Warp effect's Bend property.

1 Still at 6:09, change the Warp effect's Vertical Distortion to **–65** in the Effect Controls panel.

2 Select the Orange Dot layer in the Timeline panel and press the U key to display its animated properties—in this case, the Bend property of the Warp effect.

3 Go to 7:12 and change the Bend property to **100** in the Timeline panel. After Effects adds a keyframe, and the sphere appears in the cube in the Composition panel.

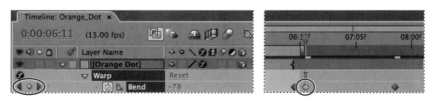

4 Go to 6:11, which is two frames after the first Bend keyframe.

5 Click the Add/Remove Keyframe switch in the Timeline panel's A/V Features column to add a Bend keyframe at 6:11. A yellow diamond icon (◆) appears in the switch and in the time ruler.

6 Press the Page Down key twice to advance two frames to 6:13, and then click the Add/Remove Keyframe switch to add another keyframe.

7 Repeat step 6 until you've added keyframes every two seconds between the first and last Bend keyframes.

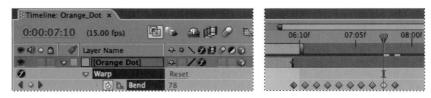

Now that you have the keyframes, adjust the Bend property value for every other one.

8 Go to 6:11, the location of the second Bend keyframe. Change the Bend value to **–42**.

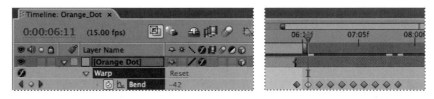

💡 *Pressing the K key moves the current-time indicator to the next visible keyframe; pressing the J key moves the current-time indicator to the previous keyframe. Use the J and K keys to navigate to the correct Bend keyframes in steps 9 through 11.*

9 Press the K key twice to go to the Bend keyframe at 7:00, and then change the Bend value to **30**.

10 Press the K key two more times to go to the Bend keyframe at 7:04, and then change the Bend value to **55**.

11 Press the K key two more times to go to the Bend keyframe at 7:08, and then change the Bend value to **96**.

12 Choose File > Save to save your work.

Making the sphere bulge

To get the results you need for the Orange Dot animation, you must to finesse the sphere's final moments in the cube.

1 With the Orange Dot layer selected in the Timeline panel, press the E key to display its effects properties.

2 Expand the layer's Warp effect properties.

3 Go to 7:12.

4 Click the Vertical Distortion stopwatch (🕑) to add a keyframe to the property.

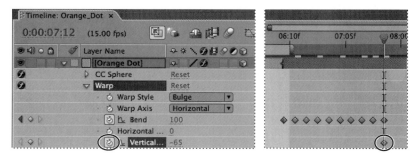

5 Select the Orange Dot layer in the Timeline panel, and then press Shift+P to also display the layer's Position property underneath its effects properties.

6 Click the Position stopwatch (🕑) to add a keyframe to the property.

7 Select the Orange Dot layer in the Timeline panel, and then press Shift+S to also display the layer's Scale property.

8 Click the Scale stopwatch (🕑) to add a keyframe to the property.

9 Select the Orange Dot layer in the Timeline panel, and then press the U key to display just the layer's keyframed properties in the Timeline panel.

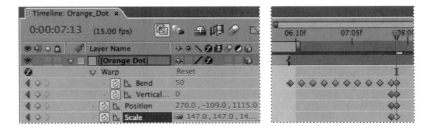

10 Press the Page Down key once to go forward one frame to 7:13.

11 Set the following properties for the Orange Dot layer in the Timeline panel:

- Bend: **0**

- Vertical Distortion: **0**

- Position: **270.0, –109.0, 1115.0**

- Scale: **147.0, 147.0, 147.0%**

After Effects adds keyframes for all four properties.

12 Click the triangle in the Label column of the Orange Dot layer in the Timeline panel to hide the layer's properties.

Previewing the animated sphere

It's time to preview the sphere's animation to see how it looks.

1 Go to 6:04, and then drag the work area start marker to the same time. Then, drag the work area end marker to about 8:04. This gives a cushion of time around the actual animation.

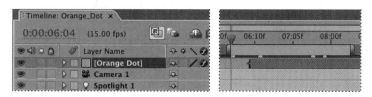

2 Deselect all layers in the Timeline panel, and then press the spacebar to preview the work area. The orange sphere should initially be out of sight, then rise and fall a few times inside the box as if being inflated, and then stop when it is bulging out of the box.

3 Press the spacebar to stop the playback when you're ready. Then, drag the work area start marker to the beginning of the time ruler and drag the work area end marker to the end of the time ruler.

4 Choose File > Save to save your work.

Adding the logo

You'll create the animated logo that appears at the end of the animation by applying a text animation preset.

Creating the text layer

For the logo, you'll use a Text Path animation preset. As you may recall from Lesson 3, "Animating Text," the Path presets use placeholder text. So for this exercise, you'll create an empty text layer, apply the preset, and then customize the type.

1 Deselect all layers in the Timeline panel and then choose Layer > New > Text. After Effects adds the new layer, Text 1, to the Timeline and Composition panels.

2 Go to 7:13, which is when the Orange Dot finishes bulging out of the cube.

3 Make sure the text layer (now named Empty Text Layer) is selected in the Timeline panel, and then choose Animation > Browse Presets to jump to Bridge.

4 In Bridge, double-click the Text folder, then the Paths folder.

5 Preview the Spiral Long preset, and then double-click it to apply it to the empty text layer in After Effects.

Back in After Effects, the preset appears in the Composition panel with its name, Spiral Long, along the spiral path. The empty text layer name changes to spiral long in the Timeline panel, which also displays the properties of the animation preset.

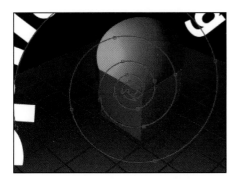

Reversing the animation direction

As you saw in the Preview panel in Bridge, the Spiral Long preset animates the text inward along the spiral until it disappears. You want the text to spiral outward, so you need to reverse the keyframes that the preset applied.

1 Select the Spiral Long layer in the Timeline panel and press the U key to reveal just its keyframed properties.

2 Shift-click the First Margin, Scale, and Tracking Amount property names to select all of their keyframes.

3 Choose Animation > Keyframe Assistant > Time-Reverse Keyframes.

Positioning the text

For this part of the project, you can scale the 2D layer to get the text into position; you don't need to make a it 3D layer and position it along the *z* axis.

1 Select the spiral long layer in the Timeline panel and press the S key to reveal just its Scale property.

2 Change the Scale values to **32.0, 32.0%**.

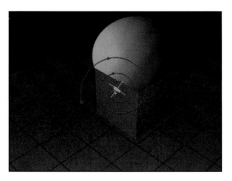

3 Select the Spiral Long layer in the Timeline panel and press the P key to reveal just its Position property.

4 Change the Position values to **191.0, 79.0** so that the spiral is roughly centered in the sphere.

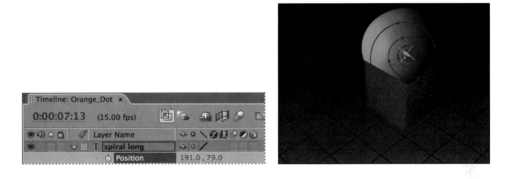

Customizing the text

Finally, replace the placeholder text with the company name, Orange Dot, Inc.

1 Go to 9:13, which is when the spiral animation finishes.

2 Select the Spiral Long layer in the Timeline panel.

3 Select the Horizontal Type tool (**T**) in the Tools panel.

4 Select the placeholder text in the Composition panel, and then type **Orange Dot, Inc.** Then, press Enter on the numeric keypad.

5 If desired, choose Window > Character and choose a different typeface for the logo. Or, accept the default sans serif typeface for the Spiral Long preset.

6 Select the newly named Orange Dot, Inc. text layer in the Timeline panel and hide its properties.

Finishing up

Congratulations. You've completed the two-part 3D animation for this *Adobe Classroom in a Book*. After all that hard work, you should definitely preview the entire animation.

1 Deselect all layers in the Timeline panel.

2 Press the Home key to go to the beginning of the time ruler.

3 Press 0 on the numeric keypad to watch a RAM preview of the entire composition.

4 Choose File > Save to save your project.

5 Close Bridge.

If you'd like to render the piece, see Lesson 12, "Rendering and Outputting," for instructions. Alternatively, you can export the animation as a Macromedia Flash (SWF) file for use on the web. See Lesson 2, "Creating a Basic Animation with Preset Effects," for instructions on exporting Flash animations.

Review

▶ **Review questions**

1 How are 3D lights handled in After Effects?

2 What is a camera layer?

3 What is a point of interest?

▶ **Review answers**

1 In After Effects, a light is a type of layer that shines light on other layers. You can choose from among four different types of lights—Parallel, Spot, Point, and Ambient—and modify them with various settings.

2 You can view After Effects 3D layers from any number of angles and distances using layers called *cameras*. When you set a camera view for your composition, you look at the layers as though you were looking through that camera. You can choose between viewing a composition through the active camera or through a named, custom camera. If you have not created a custom camera, then the active camera is the same as the default composition view.

3 Cameras and lights include a property that specifies the point in the composition at which the camera or light points. By default, this point of interest is set at the center of the composition, and the camera or light's view is automatically oriented toward it. You can move the point of interest at any time.

Petals

*After Effects Professional Edition
offers all of the features of the
Standard Edition, plus advanced
motion stabilization, motion tracking,
high-end effects, and other features
for the most demanding production
environments.*

11 | Advanced Editing Techniques

Lesson overview

In this lesson, you'll learn how to do the following:

- Use motion stabilization to smooth out a shaky camera shot.

- Use single-point motion tracking to track one object in a shot to another object in a shot.

- Perform multipoint tracking using perspective corner-pinning.

- Create a particle system.

- Do the Timewarp.

After Effects 7.0 Standard Edition provides the essential 2D and 3D tools you need for motion graphics design. After Effects 7.0 Professional Edition adds motion stabilization, motion tracking, advanced keying tools, distortion effects, the capability to retime footage using the Timewarp effect; support for high dynamic range (HDR) color images, network rendering, and much more.

In this lesson, you will learn how to use the motion-stabilization and motion-tracking features of After Effects Professional to stabilize a handheld camera shot and to track one object to another in an image so that their motion is synchronized. Then, you will use corner-pinning to track an object with perspective. Finally, you will explore some of the high-end digital effects available in the Professional Edition of the software: a particle system generator and the Timewarp effect.

If you have only the Standard Edition of After Effects, you may download a trial version of After Effects 7.0 Professional Edition from the Adobe website (www.adobe.com) to try it out for this lesson. Then, you may license the Professional version of the software for ongoing use.

This lesson will take approximately 2 hours to complete.

Getting started

Make sure the following files are in the AE7_CIB > Lessons > Lesson 11 folder on your hard disk, or copy them from the *Adobe After Effects 7.0 Classroom in a Book* DVD now.

• In the Assets folder: banner.ai, building.mov, flowers.mov, Group_Approach[DV].mov, petals.ai

• In the Sample_Movies folder: Lesson_11_Stabilize_and_Track.mov, Lesson11_Multipoint.mov, Lesson_11_Particles.mov, Lesson11_Timewarp.mov

1 Open and play the four sample movies in the Lesson11 > Sample_Movies folder to see the four projects you will create in this lesson. When you're done, quit the QuickTime player. You may delete these sample movies from your hard disk if you have limited storage space.

Note: You can view these movies all at once or, if you don't plan to complete these exercises in one session, you can watch each sample movie just before you are ready to complete the associated exercise.

Using motion stabilization

If you shoot footage using a handheld camera, you will probably end up with shaky shots. Unless this look is intentional, you will want to stabilize your shots to eliminate unwanted shaky motion.

To stabilize footage, After Effects first tracks the motion in the shot. It then shifts the position and rotation of each frame as necessary to remove the movement. When played back, the motion appears smooth because the layer itself moves incrementally to offset the unwanted motion.

Setting up the project

When you begin the lesson, restore the default application settings for After Effects. See "Restoring default preferences," page 5.

1 Press Ctrl+Alt+Shift (Windows) or Command+Option+Shift (Mac OS) while starting After Effects 7.0 Professional to restore default preferences. When asked whether you want to delete your preferences file, click OK.

After Effects opens to display a new, untitled project.

2 Choose File > Save As.

3 In the Save Project As dialog box, navigate to the AE7_CIB > Lessons > Lesson11 > Finished_Projects folder.

4 Name the project **Lesson11_Stabilize_and_Track.aep**, and then click Save.

Importing the footage

You need to import one footage item to start this project.

1 Double-click an empty area of the Project panel to open the Import File dialog box.

2 Navigate to the AE7_CIB > Lessons > Lesson11 > Assets folder. Select the flowers. mov file and then click Open.

Creating the composition

Now, you will create the composition.

1 Choose Composition > New Composition, or press Ctrl+N (Windows) or Command+N (Mac OS).

2 In the Composition Settings dialog box, type **Stabilize_and_Track** in the Composition Name field.

3 Make sure the Preset pop-up menu is set to NTSC DV. This automatically sets the width, height, pixel aspect ratio, and frame rate for the composition.

4 In the Duration field, type **1000** to specify 10 seconds, which matches the length of the flowers.mov file, then click OK.

Now, add the footage item to the composition and preview it.

5 Drag the Flowers.mov file from the Project panel to the Timeline panel. The flowers image appears in the Composition panel.

6 Drag the current-time indicator across the time ruler to manually preview the footage. This clip was shot by a handheld camera in the late afternoon. A slight breeze rustles the vegetation, and the camera moves unsteadily.

To stabilize this image, your first task is to identify two areas in the shot that are stationary within the context of the frame. These areas are called the *feature regions*. The following figure shows two feature regions that will work for this project.

It is important to locate and size feature regions carefully. For the smoothest tracking, try to select areas that:

• Are visible for the entire shot.

• Have a contrasting color from the surrounding area.

• Have a distinct shape (at least within the search region).

• Have a consistent shape and color throughout the shot.

Positioning the track points

After Effects tracks motion by matching subpixels from a selected area in a frame to subpixels in each succeeding frame. You specify the area to track by using the *track point*. The track point contains the feature region as well as a search region and an attach point. After Effects displays the track point during tracking in the Layer panel.

You will now open the Tracking Controls panel and apply track points to the clip.

1 Press the Home key to make sure the current-time indicator is at the beginning of the time ruler.

Note: This step is very important for accurate tracking. The motion tracking will be based on the frame where the current-time indicator is positioned.

2 Choose Window > Workspace > Motion Tracking to open the Tracker Controls panel along the right side of the application window. The Tracker Controls panel is where you specify your motion source and motion target layers, the type of tracking you want to use, and other tracking options.

3 Click the Stabilize Motion button in the Tracker Controls panel, and make sure that Flowers.mov is chosen in the Motion Source pop-up menu. This tells After Effects that you want to stabilize the motion in the Flowers layer. When you set these options, the Layer panel opens, and in the Tracker Controls panel, the Current Track pop-up menu shows Tracker 1 and the Track Type is set to Stabilize.

When you manually previewed the footage, you may have noticed that the camera not only moved left, right, up, and down, but also rotated slightly. So you need to stabilize the shot's rotation as well as its position.

4 Make sure the Position and Rotation boxes are both checked in the Tracker Controls panel. You should see two track point indicators in the Layer panel.

5 Notice that Motion Target is the Flowers.mov layer. When you stabilize a shot, the resulting data can be applied to the original layer, as specified here, or you can select another layer by clicking the Edit Target button. Leave it set to Flowers.mov.

Now, you're ready to set your track points.

6 Using the Selection tool (⬉), drag the Track Point 1 indicator (from the center) in the Layer panel to position it over the first feature region, which is the light green, closed flower bud below and to the left of the orange flower in the foreground.

7 Drag the Track Point 2 indicator (from the center) to the second feature region, which is the light green leaf to the right of the orange foreground flower.

Moving and resizing the track points

In setting up motion tracking, it's often necessary to refine your track point by adjusting the feature region, search region, and attach point. You can resize or move these items independently or in groups by dragging with the Selection tool, whose pointer icon changes to reflect one of many different activities.

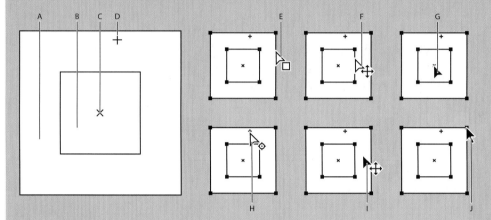

Track point components (left) and Selection tool pointer icons (right)
A. *Search region* **B.** *Feature region* **C.** *Keyframe marker* **D.** *Attach point* **E.** *Moves search region* **F.** *Moves both regions* **G.** *Moves entire track point* **H.** *Moves attach point* **I.** *Moves entire track point* **J.** *Resizes region*

• To turn feature region magnification on or off, choose Magnify Feature When Dragging from the Tracker Controls panel menu. A check mark appears next to the option when it's on.

• To move the feature region, search region, and attach point together, drag with the Selection tool inside the track point area (avoiding the region edges and the attach point); the Move Track Point pointer (▷₀) appears.

• To move just the feature and search regions together, drag the edge of the feature region with the Selection tool; the Move Both Regions pointer (▷₊) appears.

• To move just the feature and search regions together, Alt-drag (Windows) or Option-drag (Mac OS) with the Selection tool inside the feature or search region; the Move Both Regions pointer (▷₊) appears.

• To move only the search region, using the Selection tool, drag the edge of the search region; the Move Search Region pointer (▷□) appears.

• To move only the attach point, using the Selection tool, drag the attach point; the Move Attach Point pointer (▷◇) appears.

• To resize the feature or search region, drag a corner handle.

For more information about track points, see After Effects Help.

Analyzing and applying stabilization

Now that the two track points are defined, After Effects can analyze the data and then apply the stabilization tracker.

1 Click the Analyze Forward button (▶) in the Tracker Controls panel. After Effects analyzes the motion stabilization for the duration of the clip.

2 When the analysis is complete, click the Apply button.

3 In the Motion Tracker Apply Options dialog box, click OK to apply the stabilization to the *x* and *y* dimensions.

The motion-tracking data is added to the Flowers layer in the Timeline panel, where you can see the track points, their properties, and their keyframes. You can also see the Anchor Point, Position, and Rotation keyframes that were applied to the layer. Keyframes are created at every frame, so 300 are created for this 10-second shot. After Effects also opens the Flowers image in the Composition panel again.

4 Close the properties for the Flowers layer in the Timeline panel, and then watch a RAM preview of the stabilized shot. Press the spacebar to stop the playback when you're ready.

Scaling the layer

You've stabilized the footage, but there's still a problem. The tracking was applied to the Anchor Point and Rotation properties of the layer, but the entire layer is moving and rotating. This means you can see the edge of the shot and the empty space around it in some frames. The only way to fix this is to scale the layer.

1 Press the Home key to go to the beginning of the time ruler.

2 With the Flowers layer selected in the Timeline panel, press the S key to display its Scale property.

3 Drag the current-time indicator across the time ruler until you find the frame where the layer displacement is the greatest (around 7:16).

4 Increase the Scale values to **110.0, 110.0**%. The clip fills the frame completely.

5 Go to 2:16, where you can still see some of the empty area outside of the shot.

Because the tracking data is applied to the anchor point of the layer, you can reposition the entire layer without destabilizing it.

6 With the Flowers layer selected in the Timeline panel, press the P key to reveal its Position property. The tracker added an initial Position keyframe to the layer. You don't need it, so click the stopwatch icon (🕑) to delete the keyframe.

7 Change the Position values to **325.0, 375.0**.

8 Manually preview the clip once more to check for additional edge slips. You may need to scale the layer another percentage or two. When you're done, go to 0:00.

Note: The greater you scale the layer, the more the image quality will degrade, so keep the scale operation to a minimum.

9 Watch another RAM preview. The shot should now look rock-steady, with only movement being caused by the wind rustling the flowers.

10 Press the spacebar to stop playback when you're done.

11 Close the properties for the Flowers layer in the Timeline panel, press the Home key to go to the beginning of the time ruler, and choose File > Save to save your work.

As you have discovered, stabilizing a shot is not without its drawbacks. To compensate for the movement or rotation data applied to the layer, you need to adjust the Scale and Position properties, which could ultimately degrade the footage. It is a fine line, but if you really need to use the shot in your production, this may be the best compromise.

Using single-point motion tracking

With the increase in the number of productions that incorporate digital elements into final shots, compositors need an easy way to synchronize computer-generated effects with film or video backgrounds. After Effects lets you do this with the capability to follow, or track, a defined area in the shot and apply that movement to other layers. These layers can contain text, effects, images, or other footage. The resulting visual effect precisely matches the original moving footage.

When you track motion in an After Effects composition that contains multiple layers, the default tracking type is Transform. This type of motion tracking tracks position and/or rotation to apply to another layer. When tracking position, this option creates one track point and generates Position keyframes. When tracking rotation, this option creates two track points and produces Rotation keyframes.

In this exercise, you will continue working on the flower shot captured by the handheld camera. You will add a text layer to the composition and track the text to one of the swaying flowers.

Note: This exercise continues where the previous exercise left off. Before you begin, make sure you have completed the previous exercise, that the project Lesson11_Stabilize_and_Track.aep is open in After Effects Professional, and that After Effects displays the Motion Tracking workspace.

Preparing the text layer

You will start by importing the text for this exercise from an Illustrator file.

1 Double-click an empty area of the Project panel to open the Import File dialog box.

2 Navigate to the AE7_CIB > Lessons > Lesson11 > Assets folder, select the petals.ai file, and click Open.

3 Drag the Petals.ai file from the Project panel to the Timeline panel, placing it above the Flowers layer in the layer stack.

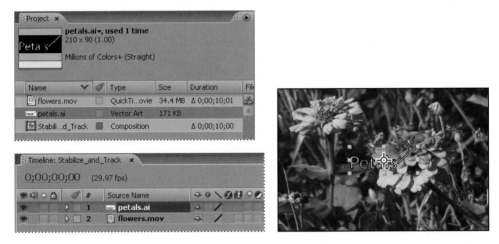

Positioning the track point

With the Petals text added to the Stabilize_and_Track composition, you are ready to position the track point.

1 Press the Home key to make sure the current-time indicator is at the beginning of the time ruler.

2 Select the Flowers layer in the Timeline panel.

3 Click the Track Motion button in the Tracker Controls panel. The Layer panel opens, with a Track Point 1 indicator in the center of the image. Notice the settings in the Tracker Controls panel: The Motion Source is set to Flowers.mov. The Current Track is Tracker 2, and the Motion Target is Petals.ai, because After Effects automatically sets the Motion Target to the layer immediately above the source layer.

Now, position your track point.

4 Using the Selection tool ([cursor icon]), move the Track Point 1 indicator (from the center) in the Layer panel over the shadow area of the large foreground flower.

5 Adjust the size and position of the feature and search region boxes as needed to encompass the entire shaded area, but try to keep both boxes as small as possible to minimize the time needed to track the shot.

Next, move the attach point to the location where you want the Petals layer to be positioned.

6 Drag the attach point below and to the left of the foreground flower.

Analyzing and applying tracking

Now that the feature region and attach point are defined, you can apply the tracker.

1 Click the Analyze Forward button (▶) in the Tracker Controls panel.

2 When the analysis is complete, click the Apply button.

3 In the Motion Tracker Apply Options dialog box, click OK to apply the tracking to the x and y dimensions.

Checking for drift

As an image moves in a shot, the lighting, surrounding objects, and angle of the object can all change, making a once-distinct feature no longer identifiable at the subpixel level. It takes time to develop an eye for choosing a trackable feature. Even with careful planning and practice, you will often find that the feature region drifts away from the desired feature. Readjusting the feature and search regions, changing the tracking options, and trying again are a standard part of digital tracking. When you notice drifting occurring, try the following:

1 Immediately stop the analysis by clicking the Stop button in the Tracker Controls panel.

2 Move the current-time indicator back to the last good tracked point. You can see this in the Layer panel.

3 Reposition and/or resize the feature and search regions, being careful to not accidentally move the attach point. Moving the attach point will cause a noticeable jump in your tracked layer.

4 Click the Analyze Forward button to resume tracking.

The motion-tracking data is added to the Timeline panel, where you can see that the track data is in the Flower layer, but the results are applied to the Position property of the Petals layer. This is another difference between tracking and stabilization: Resulting data is applied to a layer's position, rather than to its anchor point.

Also, notice that the Petals layer has moved to the location of the attach point.

4 Watch a RAM preview. The Petals layer now moves and sways with the movement of the flower, as if the word were attached to the flower.

5 When you're ready, press the spacebar to stop playback.

6 Close the properties for both layers in the Timeline panel, choose File > Save, and then choose File > Close Project.

Motion tracking an element onto background footage can be fun. As long as you have a stable feature to track, single-point motion tracking is quite easy.

Using multipoint tracking

After Effects also offers two more advanced types of tracking that use multiple tracking points: parallel corner-pinning and perspective corner-pinning.

When you track using parallel corner-pinning, you simultaneously track three points in the source footage. After Effects calculates the position of a fourth point to keep the lines between the points parallel. When the movement of the points is applied to the target layer, the Corner Pin effect distorts the layer to simulate skew, scale, and rotation, but not perspective. Parallel lines remain parallel, and relative distances are preserved.

When you track using perspective corner-pinning, you simultaneously track four points in the source footage. When applied to the target footage, the Corner Pin effect uses the movement of the four points to distort the layer, simulating changes in perspective.

In this exercise, you will attach a banner to the side of a building using perspective corner-pinning. If you haven't already watched the sample movie for this exercise, do so now before continuing to see what you will create. (See "Getting started," page 364.)

Setting up the project

Start by launching After Effects and creating a new project.

1 Start After Effects Professional if it is not already open. Press Ctrl+Alt+Shift (Windows) or Command+Option+Shift (Mac OS) as you start it to restore default preferences. Click OK when asked whether you want to delete your preferences file. After Effects opens to display an empty, untitled project.

Note: If you're continuing from the previous exercise and After Effects is already open, choose Window > Workspace > Standard instead of performing step 1. Then, choose File > New > New Project if a blank, untitled project is not open in the application window.

2 Choose File > Save As.

3 In the Save Project As dialog box, navigate to the AE7_CIB > Lessons > Lesson11 > Finished_Projects folder.

4 Name the project **Lesson11_Multipoint_Finished.aep,** and then click Save.

Importing the footage

You need to import two footage items for this exercise.

1 Double-click an empty area of the Project panel to open the Import File dialog box.

2 Navigate to the AE7_CIB > Lessons > Lesson11 > Assets folder.

3 Ctrl-click (Windows) or Command-click to select the banner.ai and building.mov files, and then click Open.

4 In the Banner.ai dialog box that appears, make sure Import Kind is set to Footage and Merged Layers is selected under Layer Options, and then click OK.

Creating the composition

Now, create a new composition.

1 Press Ctrl+N (Windows) or Command+N (Mac OS).

2 In the Composition Settings dialog box, type **Multipoint_Tracking** in the Composition Name field.

3 Make sure the Preset pop-up menu is set to NTSC DV. This automatically sets the width, height, pixel aspect ratio, and frame rate for the composition.

4 Set the Duration to **10:00**, which matches the length of the Building.mov file, and then click OK.

You will now add the footage items to the Timeline panel, one at a time.

5 Drag the Building.mov file from the Project panel to the Timeline panel. It automatically appears in the Composition panel.

6 Manually preview the footage, which is shaky because it was shot with a handheld camera. With a building of this size, it would be extremely difficult (and impractical) to place tracking points on the subject. Therefore, you need to identify other potential features to track. Remember, the feature region box doesn't need to be in the same location as the attach point. Since the tracker by default tracks by luminance, you will use areas in this image that have high contrast differences for tracking.

7 Press the Home key to return to the beginning of the time ruler.

8 Drag the Banner.ai file from the Project panel to the Timeline panel, placing it at the top of the layer stack.

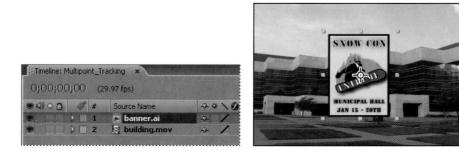

Positioning the track points

Now, it is time to add the track points to the building layer.

1 Select the Building layer in the Timeline panel.

2 Choose Window > Workspace > Motion Tracking.

3 In the Tracker Controls panel, choose Motion Source > Building.mov, and then click the Track Motion button. The building image opens in the Layer panel, with a track point indicator in the center of the image. However, you will be tracking four points in order to attach the banner to the side of the building.

4 Choose Track Type > Perspective Corner Pin. Three more track point indicators appear in the Layer panel.

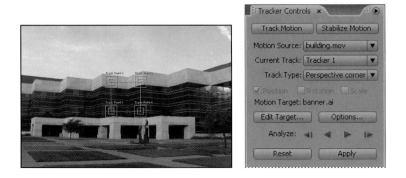

5 Drag the track points to four different high-contrast areas of the image. Use the following image as a guide.

6 Now, drag the attach point for each track point onto one wall surface. Since the banner is rectangular, try to closely follow the edges of the wall. Your feature and search region boxes, as well as your attach points, should look like the following image.

It may be helpful to zoom in to the image when placing and adjusting the track points. Zoom out again when you're finished.

Applying the multipoint tracker

Now, analyze the data and apply the tracker.

1 Click the Analyze Forward button (▶) in the Tracker Controls panel. Then, when the analysis is complete, click the Apply button to calculate the tracking.

2 Notice the results in the Timeline panel: You can see the Corner Pin and Position property keyframes for the Banner layer and the track point data for the Building layer.

3 Watch a RAM preview to see the results of the tracker.

4 When you're done watching the preview, press the spacebar to stop playback.

If you don't like the results, return to the Tracker Controls panel, click the Reset button, and try again. With practice, you will become adept at identifying good feature regions.

5 Press the Home key to go to 0:00, close the Building and Banner layer properties to keep the Timeline panel neat, and choose File > Save to save your work.

Adding a drop shadow and blur effect

The banner now appears to be attached to the building and follows the movement of the handheld camera. But because the banner was created in Illustrator, it doesn't appear to be realistic against the photographic background. Let's take care of that next.

1 Select the Banner layer in the Timeline panel. The Effect Controls panel, which is open, displays the Corner Pin Effect settings for the layer.

2 Choose Effect > Perspective > Drop Shadow.

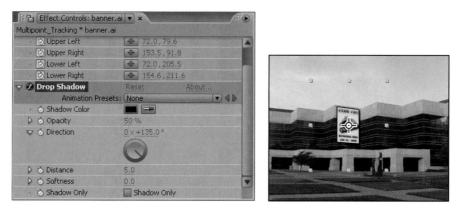

3 Using the Shadow Color eyedropper (🖋) in the Drop Shadow area of the Effect Controls panel, click a shadow area under one of the building overhangs in the Composition panel.

4 Adjust the Direction control until the shadow angle matches the surroundings (approximately 113.0°).

5 Change the Distance to **4.0** and the Softness to **5.0**.

6 Reduce the Opacity until the shadow blends with its surroundings. A value of about **40%** works well.

The banner still looks too crisp for this shot. You'll blur the layer slightly to fix that.

7 Close the Drop Shadow settings in the Effect Controls panel to make room for the next effect you're going to apply.

8 Make sure the Banner layer is selected in the Timeline panel, and then choose Effect > Blur & Sharpen > Fast Blur. The Fast Blur effect is similar to the Gaussian Blur effect, but it blurs large areas more quickly.

9 Set the Blurriness value to **0.3**.

That's better.

10 Watch another RAM preview of your work.

11 When you're done, press the spacebar to stop playback.

12 Choose File > Save to save your work, and then choose File > Close Project.

Creating a particle system

After Effects Professional includes several effects that do an excellent job of creating particle simulations. Two of them—Particle Systems II and Particle World—are based on the same engine. The major difference between the two is that Particle World allows you to move the particles in 3D space, as opposed to in a 2D layer.

In this exercise, you will learn how to use the Particle Systems II effect to create a supernova that could be used as the opening of a science program or as a motion background. If you haven't already watched the sample movie for this exercise, do so now before continuing to see what you will create. (See "Getting started," page 364.)

Note: Particle Systems II and Particle World are part of the Cycore Effects bundle that comes with After Effects Professional. Make sure you have installed Cycore Effects before you start this exercise.

5 Go to 4:00 to see the particle system.

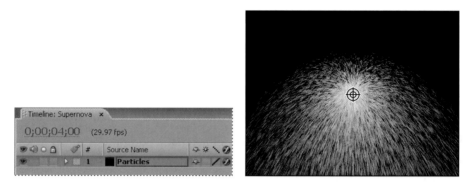

A large stream of yellow particles appears in the Composition panel.

Customizing the particle effect

You will turn this stream of particles into a supernova by customizing the settings in the Effect Controls panel.

1 Expand the Physics property group in the Effect Controls panel. The Explosive Animation setting works fine for this project, but instead of the particles falling down, you want them to flow out in all directions, so change the Gravity value to **0.0**.

3 Watch a RAM preview to see the results of the tracker.

4 When you're done watching the preview, press the spacebar to stop playback.

If you don't like the results, return to the Tracker Controls panel, click the Reset button, and try again. With practice, you will become adept at identifying good feature regions.

5 Press the Home key to go to 0:00, close the Building and Banner layer properties to keep the Timeline panel neat, and choose File > Save to save your work.

Adding a drop shadow and blur effect

The banner now appears to be attached to the building and follows the movement of the handheld camera. But because the banner was created in Illustrator, it doesn't appear to be realistic against the photographic background. Let's take care of that next.

1 Select the Banner layer in the Timeline panel. The Effect Controls panel, which is open, displays the Corner Pin Effect settings for the layer.

2 Choose Effect > Perspective > Drop Shadow.

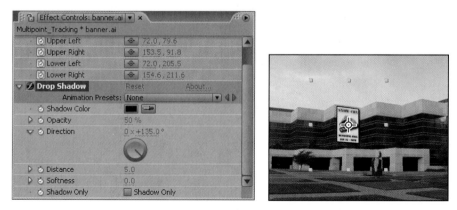

3 Using the Shadow Color eyedropper (⬤) in the Drop Shadow area of the Effect Controls panel, click a shadow area under one of the building overhangs in the Composition panel.

4 Adjust the Direction control until the shadow angle matches the surroundings (approximately 113.0°).

5 Change the Distance to **4.0** and the Softness to **5.0**.

6 Reduce the Opacity until the shadow blends with its surroundings. A value of about **40%** works well.

The banner still looks too crisp for this shot. You'll blur the layer slightly to fix that.

7 Close the Drop Shadow settings in the Effect Controls panel to make room for the next effect you're going to apply.

8 Make sure the Banner layer is selected in the Timeline panel, and then choose Effect > Blur & Sharpen > Fast Blur. The Fast Blur effect is similar to the Gaussian Blur effect, but it blurs large areas more quickly.

9 Set the Blurriness value to **0.3**.

That's better.

10 Watch another RAM preview of your work.

11 When you're done, press the spacebar to stop playback.

12 Choose File > Save to save your work, and then choose File > Close Project.

Creating a particle system

After Effects Professional includes several effects that do an excellent job of creating particle simulations. Two of them—Particle Systems II and Particle World—are based on the same engine. The major difference between the two is that Particle World allows you to move the particles in 3D space, as opposed to in a 2D layer.

In this exercise, you will learn how to use the Particle Systems II effect to create a supernova that could be used as the opening of a science program or as a motion background. If you haven't already watched the sample movie for this exercise, do so now before continuing to see what you will create. (See "Getting started," page 364.)

Note: Particle Systems II and Particle World are part of the Cycore Effects bundle that comes with After Effects Professional. Make sure you have installed Cycore Effects before you start this exercise.

Setting up the project

Start by launching After Effects and creating a new project.

1 Start After Effects Professional if it is not already open. Press Ctrl+Alt+Shift (Windows) or Command+Option+Shift (Mac OS) as you start it to restore default preferences. Click OK when asked whether you want to delete your preferences file. After Effects opens to display an empty, untitled project.

Note: If you're continuing from the previous exercise and After Effects is already open, choose Window > Workspace > Standard instead of performing step 1. Then, choose File > New > New Project if a blank, untitled project is not open in the application window.

2 Choose File > Save As.

3 In the Save Project As dialog box, navigate to the AE7_CIB > Lessons > Lesson11 > Finished_Projects folder.

4 Name the project **Lesson11_Particles_Finished.aep**, and then click Save.

Creating the composition

You do not need to import any footage items for this exercise, so the first thing to do is to create the composition.

1 Press Ctrl+N (Windows) or Command+N (Mac OS).

2 In the Composition Settings dialog box, type **Supernova** in the Composition Name field.

3 Choose NTSC D1 from the Preset pop-up menu. This automatically sets the width, height, pixel aspect ratio, and frame rate for the composition.

4 Set the Duration to **10:00**, then click OK.

Creating a particle system

You will build the particle system from a solid layer, so you will create it next.

1 Choose Layer > New > Solid or press Ctrl+Y (Windows) or Command+Y (Mac OS) to create a new slid layer.

2 In the Solid Settings dialog box, type **Particles** in the Name field.

3 Click on the Make Comp Size button to make the layer the same size as the composition. Then, click OK.

4 With the Particles layer selected in the Timeline panel, choose Effect > Simulation > CC Particle Systems II.

5 Go to 4:00 to see the particle system.

A large stream of yellow particles appears in the Composition panel.

Customizing the particle effect

You will turn this stream of particles into a supernova by customizing the settings in the Effect Controls panel.

1 Expand the Physics property group in the Effect Controls panel. The Explosive Animation setting works fine for this project, but instead of the particles falling down, you want them to flow out in all directions, so change the Gravity value to **0.0**.

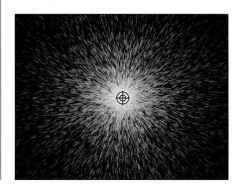

Understanding Particle Systems II properties

Particle systems have a unique vocabulary. Some of the key settings are explained here for your reference. They're listed in the order in which they appear (top to bottom) in the Effect Controls panel.

Birth Rate Controls the number of particles generated per second. This is an arbitrary value and does not reflect the actual number of particles being generated. The higher the number, the more densely packed the particles become.

Longevity Determines how long the particles live.

Producer Position Controls the center point or origin of the particle system. The position is set based on the x, y coordinates. All particles emanate from this single point. You can control the size of the producer by making adjustments to the x and y radius settings. The higher these values, the larger the producer point will be. A high x value and a 0 (zero) y value will result in a line.

Velocity Controls the speed of particles. The higher the number, the faster the particles move.

Inherent Velocity % When the Producer Position is animated, this value determines how much of the velocity is passed along to the particles. A negative value causes the particles to move in the opposite direction.

Gravity The higher the value, the faster the particles fall. A negative value causes particles to rise.

Air Resistance Simulates particles interacting with air or water.

Direction Determines which directions the particles flow. Use with the Direction Animation type.

Extra Introduces randomness into the movement of the particles.

Birth/Death Size Determines the size of the particles when they are created and when they expire.

Opacity Map Controls opacity changes for the particle of the lifetime.

Color Map Use with the Birth and Death colors to shade the particles over time.

2 Close the Physics property group and open the Particle property group. Then, change the Death Size to **1.50** and increase the Size Variation to **100.0%**. This allows the particles to change their birth size at random.

3 Reduce the Max Opacity to **55.0%**. This make the particles semi-transparent.

Currently, the particles don't look very dramatic because the Particle Type is a line.

4 Choose Particle Type > Faded Sphere.

Wow! Now the particles look intergalactic. Don't stop there, though.

5 Click the Birth Color swatch and change the color to RGB **255, 200, 50** to give the particles a yellow hue on birth, then click OK.

6 Click the Death Color swatch and change the color to RGB **180, 180, 180** to give the particles a light gray hue as they fade out, then click OK.

7 To keep the particles from staying on-screen too long, decrease the Longevity value to **0.8** seconds.

Note: Even though they're at the top of the Effect Controls panel, it is often easier to adjust the Longevity and Birth Rate settings after you have set the other particle properties.

The Faded Sphere particle type softened the look, but the particle shapes are still too sharply defined. You will fix that by blurring the layer to blend the particles with one another.

8 Choose Effect > Blur & Sharpen > Fast Blur.

9 In the Fast Blur area of the Effect Controls panel, increase the Blurriness value to **10.0**. Then, check the Repeat Edge Pixels box to keep the particles from being cropped at the edge of the frame.

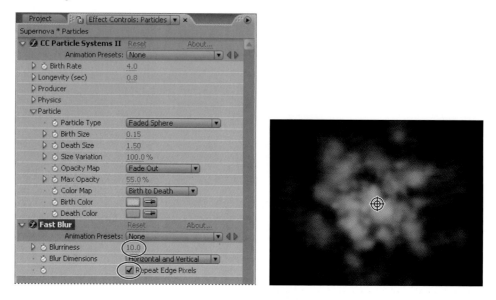

Here comes the sun

You will now create a bright halo of light that will go behind the particles.

1 Go to 0:07.

2 Press Ctrl+Y (Windows) or Command+Y (Mac OS) to create a new solid layer.

3 In the Solid Settings dialog box do the following:

• Type **Sun** in the Name field.

• Click the Make Comp Size button to make the layer the same size as the composition.

• Click the color swatch make the layer the same yellow as the Birth Color of the particles (RGB=255, 200, 50).

- Click the OK button to close the Solid Settings dialog box.

4 Drag the Sun layer below the Particles layer in the Timeline panel.

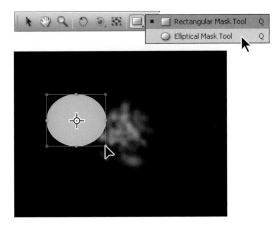

5 Select the Elliptical Mask tool ( ) in the Tools panel and Shift-drag in the Composition panel to draw a circle with a radius of roughly 100 pixels, or one-fourth the width of the composition.

6 Using the Selection tool (➤), drag the mask shape to the center of the Composition panel.

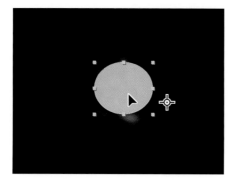

7 With the Sun layer selected in the Timeline panel, press the F key to reveal its Mask Feather property. Increase the Mask Feather amount to **100.0, 100.0** pixels.

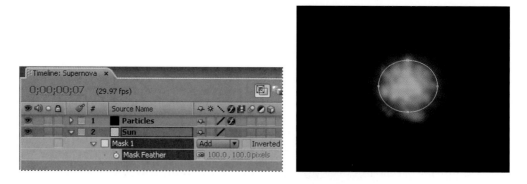

8 Press Alt+[(Window) or Option+[(Mac OS) to set the In point of the layer to the current time.

9 Click the triangle in the Label column for the Sun layer to close its properties.

Lighting the darkness

Since the sun is bright, it should illuminate the surrounding darkness.

1 Make sure the current-time indicator is still at 0:07.

2 Press Ctrl+Y (Windows) or Command+Y (Mac OS) to create a new solid layer.

3 In the Solid Settings dialog box, name the layer **Background**, click the Make Comp Size button to make the layer the same size as the composition, and then click OK to create the layer.

4 In the Timeline panel, drag the Background layer to the bottom of the layer stack.

5 With the Background layer selected in the Timeline panel, choose Effect > Generate > Ramp.

The Ramp effect creates a color gradient, blending it with the original image. You can create linear or radial ramps, and vary the position and colors of the ramp over time. Use the Start of Ramp and End of Ramp settings to specify the start and end positions. Use the Ramp Scatter setting to disperse the ramp colors and eliminate banding.

6 In the Ramp area of the Effect Controls panel, do the following:

- Change the Start of Ramp to **360.0, 240.0** and the End of Ramp to **360.0, 525.0**.

- Choose Ramp Shape > Radial Ramp.

- Click the Start Color swatch and set the start color to dark blue (RGB=0, 25, 135).

- Set the End Color to black (RGB=0, 0, 0).

7 Press Alt+[(Windows) or Option+[(Mac OS) to set the In point of the layer to the current time.

Adding a lens flare

To tie all the elements together, add a lens flare to simulate an explosion.

1 Press the Home key to make sure the current-time indicator is at the beginning of the time ruler.

2 Press Ctrl+Y (Windows) or Command+Y (Mac OS) to create a new solid layer.

3 In the Solid Settings dialog box, name the layer **Nova**, click the Make Comp Size button to make the layer the same size as the composition, set the Color to black (RGB=0, 0, 0), and then click OK. The Nova layer should be at the top of the layer stack in the Timeline panel.

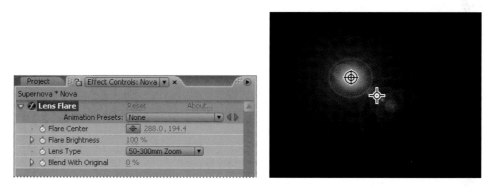

4 With the Nova layer selected in the Timeline panel, choose Effect > Generate > Lens Flare.

5 In the Lens Flare area of the Effect Controls panel, do the following:

• Change the Flare Center to **360.0, 240.0**.

• Make sure the Lens Type is set to 50-300mm Zoom.

• Decrease the Flare Brightness to **0%**, and then click the Flare Brightness stopwatch icon (⏱) to create an initial keyframe.

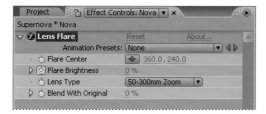

6 Go to 0:10.

7 Increase the Flare Brightness to **240%**.

8 Go to 1:04 and decrease the Flare Brightness to **100%**.

9 With the Nova layer selected in the Timeline panel, press the U key to see the animated Lens Flare property.

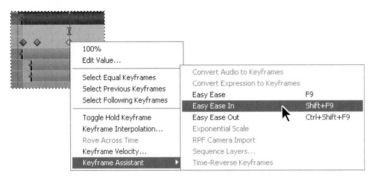

10 Right-click (Windows) or Ctrl-click (Mac OS) the ending Flare Brightness keyframe and choose Keyframe Assistant > Easy Ease In from the contextual menu.

11 Right-click (Windows) or Ctrl-click (Mac OS) the beginning Flare Brightness keyframe and choose Keyframe Assistant > Easy Ease Out from the contextual menu. Finally, you need to make the layers under the Nova layer visible in the composition.

12 Choose Columns > Modes from the Timeline panel menu, and then choose Screen for the Nova layer's blend mode.

Now, preview your work.

13 Watch a RAM preview. When you're done, choose File > Save and then choose File > Close Project.

About high dynamic range (HDR) footage

Another advanced feature available in After Effects Professional is support for high dynamic range (HDR) color.

The dynamic range (ratio between dark and bright regions) in the physical world far exceeds the range of human vision and of images that are printed or displayed on a monitor. But while human eyes can adapt to very different brightness levels, most cameras and computer monitors can capture and reproduce only a limited dynamic range. Photographers, motion-picture artists, and others working with digital images must be selective about what's important in a scene because they are working with a limited dynamic range.

HDR images open up a world of possibilities because they can represent a very wide dynamic range through the use of 32-bit floating-point numeric values. Floating-point numeric representations allow the same number of bits to describe a much larger range of values than integer (fixed-point) values. HDR values can contain brightness levels, including objects as bright as a candle flame or the sun, that far exceed those in 8-bit-per-channel (bpc) or 16-bpc (non-floating-point) mode. Lower dynamic range 8-bpc and 16-bpc modes can represent RGB levels only from black to white, which represents an extremely small segment of the dynamic range in the real world.

Currently, HDR images are used mostly in motion pictures, special effects, 3D work, and some high-end photography. After Effects Professional supports HDR images in a variety of ways. For example, you can create 32-bpc projects to work with HDR footage, and you can adjust the exposure, or the amount of light captured in an image, when working with HDR images in After Effects. For more information about support in After Effects for HDR images, see After Effects Help.

Let's do the Timewarp

The Timewarp effect in After Effects Professional gives you precise control over a wide range of parameters when changing the playback speed of a layer, including interpolation methods, motion blur, and source cropping to eliminate unwanted artifacts. The Timewarp effect works independently of the Frame Blend switch in the Timeline panel.

In this exercise, you will use the Timewarp effect to change the speed of a clip for a dramatic slow-motion playback. If you haven't already watched the sample movie for this exercise, do so now before continuing to see what you will create. (See "Getting started," page 364.)

Setting up the project

Start by launching After Effects and creating a new project.

1 Start After Effects Professional if it is not already open. Press Ctrl+Alt+Shift (Windows) or Command+Option+Shift (Mac OS) as you start it to restore default preferences. Click OK when asked whether you want to delete your preferences file. After Effects opens to display an empty, untitled project.

Note: If you're continuing from the previous exercise and After Effects is already open, make sure it displays the Standard workspace instead of performing step 1. Then, choose File > New > New Project if a blank, untitled project is not open in the application window.

2 Choose File > Save As.

3 In the Save Project As dialog box, navigate to the AE7_CIB > Lessons > Lesson11 > Finished_Projects folder.

4 Name the project **Lesson11_Timewarp_Finished.aep**, and then click Save.

Importing the footage and creating the composition

You need to import one footage item for this exercise.

1 Double-click an empty area of the Project panel to open the Import File dialog box.

2 Navigate to the AE7_CIB > Lessons > Lesson11 > Assets folder on your hard disk, select the Group_Approach[DV].mov, and click Open.

3 Click OK in the Interpret Footage dialog box.

Now, create a new composition based on the footage's aspect ratio and duration.

4 Drag the Group_Approach[DV].mov file onto the Create A New Composition button (▣) at the bottom of the Project panel. After Effects creates a new composition named for the source file and displays it in the Composition and Timeline panels.

5 Choose File > Save to save your work.

Using Timewarp

In the source footage, a group of young people approaches the camera at a steady pace. At around 2 seconds, the director would like the motion to begin to slow down to 10%, then ramp back up to full speed at 7:00.

1 With the Group_Approach layer selected in the Timeline panel, choose Effect > Time > Timewarp.

2 In the Timewarp area of the Effect Controls panel, make sure Method is set to Pixel Motion. This instructs Timewarp to create new frames by analyzing the pixel movement in nearby frames and creating motion vectors. Also, make sure Adjust Time By is set to Speed to control the time adjustment by percentage, rather than by a specific frame.

3 Go to 2:00.

4 In the Effect Controls panel, set the Speed to **100.00** and click the stopwatch (⏱) to set a keyframe. This tells Timewarp to keep the speed of the clip at 100% until the 2-second mark.

5 Go to 5:00 and change the Speed to **10.00**. After Effects adds a keyframe.

6 Go to 7:00 and set the Speed to **100.00**. After Effects adds a keyframe.

7 Press the Home key to go to the beginning of the time ruler, and then watch a RAM preview of the effect.

Note: Be patient. The RAM preview might take some time to calculate, but it will provide a more accurate playback than a spacebar preview.

You will see that the speed adjustments are rather abrupt, not a smooth, slow-motion curve you would expect to see in a professional effect. This is because the keyframes are linear instead of curved. You will fix that next.

8 Press the spacebar to stop the playback when you're ready.

9 With the Group_Approach[DV] layer selected in the Timeline panel, press the U key to see the animated Timewarp Speed property.

10 Click the Graph Editor button (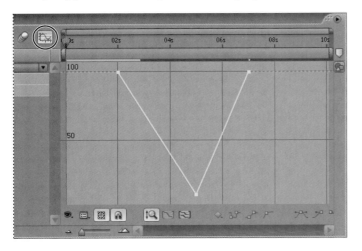) in the Timeline panel to see the Graph Editor instead of the layer bars in the time ruler. Then, select the Speed property name for the Group_Approach[DV] layer to see its graph.

11 Click to select the first Speed keyframe (at 2:00), and then click the Easy Ease button (⊰) at the bottom of the Graph Editor. This adjusts the influence into and out of the keyframe to smooth out sudden changes.

💡 *You can also apply an Easy Ease adjustment by pressing the F9 key.*

12 Repeat step 11 for the other two Speed keyframes in the motion graph, at 5:00 and 7:00.

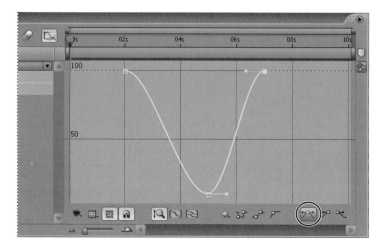

The motion graph is now smoother, but you can tweak it even more by dragging the bezier handles.

13 Using the bezier handles for the keyframes at 2:00 and 5:00, adjust the curve so that it resembles the following image.

Note: If you need a refresher on using bezier handles, see Lesson 6, "Working with Masks."

15 Watch another RAM preview. Now, the slow-motion Timewarp effect looks professional.

16 Choose File > Save to save the project, and then choose File > Close Project to close the project.

Good job. You've now experimented with some of the advanced features in After Effects Professional, including motion stabilization, motion tracking, particle systems, and the Timewarp effect. To render any or all of the projects you completed in this lesson, see Lesson 12, "Rendering and Outputting," for instructions.

Review

▶ **Review questions**

1 What is *motion stabilization* and when do you need to use it?

2 What is *drifting?*

3 What is the difference between parallel and perspective corner-pinning?

▶ **Review answers**

1 Shooting footage using a handheld camera typically results in shaky shots. Unless this look is intentional, you will want to stabilize the shots to eliminate unwanted shaky motion. Motion stabilization in After Effects works by analyzing the movement and rotation of the target layer, then applying the opposite values to the anchor point and rotation of that layer. When played back, the motion appears smooth because the layer itself moves incrementally to offset the unwanted motion.

2 Drifting occurs when the feature region loses the feature that's being tracked. As an image moves in a shot, the lighting, surrounding objects, and angle of the object can change, making a once-distinct feature unidentifiable at the subpixel level. Even with careful planning and practice, the feature region often drifts away from the desired feature. Readjusting the feature and search regions, changing the tracking options, and trying again are a standard part of digital tracking.

3 When you track using parallel corner-pinning, you simultaneously track three points in the source footage. After Effects calculates the position of a fourth point to keep the lines between the points parallel. When the movement of the points is applied to the target layer, the Corner Pin effect distorts the layer to simulate skew, scale, and rotation, but not perspective. Parallel lines remain parallel, and relative distances are preserved. When you track using perspective corner-pinning, you simultaneously track four points in the source footage. When applied to the target footage, the Corner Pin effect uses the movement of the four points to distort the layer, simulating changes in perspective.

TOOL TIPS FROM THE PROS: Patrick Siemer

Patrick Siemer is a visual effects artist at Pixar Animation Studios.

Creative ways to use the Timewarp effect

In the AE7_CIB > Lessons > Lesson11 > Patrick Siemer folder you'll find two QuickTime movies produced by Patrick Siemer. In the movie shown above, left, Siemer uses Timewarp to create a stylized morph effect. In the movie shown above, right, he applies the Timewarp effect to a collection of still images so that they appear to be a surrealistic motion-video clip. Following are some tips from Siemer on how you can create similar effects.

> **How to turn a handful of digital pictures into surreal motion-picture clip:**

• Create high-quality HD movies with an inexpensive 4-megapixel digital camera. Using a still camera enables effects you can't achieve with a video camera, such as timed exposures.

• Take at least 30 pictures of the subject. You will probably discard some. To create smoother footage, take more pictures. Animate with your camera: If the subject isn't moving, move the camera. High-res is better.

• For extra strangeness, use Photoshop to alter the image. Import images into After Effects as an image sequence.

• Apply the Timewarp effect and experiment with the settings.

• Add motion blur to decrease the "ripping" or "tearing" of the picture.

• The effect will increase with the "differentness" of the pictures.

> **A personal note to other shutterbugs:**

I love taking pictures, too—maybe a bit too much. I blame the After Effects Timewarp feature for fueling my addiction to bigger, larger, more gigantic hard drives and newer, faster computers.

Be careful: Compared to most effects, Timewarp can be really fun. It can also take a *really* long time to render high-resolution footage, so work with smaller pictures until you have an idea of what is possible.

Beware: Once your addiction sets in, you won't stop until your hard drive is completely full....

WEB

BROADCAST

The success of any project depends on your ability to deliver it in the format or formats your clients need, whether it's for the web or broadcast output. In this final lesson, you'll create time-saving templates and then render a final composition in a variety of formats and resolutions.

12 | Rendering and Outputting

Lesson overview

In this lesson, you'll learn how to do the following:

- Create render-settings templates.

- Create output-module templates.

- Render multiple output modules.

- Select the appropriate compressor for your delivery format.

- Use pixel aspect correction.

- Render the final animation for NTSC broadcast video output.

- Render a test version of a composition.

- Render a web version of the final animation.

In this lesson, you'll delve more deeply into rendering. In order to produce several versions of the animation for this lesson, you'll explore options available within the Render Queue panel. After creating render-settings and output-module templates, you'll render both a broadcast version and a web version of the final movie.

The total amount of time required to complete this lesson depends in part on the speed of your processor and on the amount of RAM available for rendering. The amount of hands-on time required is less than 1 hour.

Getting started

Make sure the following files are in the AE7_CIB > Lessons > Lesson12 folder on your hard disk, or copy them from the *Adobe After Effects 7.0 Classroom in a Book* DVD now:

- In the Sample_Movies folder: Lesson12_Sorenson_Final.mov, Lesson12_Cinepak_Final.mov, Lesson12_NTSC_Final.mov

- In the Start_Project_File folder: Lesson12_Start.aep

- Car_Ride_Flatter.psd, GordonsHead.mov, HeadShape.ai, piano.wav, studer_Corporate_Politics.jpg, studer_Crash1.jpg, studer_Full_Speed.jpg, studer_Red_Herring_Cover2.jpg, and studer_Schwab.jpg

1 Open and play the sample movies for Lesson 12. These movies represent different final versions of the animation that you created in Lesson 4, the Gordon Studer multimedia portfolio. When you are done viewing the sample movies, quit the QuickTime player. You may delete the sample movies from your hard disk if you have limited storage space.

Setting up the project

This lesson continues from the point at which all preceding lessons end: when you're ready to render the final composition. For this lesson, we provide you with a starting project file that is essentially the final composition from Lesson 4 of this book. As always, when you begin the lesson, restore the default applications settings for After Effects. See "Restoring default preferences," page 5.

1 Press Ctrl+Alt+Shift (Windows) or Control+Option+Shift (Mac OS) while starting After Effects. When asked whether you want to delete your preferences file, click OK.

2 Choose File > Open Project.

3 Navigate to the AE7_CIB > Lessons > Lesson12 > Start_Project_File folder, select the Lesson12_Start.aep file, and click Open.

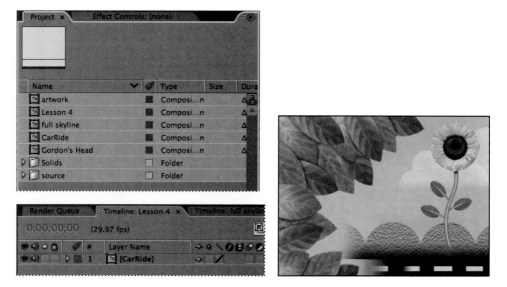

4 Choose File > Save As.

5 In the Save As dialog box, navigate to the AE7_CIB > Lessons > Lesson12 > Finished_Project folder.

6 Name the project **Lesson12_Finished.aep**, and then click Save.

7 Choose Window > Render Queue to open the Render Queue panel.

8 Drag the lower edge of the Composition panel up to enlarge the Render Queue panel so that you can see its contents better.

Creating templates for the rendering process

In previous lessons, you selected individual render and output-module settings on those occasions when you rendered your composition. In this lesson, you'll create templates for both render settings and output-module settings. These templates are presets that you can use to streamline the setup process when you render items for the same type of delivery format. After you define these templates, they appear in the Render Queue panel on the appropriate pop-up menu (Render Settings or Output Module). Then, when you're ready to render a job, you can simply select the template that is appropriate for the delivery format that your job requires, and the template applies all the settings.

Creating a render-settings template for full resolution

The first template you'll create is for full-resolution output.

1 Choose Edit > Templates > Render Settings to open the Render Settings Templates dialog box.

2 Under Settings, click New to open the Render Settings dialog box.

3 Under Render Settings, choose Quality > Best and Resolution > Full.

4 Under Time Sampling, do the following:

- For Frame Blending, choose On For Checked Layers.

- For Motion Blur, choose On For Checked Layers.

- For Time Span, choose Length Of Comp.

- Under Frame Rate, make sure that the Use Comp's Frame Rate option is selected.

5 Click OK to return to the Render Settings Templates dialog box. All the settings you selected appear in the lower half of the dialog box. If you need to make any changes, click the Edit button and then adjust your settings.

6 For Settings Name, type **Final Render_fullres** (for *full resolution*).

7 At the top of the dialog box, under Defaults, choose Movie Default > Final Render_
fullres. Then click OK to close the dialog box.

Final Render_fullres is now the default Render Settings option and will appear (instead
of Current Settings) when you add a composition to the Render Queue panel to make a
movie (which you'll do later in this lesson).

*If you want to save a render-settings template for use on another system, you can
click the Save All button in the Render Settings Templates dialog box before you close
it in step 7 (or, reopen the dialog box later by choosing Edit > Templates > Render
Settings). Save the file in an appropriate location on your hard disk, such as in the After
Effects application folder. All the currently loaded render settings are saved in a file with
the .ars extension. Then, copy this file to the disk of the other system. When you start
After Effects on that system, choose Edit > Templates > Render Settings, click the Load
button, and select the new .ars file to load the settings you saved.*

Creating a render-settings template for test renderings

Next, you'll create a second render-settings template, selecting settings appropriate
for rendering a test version of your final movie. A test version is smaller—and
therefore renders faster—than a full-resolution movie. When you work with complex
compositions that take relatively long times to render, it is a good practice to render a
small test version first. This helps you find any final tweaks or blunders that you want
to adjust before you take the time to render the final movie.

1 Choose Edit > Templates > Render Settings. The Render Settings Templates dialog box appears.

2 Under Settings, click New to open the Render Settings dialog box.

3 Select the following settings:

• For Quality, choose Best.

• For Resolution, choose Third, which reduces the linear dimension of the composition by one-third.

4 Under Time Sampling, do the following:

• For Frame Blending, choose Current Settings.

• For Motion Blur, choose Current Settings.

• For Time Span, choose Length Of Comp.

5 Under Frame Rate, select Use This Frame Rate, and type **12** (fps). Then click OK to return to the Render Settings Templates dialog box.

6 For Settings Name, type **Test_lowres** (for *low resolution*).

7 Examine your settings, which now appear in the lower half of the dialog box. If you need to make any changes, click the Edit button to adjust the settings. Then click OK.

The Test_lowres option will now be available on the Render Settings pop-up menu in the Render Queue panel.

You have now created two render-settings templates. One is for a full-resolution final version, and one is for a low-resolution test version of your final composite.

Creating templates for output modules

Using processes similar to those in the previous section, you'll now create templates to use for output-module settings. Each will include unique combinations of settings that are appropriate for a specific type of output.

Creating an output-module template for broadcast renderings

The first template you'll create for output-module settings is appropriate for an NTSC broadcast-resolution version of your final movie.

1 Choose Edit > Templates > Output Module.

2 Under Settings, click New to open the Output Module Settings dialog box.

3 In the Output Module Settings dialog box, under Output Module, do the following:

• For Format, choose QuickTime Movie. In Windows, if the Compression Settings dialog box appears, click OK to close it for the moment.

• For Post-Render Action, choose Import.

• Under Video Output, click the Format Options button to open the Compression Settings dialog box.

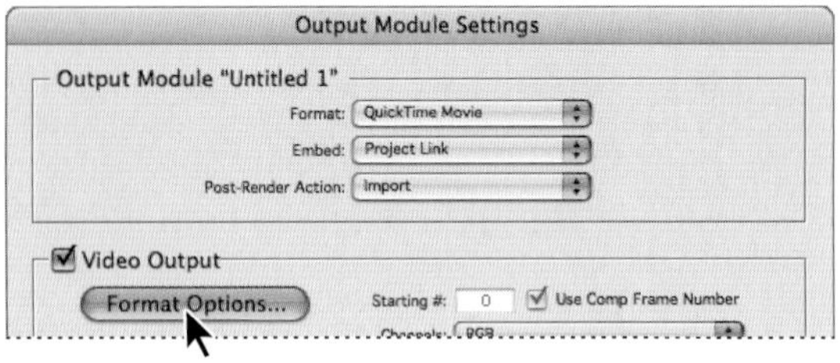

4 At the top of the Compression Settings dialog box, choose Compression Type > Animation. Under Compressor, choose Depth > Millions Of Colors. Click OK to close the dialog box.

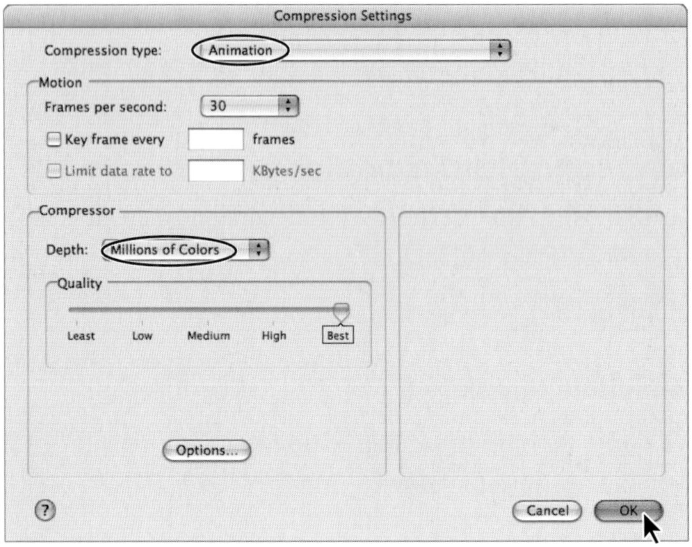

Mac OS

Windows

5 Review the settings in the Output Module Settings dialog box to make sure that the Channels pop-up menu is set to RGB and Depth is set to Millions Of Colors.

6 Check the Audio Output option, and make sure that the pop-up menus are set (from left to right) to 44.100 kHz, 16 Bit, Stereo.

7 Click OK to return to the Output Module Templates dialog box. Review the settings in the lower half of the dialog box and click the Edit button if you need to adjust your settings.

8 For Settings Name, type **Final Render_QT_audio** (to remind you that this template for QuickTime includes audio).

9 Under Defaults, choose Movie Default > Final Render_QT_audio. Then click OK.

The Final Render_ QT_audio template is now the default selection for the Output Module pop-up menu and will appear (instead of Lossless) each time you add a composition to the Render Queue panel.

> *As with the render-settings templates, you can save output-module templates for use on other systems. Click the Save All button in the Output Module Templates dialog box. Name the file and save it to an appropriate location on your hard disk, such as in the After Effects application folder. All loaded output modules are saved in a file with the .aom extension. Transfer this file to the disk of another system and launch After Effects. Choose Edit > Templates > Output Module, click the Load button, and select the .aom file to load the settings.*

Creating a low-resolution output-module template

Next, you'll create a second output-module template with settings appropriate for rendering a low-resolution test version of the movie. In this case, the settings that you'll select are also appropriate for a World Wide Web version of the movie.

1 Choose Edit > Templates > Output Module to open the Output Module Templates dialog box.

2 Under Settings, click New to create a new template and to open the Output Module Settings dialog box.

3 For Format, choose QuickTime Movie. Close the Compression Settings dialog box if it opens in Windows.

4 For Post-Render Action, choose Import.

5 Click Format Options (under Video Output) and select the following settings in the Compression Setting dialog box:

• Choose Compression Type > Sorenson Video. This compressor automatically determines the color depth.

• Set the Quality slider to High.

• Under Motion, select the Key Frame Every option, and then type **30** (frames).

• Select Limit Data Rate To, and type **150** (KBytes/sec).

6 Click OK to close the Compression Settings dialog box and return to the Output Module Settings dialog box.

7 Under Audio Output, click the Format Options button to open the Sound Settings dialog box and select the following:

- For Compressor, choose IMA 4:1.

- For Rate, choose 22.050.

- For Size, choose 16 Bit.

- For Use, select Stereo, and then click OK to close the Sound Settings dialog box. Your sound settings now appear under Audio Output in the Output Module Settings dialog box. Click OK to close the Output Module Settings dialog box.

8 In the lower half of the Output Module Templates dialog box, examine your settings, and click Edit if you need to make any changes.

9 For Settings Name, type **Test_Sorenson**, and then click OK. Now this output template will be available on the Output Module pop-up menu in the Render Queue panel.

Note: *The Sorenson Video compressor is available with QuickTime 4.0 or later. QuickTime is included on the After Effects application disc and is also available for download from the Apple website. The IMA 4:1 compressor is commonly used when compressing audio for web or desktop playback.*

As you might expect, greater compression and lower audio sample rates create smaller file sizes, but they also reduce the quality of the output. However, this low-resolution template is fine for creating test movies or movies for the web.

To render with OpenGL

If you have an OpenGL card that supports OpenGL 1.5 or later, you can use OpenGL to render in After Effects by using hardware acceleration. You can view information about your OpenGL card by choosing Edit > Preferences > Previews (Windows) or After Effects > Preferences > Previews (Mac OS) and clicking the OpenGL Info button.

Note that only features supported by OpenGL and your graphics card will be rendered into the final movie. If your card doesn't support advanced OpenGL features, don't use OpenGL to render. For a list of features supported by OpenGL, see After Effects Help.

To render using OpenGL support, do one of the following:

• Add a composition to the Render Queue panel, and then click the underlined text next to Render Settings and select Use OpenGL Renderer, or

• Select a composition in the Project panel, choose Composition > Composition Settings, click the Advanced tab, and choose Rendering Plug-In > OpenGL Hardware. Then, render the composition.

Rendering to different output media

Now that you have created templates for your render settings and output modules, you can use them to render different versions of the movie.

Preparing to render a test movie

First, you'll render the test version, selecting the Test_lowres render-settings template and the Test_Sorenson output-module template that you created.

About compression

Compression is essential to reduce the size of movies so that they can be stored, transmitted, and played back effectively. When exporting or rendering a movie file for playback on a specific type of device at a certain bandwidth, you choose a compressor/decompressor (also known as an encoder/decoder), or codec, to compress the information and generate a file readable by that type of device at that bandwidth.

A wide range of codecs is available; no single codec is the best for all situations. For example, the best codec for compressing cartoon animation is generally not efficient for compressing live-action video. When compressing a movie file, you can fine-tune it for the best-quality playback on a computer, video playback device, the web, or from a DVD player. Depending on which encoder you use, you may be able to reduce the size of compressed files by removing artifacts that interfere with compression, such as random camera motion and excessive film grain.

The codec you use must be available to your entire audience. For instance, if you use a hardware codec on a capture card, your audience must have the same capture card installed, or a software codec that emulates it.

For web or desktop playback Both Sorenson Video and Cinepak are standard compressors for items intended to be played back on the desktop, from a CD, or posted on a website. Both do a reasonably good job of decreasing the size of the file so that it can be played back efficiently, without reducing image quality too severely.

For streaming video over the web The data rate should account for real-world performance at the target data rate. For broadband connections, set the data rate for streaming video to 128 kilobits per second.

For video-resolution playback or output If you have a video-capture or playback card (or both) installed in your system, you'll want to render your animation using the compressor or codec for that card. Most manufacturers' video-capture and playback cards are based upon one of the following compression algorithms: DV compression, Motion JPG, MPEG-2, or Uncompressed Serial Digital output. By rendering with the appropriate compressor (and using the frame size that correlates to your compressor), you can take advantage of the hardware installed—playing the animation back at real time and at video resolution on an external NTSC or PAL monitor. Then, if your system is hooked up to a deck, you can also use this hardware to lay off the animation to video tape.

For DVD production The data rate should maximize quality while fitting the entire program within the space available on the DVD. In After Effects, you can create MPEG video, including MPEG-2 in Windows and MPEG-4 on Mac OS (requires QuickTime). After Effects offers a number of MPEG presets to optimize the output quality for various project types. If you're experienced with MPEG encoding, you can fine-tune projects for specific playback situations by customizing the presets in the Export Settings dialog box.

For more about compression and codecs, see After Effects Help.

1 Drag the Lesson 4 composition from the Project panel to the Render Queue panel.

💡 *Alternatively, you can select the Lesson 4 composition in the Project panel and choose Composition > Add To Render Queue.*

The Lesson 4 composition is added to the Render Queue panel. Notice the default settings in the Render Settings and Output Module pop-up menus. Next, change those settings to your low-resolution templates.

2 Choose Render Settings > Test_lowres.

3 Choose Output Module > Test_Sorenson.

4 Next to Output To, click the blue, underlined words *Not Yet Specified*.

5 In the Output Movie To dialog box, locate the AE7_CIB folder and click the New Folder button.

6 Type **Final_Renders** to name the new folder, click Create, and then open the folder, if necessary.

7 Name the file **Final_Sorenson.mov**, and then click Open (Windows) or Save (Mac OS) to return to the Render Queue panel.

8 Choose File > Save to save your work.

You'll do a few more things before you render the movie. Leave the Render Queue panel open for the next exercise.

Working with multiple output modules

Next, you'll add another output module to this render queue so that you can compare the results of two compressors. You'll set this one for Cinepak compression.

1 With the Lesson 4 composition still selected in the Render Queue panel, choose Composition > Add Output Module. A second set of Output Module and Output To options appears directly beneath the first.

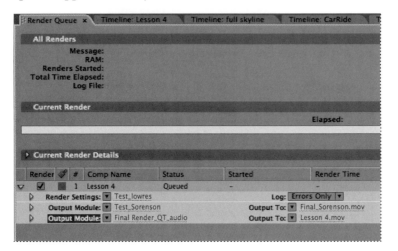

2 From the lower Output Module pop-up menu, choose Test_Sorenson.

3 Click the blue, underlined words *Test_Sorenson* to open the Output Module Settings dialog box, and then click the Format Options button under Video Output.

4 In the Compression Settings dialog box, do the following:

• For Compression Type, choose Cinepak.

• For Depth, choose Millions Of Colors.

• Make sure that the following settings are selected: Quality slider at High, Frames Per Second at 12, Key Frame Every at 30 frames, and Limit Data Rate at 150 KBytes/sec. Then click OK to close the dialog box.

5 Click OK again to close the Output Module Settings dialog box.

6 Next to Output To, click the blue, underlined words *Lesson 4.mov* to open the Output Movie To dialog box.

7 Name the movie **Final_Cinepak.mov** and save it in the AE7_CIB > Final_Renders folder.

8 Choose File > Save to save the project, and then click the Render button in the Render Queue panel. After Effects renders both of these formats simultaneously.

When the render is complete, both the Final_Sorenson.mov and Final_Cinepak movies appear in the Project panel.

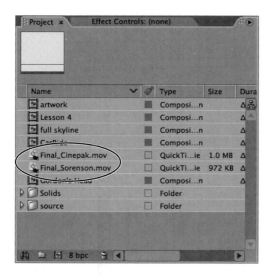

You can double-click each movie to preview it in the Footage panel and compare the results. Then, select the movie that looks better to you and rename it **Final_Web.mov** (on the desktop; do not rename it within After Effects). This version is ready for Gordon Studer's prospective clients to view on the web.

Note: When the render is complete, you may find it helpful to further reduce the size of the movie before posting it to a website. You may want to create streaming video, or simply reduce the size based on the majority of the audience's available bandwidth. You can do this with a media-compression or media-cleaner application specifically designed for this purpose.

If you need to make any final changes to the animation, reopen the composition and make those adjustments now. Remember to save your work when you finish, and then render the test movie again using the appropriate settings. After examining the test render and making any necessary changes, you'll proceed with your final render.

Exporting to SWF

You can also use After Effects to export compositions as Macromedia Flash (SWF) files for playback within a web-browser application. However, certain types of artwork are more suitable than others for export to SWF. Rasterized images and some effects cannot be represented by vectors, and therefore are not efficiently saved to SWF format. You can export them, but the files will be larger in size.

Also, it is helpful when exporting items to SWF to place all your layers within a single composition rather than using precompositions or nested compositions. Using a single composition also tends to reduce the size of the exported file.

To learn how to export a composition to SWF format, see Lesson 2, "Creating a Basic Animation Using Effects and Presets."

Preparing the composition for full-resolution rendering

Next, you'll prepare to render the final composite comp. This animation is intended primarily for NTSC video output. You'll begin by placing the final composite comp in a new composition that you create at the appropriate size for your final delivery format.

1 Choose Composition > New Composition.

2 In the Composition Settings dialog box, do the following:

• For Name, type **Final Comp NTSC**.

• Choose Preset > NTSC D1. This automatically sets the dimensions (720 x 486), pixel aspect ratio (D1/DV NTSC), and frame rate (29.97).

• For Resolution, choose Full (or lower if necessary for your system).

• Make sure that Start Timecode is 0:00.

• For Duration, type **2000** to specify 20 seconds, and then click OK.

The new, empty composition opens in the Composition and Timeline panels.

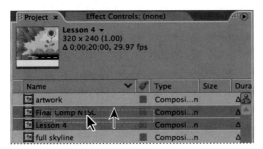

3 In the Project panel, select the Lesson 4 composition and place it in the new composition by dragging it to the Final Comp NTSC composition icon.

Using pixel aspect correction

As you scrub through or preview the animation, you may notice that the items in the Composition panel now appear a bit wider than before. That's becuase this D1 NTSC composition has a nonsquare pixel aspect ratio. However, your computer monitor displays images using square pixels. Therefore, the images that you see in the Composition panel appear stretched unless you enable a feature called *pixel aspect correction*. Pixel aspect correction squeezes the view of the composition slightly to display the image as it will appear on a video monitor. By default, this feature is turned off. Follow these steps to turn it on.

1 Go to 3:00, where there are a few elements, including Gordon Studer's masked head, in the Composition panel.

2 Choose View Options from the Composition panel menu.

3 In the View Options dialog box, under Window, select Pixel Aspect Ratio Conversion. Then, click OK to close the dialog box.

The image in the Composition panel is squeezed, appearing (at a modified pixel aspect ratio) as it will when this item is rendered, laid off to tape, and viewed on a video monitor. The layers in the Composition panel may appear a bit jagged while you have this view turned on. You'll want to turn it off to see your images with full anti-aliasing. This view does not effect rendering.

4 Turn pixel aspect correction off and on a couple of times by clicking the Toggle Pixel Aspect Ratio Correction button ( ) at the bottom of the Composition panel.

Using pixel aspect correction, you can work in a composition with a nonsquare pixel aspect ratio but still view your images as they would appear on a video monitor.

Rendering the final movie for broadcast

Now, you'll render the NTSC broadcast version of your final animation. This may take half an hour or more, depending on your system.

1 Click the Render Queue panel name to bring the panel forward, and then drag the Final Comp NTSC composition from the Project panel to the Render Queue panel below the Lesson 4 composition.

2 Next to Output To, click the blue, underlined words *Final Comp NTSC.mov* to open the Output Movie To dialog box.

3 Name the movie **Final_NTSC.mov** (indicating that this item will be rendered at NTSC D1 resolution) and specify the AE7_CIB > Final_Renders folder. Then click Save to return to the Render Queue panel.

The Final Render_fullres Render Setting appears selected in the Render Settings pop-up menu because you set this as the default movie setting when you created the template.

The Final Render_QT_audio setting appears selected in the Output Module menu, again because you set this as the default earlier in this lesson. The composition is now ready to render.

4 Save the project one more time, and then click the Render button.

5 When the render is finished, close the Render Queue panel.

6 In the Project panel, double-click Final_NTSC.mov to open it in the Footage panel.

As you play the movie, compare your final rendered output to the NTSC sample movie you watched at the beginning of this lesson. If necessary, reopen the composition and make any necessary changes. Then save the project and render the movie again, using the preceding steps.

Note: *Because this movie is so large, it may not play back at real time in the QuickTime Player. If you have a video playback card installed on your system, render the movie choosing the appropriate compressor and frame size for that card in the Compression Settings dialog box. Import the movie into your editing software and play it back using your hardware for real-time playback.*

You now have both a web version and a broadcast version of the final animation.

Congratulations! You have now completed the *Adobe After Effects 7.0 Classroom in a Book*. To learn more about After Effects, go to the After Effects page of the Adobe website.

Review

▶ ## Review questions

1 Name two types of templates and explain when and why to use them.

2 What is compression, and what are some issues associated with it?

▶ ## Review answers

1 In After Effects, you can create templates for both render settings and output-module settings. These templates are presets that you can use to streamline the setup process when you render items for the same type of delivery format. After you define these templates, they appear in the Render Queue panel on the appropriate pop-up menu (Render Settings or Output Module). Then, when you're ready to render a job, you can simply select the template that is appropriate for the delivery format that your job requires, and the template applies all the settings.

2 Compression is essential to reduce the size of movies so that they can be stored, transmitted, and played back effectively. When exporting or rendering a movie file for playback on a specific type of device at a certain bandwidth, you choose a compressor/decompressor (also known as an encoder/decoder), or codec, to compress the information and generate a file readable by that type of device at that bandwidth. A wide range of codecs is available; no single codec is the best for all situations. For example, the best codec for compressing cartoon animation is generally not efficient for compressing live-action video. When compressing a movie file, you can fine-tune it for the best-quality playback on a computer, video playback device, the web, or from a DVD player. Depending on which encoder you use, you may be able to reduce the size of compressed files by removing artifacts that interfere with compression, such as random camera motion and excessive film grain.

Index

Contributors

Mark Christiansen is the author of *Adobe After Effects 6.5 Studio Techniques* (Adobe Press). He has created visual effects and animations for feature films, network television, computer games, and an array of high-technology companies. Recent clients include Adobe Systems, Inc., The Orphanage (for Dimension Films), Telling Pictures (for The History Channel), and the Couturie Company (for HBO), as well as Seagate, Sun, Intel, and Medtronic. Feature credits include *The Day After Tomorrow* and films by Robert Rodriguez.

Takeshi Hiraoka Plucked out of paradise, Hiraoka moved to chilly San Francisco from Honolulu, Hawaii, one cold winter in 2002. In San Francisco, attended the Academy of Art University, graduating in May 2004. This is where Hiraoka met Sheldon Callahan, with whom he directed and produced the feature-length, DV film *Origin*. In addition to being a DV producer, Takeshi is also 2D and 3D animator.

Stephen Schleicher has travelled from Kansas to Georgia to California working as an editor, graphic designer, videographer, director, and producer on a variety of small and large video productions. Currently, Stephen teaches media and web development at Fort Hays State University. He also works on video and independent projects for state and local agencies and organizations, as well as his own works. Stephen is a regular contributor to Digital Media Net (www.digitalmedianet.com).

Anna Ullrich is a pale but fine digital artist based in Seattle, Washington, although her heart resides in Minnesota, where her spry and brilliant Democratic grandmother lives. Anna earned a BFA from the University of Washington in Seattle and a MFA from the University of Notre Dame in Indiana (both in photography).

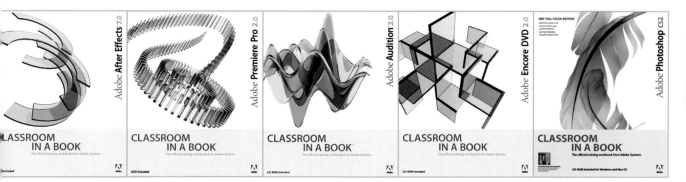